# SCARLET
# LETTERS

# SCARLET LETTERS

## THE EVER-INCREASING INTOLERANCE OF THE CULT OF LIBERALISM EXPOSED

# JACK CASHILL

**WND Books**

# SCARLET LETTERS

Published by WND Books, Washington, D.C. WND Books is a registered trademark of WorldNetDaily.com, Inc. ("WND")

Book designed by Mark Karis
Unless otherwise indicated, scripture quotations are taken from the Holy Bible, King James Version (public domain).
Scriptures marked NKJV are from the NEW KING JAMES VERSION. © 1982 by Thomas Nelson, Inc. Used by permission. All rights reserved.
Also quoted: The International Standard Version. Copyright © 1995–2014 by ISV Foundation. ALL RIGHTS RESERVED INTERNATIONALLY. Used by permission of Davidson Press, LLC.

WND Books are available at special discounts for bulk purchases. WND Books also publishes books in electronic formats. For more information call (541) 474-1776 or visit www.wndbooks.com.

Hardcover ISBN: 978-1-935071-92-1
eBook ISBN: 978-1-935071-93-8

Library of Congress Cataloging-in-Publication Data Available
Cashill, Jack.
Scarlet letters : the ever-increasing intolerance of the cult of liberalism / Jack Cashill.
pages cm
Includes bibliographical references and index.
ISBN 978-1-938067-73-0 (hardcover)
1. Liberalism--United States. 2. Fanaticism--United States. 3. United States--Social conditions.  I. Title.
JC574.2.U6C37 2015
320.51ʾ30973--dc 3
2015009445
*Printed in the United States of America*
15 16 17 18 19 MPV 9 8 7 6 5 4 3 2 1

*For Phoebe*

# CONTENTS

# ACKNOWLEDGMENTS

Many thanks to those at WND Books who made *Scarlet Letters* possible, notably Joseph and Elizabeth Farah, editor Geoff Stone, copy editor Renee Chavez, and designer Mark Karis.

Thanks, too, to those who shared their often difficult stories with me including Emil Tonkovich, John Rocker, Stephen Jimenez, Darren Wilson, Robert Zimmerman, Melissa and Aaron Klein, and Nicolle Martin.

Kudos to those many good people who stared down our Torquemadas and survived. We need more of you.

And special thanks to my wife, Joan, for understanding my mission.

# INTRODUCTION

# THE NEO-PURITAN

Jess Dooley had had enough. A coach at Concord Community High School in Elkhart, Indiana, Dooley watched the evening news out of nearby South Bend with dismay. She knew that she would have to do something.

Earlier that late March day, young ABC 57 reporter Alyssa Marino went in search of a Christian who supported Indiana's controversial Religious Freedom Restoration Act. To find one she drove twenty miles south to Walkerton, Indiana, and started knocking on doors. There, on Roosevelt Road, in this humble town of two thousand souls, she stopped at a family-owned business called Memories Pizza. "I just walked into their shop and asked how they feel. They've never been asked to cater a same-sex wedding," Marino would later admit.

The unsuspecting young woman who managed the restaurant, Crystal O'Connor, greeted her warmly and answered her hypothetical question artlessly. "If a gay couple came in and wanted us to provide pizzas for their wedding, we would have to say no," said Crystal. The idea that a gay couple anywhere would request pizzas for a wedding—let alone in Walkerton, Indiana—seemed a bit of a stretch, but Marino got what she came for. She rushed her footage back to the studio.

ABC 57 anchor Brian Dorman led the broadcast: "We went into small towns tonight for reaction to the Religious Freedom Restoration Act. We found one business just twenty miles away from a *welcoming* South Bend with a much different view." Then came Marino's fateful interview with O'Connor. It ran over the chyron, "Restaurant denies some services to same-sex couples." Deep in the report, Marino conceded, "The O'Connor family told ABC 57 news that if a gay couple or a couple belonging to another religion came in to the restaurant to eat, they would never deny them service," but if Jess Dooley or her fellow progressives heard this, it was too little, too late.

The firestorm began immediately as ABC 57 hoped it would. Left-leaning journals like *Buzzfeed* and *Politico* picked up the feed and zeroed in on the Indiana pizzeria. Thousands across the nation expressed their outrage in tweets and through trolling attacks on the pizzeria's Facebook and Yelp pages. Others posted obscenities and gay pornography. Some made death threats, causing the O'Connors to shut down the business and seek help from the local police.

Amidst the furor, it was Jess Dooley who best captured the essence of the moment. At 9:08 p.m. on the evening of the broadcast, she tweeted to her followers, many of them students at Concord High, "Who's going to Walkerton, IN to burn down #memoriespizza with me?" So righteous was Dooley's calling she used her own name. So convinced was she of the O'Connors' evil, she proposed to burn their business down. So confident was she of the national zeitgeist, she expected a mob— a mob she was prepared to lead.

America was finally beginning to notice. The spirit of Salem lives on.

# 1

# MAN'S SECOND-OLDEST FAITH

In those heady first years after the Russian Revolution, tremors from the east tripped the internal Richter scales of sensitive souls from Mitte to Montmarte to Greenwich Village. One Villager who felt the shock was crusading birth control advocate Margaret Sanger. Although she did not think Marxism the solution to her issue—"the sexual and racial chaos" then vexing liberal America—she knew many an aspiring bohemian who bought the whole package.

"The heaven of the traditional theology had been shattered by Darwinian science," she wrote in her 1922 book, *The Pivot of Civilization*, "and here, dressed up in all the authority of the new science, appeared a new theology, the promise of a new heaven, an earthly paradise, with an impressive scale of rewards for the faithful and ignominious punishments for the capitalists."[1]

Sanger was hardly alone in sensing a shift in the spiritual landscape. At about this time, a young Whittaker Chambers was coming to terms with what he would later call "man's second-oldest faith," the faith Adam embraced when he yielded to the serpent's plea, "Ye shall be as gods." To this point in history, no human cohort had committed itself to this faith more passionately than the Communist Party, and it was this passion that attracted Chambers. Communists, however, had no monopoly on the vision. As Chambers saw it, leftists of various stripes— "socialists, liberals, fellow travelers, unclassified progressives and men of good will"—shared the conviction that human reason would displace "God" as the "creative intelligence of the world."[2]

What eventually prompted Chambers to rethink his alliances were the "punishments" Sanger mentioned in passing. As a high-level operative in the Communist underground during Stalin's ruthless rise to power, Chambers could see just how arbitrary and "ignominious" those punishments could be. He saw too much, in fact, to remain a Communist. His break eventually led to a dramatic, mid-century face-off against former comrade Alger Hiss, the well-connected avatar of the evil Chambers only barely escaped. Even as Chambers rejected Communism, however, he could not deny Sanger's claim that a "new theology" had shattered the firmament. Nor could he deny that at mid-century this theology was ascendant. In fact, by choosing "Almighty God" over "Almighty Man," by rejecting Communism for freedom, Chambers thought himself on the losing side of an epic showdown.[3]

Given America's cultural and political dominance in the years after World War II, many thought Chambers unduly pessimistic. Aleksandr Solzhenitsyn was not among them. Of all the college commencement speakers in 1978, Solzhenitsyn was perhaps the only one to sense that in the near future no major university would dare ask a person like him to speak. If he had shared this concern before his address, few would have believed him. At the time, after all, he was arguably the most sought-after commencement speaker in America. The fact that Harvard recruited him was testament to that.

"In terms of the effect he has had on history, Solzhenitsyn is the dominant writer of the 20th century," *New Yorker* editor David Remnick would write some years later. "Who else compares? Orwell? Koestler?"[4] No Harvard speaker before or since saw more or suffered more than Solzhenitsyn.

The son of a Russian artillery officer, Solzhenitsyn graduated from college just in time to sign up for the "Great Patriotic War." He would serve three punishing years as a battery commander in the Eastern European bloodlands. Just as victory loomed, Solzhenitsyn, in a letter to a friend, made the seriously "incorrect" jest of referring to Stalin as "the man with the mustache." That little joke would earn him a twelve-year sojourn in the hellish outposts of what he would render infamous as the "gulag archipelago."[5]

While imprisoned, Solzhenitsyn conceived any number of short stories. In 1962, six years after his release, he put one of those stories to pen as the novella *One Day in the Life of Ivan Denisovich*. Thanks to a very brief thaw in the long Soviet literary winter, the book found a publisher, and Solzhenitsyn found an international audience. In 1970, he was awarded the Nobel Prize for Literature. In 1973, the thaw long since over, he smuggled a copy of his epic masterwork, *The Gulag Archipelago*, to publishers in the West.

In 1974, Soviet authorities decided they had had enough of Solzhenitsyn and booted him from his beloved homeland. He eventually made his way with his family to an obscure hamlet in Vermont, and there he was living and writing as something of a recluse when Harvard invited him to speak. No speaker ever brought more gravitas to the Harvard podium, certainly not recent commencement speakers, such as Oprah Winfrey, J. K. Rowling, or the serial plagiarist Fareed Zakaria.

The fact that Solzhenitsyn criticized his adopted country could not have troubled those in attendance. They expected as much. By 1978, bashing America had become de rigeur at any university to the left of Bob Jones. What surely rankled students and faculty both was that Solzhenitsyn aimed his guns at them, "the ruling groups and the intellectual elite."[6] He chastised them for their lack of courage and of self-restraint, their materialism and their self-indulgence. "Destructive and irresponsible freedom has been granted boundless space," he lectured. "Society appears to have little defense against the abyss of human decadence."

Knowing that many in the audience, faculty and students alike, played at socialism, Solzhenitsyn coldly stripped them of their illusions. "Socialism of any type and shade leads to a total destruction of the human spirit and to a leveling of mankind into death," he told them. It is the inevitable path men take when they see themselves as the master of the world, free of personal evil and confident that "all the defects of life are caused by misguided social systems, which must therefore be corrected."

All of this was disturbing enough, but Solzhenitsyn rocked the young swells when he described, much as Chambers had, the unfortunate choices America's ruling classes had made. Thinking themselves "the center of everything," they had forgotten what the nation's founding fathers well understood, namely, that "man is God's creature." For those graduates who had not heard the word *God* in the last four years, save as the first half of a swear word, this news had to shock.

As both Chambers and Solzhenitsyn recognized, the empty rationalism of the twentieth century had eroded the traditional faith of millions of Western intellectuals and replaced it with a smug, self-satisfied belief in the human will to power. At its conception, this new theology was self-righteous to the core and keen on "punishments," but initially those punishments were reserved for its class enemies. Over time, believers would broaden the roster of sinners. Indeed, contempt for these many and various sinners would become the faith's unifying core.

Although Soviet-styled communism was in the process of exhausting itself at the time of Solzhenitsyn's Harvard address, man's second-oldest faith was mutating and adapting to the environment. As a would-be 1960s radical, African American author and social critic Shelby Steele watched it happen up close. Like Solzhenitsyn, Steele noted the emergence of a narcissistic "new man, a better man than the world has seen before." This new man, teased Steele, was "so conspicuously cleansed of racism, sexism, and militarism that he would be a carrier of moral authority and legitimacy."[7]

According to the Steele, the nation had begun to address the obvious imperfections in its racial history just when the baby boomers were coming of age. As their elders struggled to atone for racial sins real and imagined, boomers sensed a crack in their moral authority and drove a wedge through it. Boomers would celebrate themselves not for honing their own character or for honoring some larger principle but for disassociating themselves from "the sins that had caused whites to lose moral authority in the first place—racism and racial discrimination, but also imperialism, ecological indifference, sexism and so on."[8]

In Great Britain, author Peter Hitchens observed a comparable loss of confidence. The "old morality," as he saw it, lacked the conviction to withstand "the sneering assault of our modern age." With the embers of their Christian heritage not quite extinguished, young Brits looked for spiritual satisfaction wherever they could find it. Many of them, perhaps most, wrote Hitchens, found "an acceptable substitute for Christian faith" in the multicultural canon, specifically "a commitment to social welfare at home and liberal anticolonialism abroad." What distinguished these secular, often atheistic evangelists from their Christian peers, Hitchens added, was a "high opinion of their own virtue."[9]

In late twentieth-century Holland, Somalian refugee Ayaan Hirsi Ali found a seeming wonderland of tolerance and functional technology. As a female, she particularly appreciated the freedoms her adopted country afforded. What surprised her, and what finally undid her, was that "nobody seemed *proud* of being Dutch."[10] Lacking confidence in their own traditions, Dutch leftists in particular found refuge in multiculturalism. The Dutch strain, like the British and American, had at its heart a contempt for the host nation's Western heritage and a blind embrace of certain select subcultures. As Hirsi Ali would discover, the blind had no mercy on those who could see.

As the new century began, liberal boomers dominated the news media, academia, and popular culture throughout the Western world. Within their "magic circle," observed Walter Russell Mead in the *American Interest*, their ideas had "never been more firmly entrenched and less contested."[11] Convinced of their own righteousness, activists were taking a more aggressive posture, culturally and politically, than the generation past. This may explain why they abandoned "liberal" and adopted "progressive" as their preferred self-designation ("multiculturalist" being too unwieldy in any case). The word switch mirrored a political reality. If old-school liberals could content themselves with honoring a fixed set of principles, progressives, like sharks, had to move forward. At the risk of tautology, progressives "progressed." Their identity depended on it.

At this intermediate stage in the movement's evolution, progressives had the power to hector and humiliate, but they had only a limited ability to enforce their values through the police arm of the state. Throughout the West, the democratic process restrained them. If within the magic circles progressive ideas seemed fabulous, outside the circles those same ideas, said Mead, often seemed "outlandish."[12] In the United States, citizens enjoyed the added protection of the Constitution. With the ascent of Barack Obama—"the next messiah," as he was called too often and too earnestly[13]— that protection began to erode. Until this point, progressives had shamed many a poor soul out of a job, but they had sent no one to a gulag. Francis Cardinal George was among those traditionalists who sensed an unhealthy shift toward the coercive in Obama's Washington. The government, George observed, was beginning to take upon itself "the mantle of a religion." In the age of Obama, he feared, a cultural-political "ruling class" was extending its sway over the nation's institutions and was "using the civil law to impose its own form of morality on everyone." From his perspective, these moral czars seemed much too eager to tell citizens "what they must personally think [and] what 'values' they must personalize in order to deserve to be part of the country."[14]

Although the national government had never before harbored such ambitions, there was an American precedent for what George witnessed, the Puritans of New England. In his classic 1850 novel, *The Scarlet Letter*, Nathaniel Hawthorne rightly described his seventeenth-century ancestors as "a people among whom religion and law were almost identical."[15] This was a reality the novel's protagonist, Hester Prynne, learned through hard experience. As the plot unfolds, the birth of Hester's child while her husband is still in England alerts civic officials to her adultery. As punishment, Hester is made to stand on a scaffold in the Boston town square for three hours and forever thereafter wear an embroidered scarlet A—for *adultery*—on her chest.

In the age of Obama, the "new theology" took a turn for the

Puritan. The enforcers of progressive orthodoxy would never call themselves "neo-puritan," but that is what they had become. In their mingling of law and morality, they mimicked the polity of those early New Englanders but were, if anything, less merciful. Dissent was no longer merely "misguided," said Mead; it was "morally wrong." In that "bad thoughts create bad actions," Mead added, "the heretics must be silenced or expelled."[16]

To be sure, not all progressives were neo-puritans, but all neo-puritans were progressives. With little resistance from their passive coreligionists, the neo-puritans made themselves the punitive arm of the progressive movement. An astute observer of the culture, prominent Catholic social critic Joseph Bottum, described them as "hungry for the identification of sinners—the better to prove the virtue of the accusers and, perhaps especially, to demonstrate the sociopolitical power of the accusers."[17]

In her HBO documentary *Fall to Grace*, Alexandra Pelosi—yes, Nancy's daughter—revealed, without intending, how the shifting progressive creed had become conflated with "sin." The documentary tracks the career of former New Jersey governor Jim McGreevey, the self-dubbed "gay-American" disgraced in a sex and security scandal. In one passing scene, McGreevey enters an Episcopal church ostensibly more welcoming than the hidebound Catholic church of his childhood. The message board on the church front reads, "Jesus liberates us from our sin of sexism, homophobia, racism and classism."[18] Had the message board been bigger, the good pastor might have had Jesus liberating "us" from xenophobia, Islamophobia, and global warming denial as well. Although there were many other ways the insensitive could go wrong, these stood for the moment as the seven new deadly sins.

Over time, neo-puritans have shown less interest in celebrating the many colors of the multicultural rainbow than they have in condemning those who resisted the celebration. The accusers insist that resistance is born out of hatred—of blacks, of gays, of immigrants, of Muslims, of women, of poor people, even, yes, of Mother Earth. "Hate" stands as the umbrella sin for all dissenters. Indeed, if there is one shared ritual among the progressive subcults, it is the imputation of "hate" to the less enlightened. Hawthorne accused his Puritan forebears of "being of the most intolerant brood that ever lived,"[19] but they were the picture of tolerance compared to the progressive neo-puritans who would flourish four centuries later.

Like Hazel Motes, the embittered protagonist of Flannery O'Connor's prescient 1952 novel *Wise Blood*, Western progressives were creating "a Church Without Christ"—a church without God, for that matter—where, in O'Connor's words, "there was no Fall because there was nothing to fall from and no redemption because there was no Fall and no Judgment because there wasn't the first two."[20] Among the many contradictions of contemporary progressivism is its avowed reluctance to pass judgment. If neo-puritans did not create the word *judgmentalism*, they created the taboo around it. "Censorious judgmentalism from the moralising wing, which treats half our countrymen as enemies must be rooted out," thundered Alan Duncan, Britain's openly gay Tory MP a few years back. In a similar vein, actress Ann Heche, speaking at a vigil for slain gay student Matthew Shepard, wished that "one day, we will all join on the opposite side of hatred where one truly connects with God."

The catch was, of course, that Duncan and Heche, like most progressives, could no more shuck the impulse to judge than could Hazel Motes. After scolding his colleagues for their judgmentalism, Duncan denounced them as the "Tory Taleban."[21] After scolding her fellow Americans for their antigay judgmentalism, Heche reminded them, "You, you are the abomination in the eyes of my God."[22]

Without meaning to, Duncan and Heche captured the paradoxical nature of what Steele called "an unforgiving social puritanism"[23] and what Peter Hitchens called "an intolerant and puritan secular fundamentalism."[24] For all of their postmodern prattle about relativism and multiculturalism, neo-puritans would prove quicker to judge and harsher in their judgments—Abomination? Tory Taleban?—than the most spiteful New England divine. "Throughout the Western world," author Mark Steyn has observed, 'tolerance' has become remarkably 'intolerant,' and 'diversity' demands ruthless conformity."[25] With the exception of Islam, an unlikely ally in the rainbow coalition, progressive neo-puritanism may well be the most judgmental, vengeful, unforgiving quasi-religious sect abroad in the Western world today.

Despite the dogmatism, progressives, like their seventeenth-century New England soul mates, exist in a perpetual state of anxiety. For the original Puritans, the anxiety derived from a Calvinist theology that spared only the "elect" from eternal damnation. The problem was that no amount of good works could assure one's "elect" status. Only faith could do that, but even the devout could not be certain their faith would suffice. This uncertainty led many a Puritan to proclaim his own worthiness and question the worthiness of others.

For progressives, the anxiety derives from never quite knowing what the boundaries of thought and language on a given subject at a given moment might be. Resident *Duck Dynasty* philosopher Phil Robertson got it right when he described their belief system as "constantly changing and evolving" and eventually "morphing into a dark maze of nonsense."[26] The further this system estranges itself from reason, the more confused progressives are about what a "perfect faith" entails. In the Judeo-Christian tradition, all virtues are compatible. One can just say no to wrath, greed, sloth, pride, lust, envy, and gluttony more or less simultaneously without semantic assistance from the Ministry of Truth. Progressivism, to say the least, lacks that kind of coherence. The biggest slacker in Logic 101 can sense the dust-up coming when the enemies of sexism and homophobia and the friends of Islam try to hammer out a multicultural "ten commandments." Heads just might roll. Literally.

Like their New England forebears, progressives cope with this anxiety by aggressively asserting their rightful place among the elect. Steele coined the phrase "zone of decency" to describe the sacred preserve in which progressives imagine themselves clustering. To distinguish themselves from lesser mortals, argued Steele, they are quick to "decertify" those who do not embrace the values du jour and to dispatch the condemned to Hester Prynne's "magic circle of ignominy." And again like the Puritans, Steele argued, progressives need "only the *display* of social justice to win moral authority."[27]

The Puritans, at least, could turn to a fixed source of authority in the Bible. As Robertson noted, "Biblical correctness has never changed."[28] When the Puritans "decertified" one of their own, the individual almost always understood why. Hester acknowledged she had committed adultery and did not protest the scarlet *A* with which she was branded. Her sin was willful. Those subject to neo-puritan scrutiny have no such assurance. If the charges against Prynne were legitimate, the charges against sinners today rarely ever are. "Even when you have no idea you're committing a hate crime, chances are you still are," Mark Steyn opined after Canadian neo-puritans dragged him before that nation's official inquisitors.[29] Neo-puritans exaggerate the sins of the targeted or concoct them out of whole cloth. In either case, like Hawthorne's Puritans, they publicly brand the sinner to render him or her, in Hawthorne's words, "the general symbol at which the preacher and moralist might point."[30]

"If there is no God," said Jean-Paul Sartre in his famous paraphrase of Dostoevsky's Ivan Karamazov, "everything is permitted."[31] Observed Obama mentor and small-*c* communist Bill Ayers, "The old gods failed and the old truths left the world. Clear conclusions were mainly delusional, a luxury of religious fanatics and fools."[32] Given this latitude, the neo-puritan clerisy add new sins regularly and new sinners daily. An awkward phrase, a misunderstood joke, a quote out of context, a frank look at data, a hacked e-mail, or a persistent belief in a revered tradition could earn a sinner any one of many scarlet letters as ablaze with "awe and horrible repugnance"[33] as Hester's own scarlet *A*—a letter progressives treat as the punch line of a joke.

Among those the neo-puritans would decertify was Aleksandr Solzhenitsyn. "When his name comes up now," wrote Remnick in 2001 of the previous century's most consequential writer, "it is more often than not as a freak, a monarchist, an anti-Semite, a crank, a has been."[34] Solzhenitsyn did not change. The rules did. Upon his death in Russia in

2008, the *New York Times* obituary recounted a conversation between leftist writer Susan Sontag and Russian poet Joseph Brodsky. "We were laughing and agreeing about how we thought Solzhenitsyn's views on the United States, his criticism of the press, and all the rest were deeply wrong, and on and on," said Sontag. "And then Joseph said: 'But you know, Susan, everything Solzhenitsyn says about the Soviet Union is true. Really, all those numbers—60 million victims—it's all true.'"[35] Solzhenitsyn never stopped telling the truth.

The West just stopped listening.

# 2

# THE SCARLET *R*: RACIST

Katherine Ann Porter had been duped, badly. In her memoir, *The Never-Ending Wrong*, published on the fiftieth anniversary of the execution of convicted murderers Nicola Sacco and Bartolomeo Vanzetti, the Pulitzer Prize–winning Porter told how this came to be. As the anarchists' final hours ticked down, Porter had been standing vigil with other artists and writers in Boston. Ever the innocent liberal, Porter approached her group leader, a "fanatical little woman" and a dogmatic Communist, and expressed her hope that Sacco and Vanzetti could still be saved. The response of this female comrade is noteworthy largely for its candor: "Saved . . . who wants them saved? What earthly good would they do us alive?"[1]

This was 1927, just five years after Margaret Sanger predicted "ignominious punishments for the capitalists," and already the scarlet *R* for *racism* was replacing the scarlet *C* for *classism* as the most grievous affront to American progressives. To this day, it remains so. As their predecessors did with Sacco and Vanzetti, neo-puritans today falsify narratives and manufacture outrage, inevitably in pursuit of some goal. That goal might be as grubby as enriching a race hustler or as grand as turning a presidential election, but rarely is it about justice, and always there is someone to accuse.

## THE RACIST, REPRESSIVE CAPITALIST STATE

Nearly a century after Sacco and Vanzetti's demise, crowds stood vigil outside the Ferguson, Missouri, police station, waiting to hear whether a grand jury would indict Officer Darren Wilson for the shooting death of black eighteen-year-old Michael Brown. In the crowd were many protestors as naïve as Porter had been. Also in the crowd were leftist agitators eager to see Wilson go uncharged. After all, what earthly good would Wilson do them in jail?

The Soviets called the practice "framing"—that is, taking a small kernel of truth and rewriting the history of a person or an event around it.[2] In Ferguson, that small kernel was the testimony of Brown's partner in crime, Dorian Johnson. Immediately after the shooting, Johnson told all who would listen that Brown raised his hands to surrender before Wilson shot him dead in a Ferguson street. The story could not withstand the least bit of scrutiny.

"It seems hard to come to any other conclusion," the *Washington Post* finally conceded some months later, "than that Dorian Johnson's version is simply made up."[3] The Department of Justice eventually came to the same conclusion. "There is no evidence upon which prosecutors can rely to disprove Wilson's stated subjective belief that he feared for his safety," read its March 2015 report.[4] In fact, Brown attacked Wilson in his car and then charged him when told to stop. For the agitators, however, Johnson's kernel trumped Wilson's testimony, the corroborating testimony of a half dozen black eyewitnesses, the forensic evidence, and the cautious judgment of a multiracial grand jury. Even while Brown's body lay sprawled on Canfield Drive, activists were rehearsing his neighbors in the "Hands up, don't shoot" gesture. With the help of an obliging media, this thoroughly corrupt iconography swept the world.

The seeds of Ferguson were planted ninety years earlier when Joseph Stalin took control of the Soviet apparatus. More of a realist than Lenin, Stalin had no delusions that either the international propaganda arm of the Communist Party, the Comintern, or the fledgling Communist Party in America could inspire a workers' revolution in America. He focused his American efforts instead, wrote author Stephen Koch, "on discrediting American politics and culture and assisting the growth of

Soviet power elsewhere."[5] For the Soviet experiment to prevail, the American experiment had to yield. The world had to see America through fresh, unblinking eyes, not as the great melting pot, but as a simmering stew of racism and xenophobia.

In 1925 the Comintern found just the victims of American injustice Stalin was looking for in Sacco and Vanzetti, a pair of Italian anarchists justly convicted of murdering an Italian American payroll clerk five years earlier. While their capital murder case worked its way through the appeals process in the Massachusetts courts, the Comintern ginned up a worldwide frenzy around the fate of the convicted killers. "Spontaneous" protests sprang up seemingly everywhere. Europe's great squares—in London, Paris, Rome, Berlin—filled with sobbing, shouting protestors, declaiming the innocence of the immigrant martyrs and denouncing the vile injustice of their persecutors.[6]

The reaction to the Ferguson grand jury decision was eerily similar. Despite Wilson's transparent innocence, hundreds gathered outside the American embassy in London with signs proclaiming "No justice, no peace" and "Solidarity with Ferguson."[7] In Berlin, protestors waved signs that read, "Ferguson is everywhere."[8] In Ferguson, outsiders took to the streets, chanting red standards like, "The only solution is a communist revolution," and, "Turn your guns around and shoot the bosses down!"[9] In Oakland, California, meanwhile, angry mobs shut down the freeways, chanting, "Indict, convict, send these killer cops to jail!"[10] Whereas once the international left contented itself with claiming the guilty innocent, neo-puritans were prepared to claim the innocent guilty, a darker turn altogether.

For progressive activists, Officer Wilson's innocence mattered no more than did Sacco and Vanzetti's guilt. Nearly seventy years after the pair's execution, a California attorney stumbled upon some letters that Upton Sinclair, the esteemed socialist author of *The Jungle*, wrote in 1927, the year the pair was executed. The letters showed Sinclair knew the duo to be guilty even before he published *Boston*, his epic novel about the case. One letter from Sinclair to his attorney,

John Beardsley, told of how Sinclair had met with Fred Moore, the anarchists' attorney, in a Denver motel room.

Moore "sent me into a panic," wrote Sinclair. "Alone in a hotel room with Fred, I begged him to tell me the full truth. . . . He then told me that the men were guilty, and he told me in every detail how he had framed a set of alibis for them." As Sinclair made clear in this and other letters, he went ahead and wrote his book about the convicted anarchists as though they were innocent. "My wife is absolutely certain that if I tell what I believe," Sinclair confided to a friend that same year, "I will be called a traitor to the movement and may not live to finish the book." Sinclair finished the book, and the myth lived on.[11] The fact that America was successfully "framed" as a nation that casually executed innocent shoemakers and fish peddlers because of their ethnicity did not trouble Sinclair enough to come clean.

Comparably, no amount of solid evidence in the Michael Brown shooting would spare Wilson his scarlet *R*. "Whatever the Grand Jury decides," CUNY professor of history Deirdre Owens tweeted, "the people have indicted Darren Wilson and the racist, repressive capitalist state he represents."[12] Or, as Chauncey DeVega wrote on AlterNet, "The absurd, unfathomable, and fantastical story which Wilson spun out of the whole cloth in order to justify killing an unarmed black teenager combines the deepest and ugliest white supremacist stereotypes and fantasies about black folks' humanity."[13]

For all the competition, the scarlet *R* for racism remains the most damning and enduring letter in the neo-puritan catalog. This is so because progressives routinely trace racism to what Barack Obama, among many others, has called "this nation's original sin of slavery."[14] Although slavery has been a feature of almost every economy in almost every era of human history, only America positioned itself as the land of the free and the home of the brave while tolerating it. To reconcile its stated principles with its reality, the nation endured a brutal civil war. That war effectively ended slavery in America, but a century of Jim Crow and a half century of retelling horror stories undid the exculpatory value of the war's human sacrifice. The result was a lingering sense of guilt, especially among those who shaped public opinion. In turn, their repeated professions of the nation's past sins led to a broad questioning by the young and alienated of America's founding principles.

Sensing an opportunity amid this loss of moral authority, progressives chipped away at those principles and challenged standards on any number of fronts—family, faith, love, marriage, language, literature, education, entertainment. For all their moral relativism, however, progressives more than held the line in one area. America, observed Shelby Steele, became "puritanical rather than relativistic around racism."[15] Progressives may have abandoned Christian content, Joseph Bottum argued in an insightful 2014 essay, "The Spiritual Shape of Political Ideas," but they carried forward the spiritual infrastructure of Christianity. "How else can we understand the religious fervor with which white privilege is preached these days," wrote Bottum, "the spiritual urgency with which its proponents describe a universal inherited guilt they must seek out behind even its cleverest masks?"[16] From the neo-puritan perspective, one wrong word, one off-color joke, one garbled explanation stripped away the surface bonhomie and showed the racist, satanic soul beneath.

## LORD OF THE FLIES

The obituaries often tell the tale. As Hawthorne wrote of Hester Prynne, "Over her grave, the infamy that she must carry thither would be her only monument."[17] So it was for Nixon-era secretary of agriculture Earl Butz, the most consequential ag secretary since the Depression. "Earl L. Butz, Secretary Felled by Racial Remark, Is Dead at 98," read the *New York Times* headline on the occasion of Butz's death in 2008.[18] He may well have been the first unsuspecting public figure so branded, but he would not be the last. For all his power outside the zone of decency, Butz had little, if any, pull within. Few Republicans did. In 1976, while on a campaign trip for incumbent president Gerald Ford, Butz told a joke to seatmate Pat Boone.

Sitting behind Butz on the plane was professional snitch John Dean. Although the joke could just as easily have been told about any rural male, Butz specified "coloreds" as those who wanted little more out of life than—in the dainty phrasing of the *New York Times*—"satisfying sex, loose shoes and a warm bathroom." Butz, of course, phrased the joke more artfully, humorously, and crudely.

For his role in helping bring down his boss Richard Nixon, Dean had been awarded a writing gig at *Rolling Stone* magazine. On its pages he promptly ratted out Butz, referring to him as a "cabinet official." The timing did not help Butz. A month to go before the election, the media were quick to dig into Dean's tale and out Butz by name. They and their political allies tattooed the scarlet *R* on Butz's forehead and forced his resignation within days. Said Butz on his departure, "The use of a bad racial commentary in no way reflects my real attitude."[19] The plea for mercy did no good. The ink was indelible. Although Butz would live an eventful thirty-two more years, he would be forever remembered for the scarlet *R*.

In the first sentence of his 1996 obituary, the *New York Times* reminded the reader that "Jimmy the Greek" Snyder had been "fired by CBS Sports for saying that black Americans were better athletes than whites because of physical traits dating back to slavery." Eight years before his death, an inebriated Snyder volunteered to a reporter his explanation for black athletic superiority. "During the slave period," said Snyder artlessly, "the slave owner would breed his big black with his big woman so that he could have a big black kid —that's where it all started." CBS immediately fired Snyder.[20]

Other reporters promptly piled on. At the squeamishly race-conscious *New York Times*, in a column hounding the NFL to hire a black coach, George Vecsey conceded that "blacks excel" in sports like football and basketball, but instead of proposing an alternate theory as to why that was so, he extrapolated from Snyder's remark a racist slam on black intelligence.[21] Snyder meant no such thing. He had no known history of racism. And yet one inelegant comment was enough to kill his career and send him to the grave with the scarlet *R* pinned to the coffin. There was much more to the man than that. In the sixteenth of seventeen paragraphs in his obituary, the *Times* noted, "The Snyders lost three children to cystic fibrosis."[22] There, one suspects, was the real story of Jimmy the Greek, but that news was apparently not fit to print.

Two years after Snyder died a marked man, Al Campanis did as well. The *Times* summed up its take on Campanis's life in the headline "Al Campanis Is Dead at 81; Ignited Baseball over Race."[23] The headline compressed Campanis's entire life into one awkward moment. A Greek immigrant, Campanis graduated from New York University, served in the Navy, and then began his long career in baseball. In 1946, in fact, he played with Jackie Robinson on the Dodgers' Montreal farm team and was among his most vocal defenders. Later, as a scout and manager in the Dodgers' system, he was known as a "Rickey man," an acolyte of the pioneering civil rights executive who signed Robinson.

On April 6, 1987, baseball's opening day and the fortieth anniversary of Robinson's debut, Ted Koppel of ABC's *Nightline* interviewed the then seventy-year-old Campanis on air. Koppel asked Campanis why baseball then had no black managers or general managers and suggested, in good liberal fashion, the answer was prejudice. "No, I don't believe it's prejudice," said Campanis. "I truly believe that they may not have some of the necessities to be, let's say, a field manager or perhaps a general manager."

Some of Campanis's following remarks suggest the confusion of age. At one point, for instance, he said of black athletes, "They certainly are short." After a commercial break, Koppel gave Campanis a chance to dig himself out. "I have never said that blacks are not intelligent," he told Koppel. "I think many of them are highly intelligent. But they may not have the desire to be in the front office." He added, "But they're outstanding athletes, very God-gifted, and they're wonderful people." So saying, Campanis ended his career in baseball. He apologized the next day for his "inability, under the circumstances, to express accurately

[his] beliefs," but no one was listening. Dodger owner Peter O'Malley forced his resignation the day after that, and O'Malley's fellow owners, none of whom employed blacks as managers or general managers, dutifully recorded their disgust. "This is the saddest moment of my career," Campanis said at the time.[24] In an instant, a lifetime of good work was erased for his failure to understand that in the neo-puritanical age, good works don't count. Only the profession of faith does. And in the faith department, Campanis had failed to keep current.

Although the *Times* has not yet had the opportunity to publish their obituaries, there are several Americans whose signature achievement, the *Times* will tell its readers, was the scarlet *R*. Southern cooking celebrity Paula Deen earned hers by referring to a bank robber who put a gun to her head as a "nigger." She did not say this in public. She admitted to it only in a deposition years later. "No one would feel favorable toward a man holding a gun to their head," preached a *Salon* editorial the day after the story broke. "But one sin, however more grave, should not justify another."[25] That "sin" cost Deen her cookery programs, publishing deals, and multiple endorsement contracts.

Something of a taboo smasher, Don Imus was fired from an early radio job for saying "hell" on the air, but as the Associated Press acknowledged, "in what became a continuing pattern—the controversy only boosted his profile and career prospects." In 2007 the veteran shock jock discovered that not all controversies boost careers. Misreading the lay of the land, Imus referred to the women's basketball team at Rutgers University as a bunch of "nappy headed hos,"[26] a term he claimed was common parlance in the world of hip-hop.

The now mandatory neo-puritan apology tour took Imus quickly to the studios where Al Sharpton hosted his own nationally syndicated radio show. This was the same Sharpton who dissed the work of "Socrates and them Greek homos"; the same Sharpton who instigated the lethal Crown Heights pogrom with the rallying cry, "If Jews want to get it on, tell them to pin their yarmulkes back and come over to my house";[27] and yes, the same Al Sharpton who called Imus's comments "abominable" and "racist" and stood in judgment over him.

"Our agenda is to be funny and sometimes we go too far. And this time we went way too far," whimpered Imus, but Sharpton was not in a merciful mood. He informed Imus that regardless of what his intentions were, his actions had "set a precedent" and that if he were to walk away from the incident "unscathed," others might be tempted to do something comparable. To make sure this did not happen, Sharpton promised to lean on the FCC and Imus's sponsors.[28] CBS radio, Imus's employer, responded the same day by suspending Imus for two weeks.[29] That move did nothing to appease the vengeful neo-puritan clerisy. Two days later, under pressure now from feminists as well as black groups, CBS fired Imus. "He says he wants to be forgiven. I hope he continues in that process," said Sharpton. Jesse Jackson, who once referred to New York City as "Hymietown," called the firing "a victory for public decency."[30]

In 2014 Los Angeles Clippers owner Donald Sterling became very nearly a household word for telling his mistress something about not wanting to see her in the presence of black men. "She blindfolded him and spun him around until he was just blathering all sorts of incoherent racist sound bites that had the news media peeing themselves with glee," said basketball legend Kareem Abdul-Jabbar.[31]

The Abdul-Jabbar op-ed was among the fair-minded few. Sports-oriented progressives who had found mercy in their hearts for dog killers, wife beaters, child deserters, child beaters, lethal DUI drivers, steroid abusers, cocaine addicts, serial baby daddies, and abortion enablers could not spare a drop of it for this cuckolded old sugar daddy whose comments on race had been so teased out of him that they were impossible to quote in any meaningful way. "The man who poisoned the Los Angeles Clippers for nearly thirty years with his ignorance and hate," sermonized the *LA Times* Bill Plaschke all too typically, "has at last been dragged away into sweet oblivion."[32]

President Obama interrupted a critical foreign tour of Malaysia to denounce Sterling's "incredibly offensive racist statements," whatever they were exactly. Lest anyone overlook the origins of Sterling's unseemly comments, Obama added, "The United States continues to wrestle with the legacy of race and slavery and segregation."[33] With the scarlet *A* having long ago lost its power to shame, Obama failed to mention that Sterling had publicly humiliated his wife of nearly sixty years and the mother of his three children. In a thoughtful essay, "Virtues, Past & Present," writer Jonathan Last took note. "It was mentioned nowhere as a defect of Sterling's character," wrote Last of Sterling's infidelity. "His private, whispered racist thoughts, however, were important enough to elicit the displeasure of the leader of the free world."[34] Not to excuse the racist comments, but it's just telling what are the accepted sins of the day.

Sterling must have had some sense of how the neo-puritans rolled. To keep the race hustlers at bay, he had been buying indulgences for years. Leon Jenkins, the Los Angeles branch NAACP president, observed that Sterling's organization "brought in numerous minorities and inner city kids to games" and also "contributed to a lot of minority charities, including the NAACP."[35] Sterling's largesse netted him an NAACP Lifetime Achievement award in 2009 and another one—almost—in 2014. Sterling's contributions, however, were too limited and too local to secure him a permanent place in the decency zone. Newsroom scolds found him more entertaining than useful. "They caught big game on a slow news day," said Abdul-Jabbar of the media, "so they put his head on a pike, dubbed him Lord of the Flies, and danced around him whooping."[36]

## FLAMES OF HATE

In the decades that followed the executions of Sacco and Vanzetti and preceded Ferguson, the hard left produced any number of racial dramas with conspicuously guilty ethnics as martyr heroes—Jewish atom bomb spies Julius and Ethel Rosenberg, the American Indian FBI-killer Leonard Peltier, and the radical black Philadelphia cop-killer Mumia Abu-Jamal among others. Tracing the inspiration for a particular leftist cause célèbre, however, has never been easy. In the Soviet world, claimed Romanian Lt. Gen. Ion Mahai Pacepa, lying was a policy of the state. Pacepa knew whereof he spoke. Before defecting to the West, he had been chief of Romania's intelligence service. The strategy the Soviets used to sell a lie they called *dezinformatsiya*, "disinformation." Pacepa described it as "a secret intelligence tool, intended to bestow a Western nongovernment cachet on government lies."[37] In other words, Western liberals made better propagandists than KGB operatives.

The strategy, like the Kremlin's intelligence service, has outlived the Soviet Union. A testament to its immortality was the church-burning hysteria of 1996. In February of that year, the NAACP sent a letter to Bill Clinton's attorney general, Janet Reno, asking her to investigate what the *Washington Post* innocently described as "a string of suspicious fires at predominantly black churches." In one charred Tennessee church, police allegedly found racial slurs spray-painted on the walls. "For many people," said the *Post* reporter, "the attacks conjured up dark memories of the most violent days of the civil rights movement."[38]

The two groups pushing this story from the beginning were the National Council of Churches (NCC) and the Center for Democratic Renewal (CDR). To give the story legs, they held a joint press conference in March 1996 at which they released a report on the "huge increase" in black church burnings. Said the Reverend Mac Charles Jones, a CDR board member, "You're talking about a well-organized white-supremacist movement."[39] From there, the story took wing, generating more than two thousand articles in the next three months, including three huge layouts on consecutive days in *USA Today*, a two-page spread in the *New York Times*, and incendiary headlines like the following from the *New York Daily News*: "Flames of Hate: Racism Blamed in Shock Wave of Church Burnings." The good guys in the *Daily News* story were, of course, the CDR and the NCC. Readers learned that these two groups had put aside their radical activism for a moment to team up on the "investigation." Said CDR program director Rose Johnson none too subtly of the alleged suspects, "Every arrest has been of a white male, age 15 to 45."[40]

Historically, Soviet intelligence had been content to pin the scarlet *R* on America, writ large. By 1996 homegrown Marxists were employing a comparable strategy, but with more precision, both in targeting and messaging. In fact, the CDR had evolved out of an outfit called the National Anti-Klan Network (NAKN), a group described by the radical publication *Workers Vanguard* as a loose coalition of Southern ministers and "the remnants of the pro-Peking Stalinists." According to its own literature at the time, the CDR worked "with progressive activists and organizations to build a movement to counter right-wing rhetoric and public-policy initiatives." The NCC was one such progressive organization. Pacepa identified the NCC as an affiliate of the World Council of Churches, an organization that had been "infiltrated and effectively controlled by Russian intelligence since 1961." Not one for hyperbole, Pacepa described the NCC and CDR as "two secretly Marxist organizations headquartered in the United States."[41]

As the church-burning saga unfolded, the targets of choice became increasingly obvious. "There's only a slippery slope between conservative religious persons and those that are really doing the burning," said Reverend C. T. Vivian, the CDR's chairman.[42] According to the *New York Times*, Vivian's take on things was pretty much the norm among black church leaders, Jesse Jackson included. For the seemingly hostile atmosphere in the South, they blamed "the assault on affirmative action and the populist oratory of Republican politicians like Patrick J. Buchanan."[43]

This was an election year, after all. President Clinton, up for reelection, used his June 10, 1996, radio address to warn America of the "disturbing rash of crimes that hearkens back to a dark era in our nation's history." Lest anyone think that he, as an Arkansas native, had anything to do with that dark history, he reminded the audience, "I have vivid and painful memories of black churches being burned in my own state when I was a child." Although uncertain as to whether there was a national conspiracy afoot, Clinton assured his radio audience that "racial hostility" was the driving force behind the outbreak. He then praised the NCC—the CDR's red roots were too obvious—for raising awareness and concluded with a grand if garbled metaphor, "We must come together, black and white alike, to smother the fires of hatred that fuel this violence."[44]

Of course this was all nonsense. Clinton was a senior at segregated Hot Springs High during the hottest year of the civil rights era, 1964, the year of the "Mississippi Burning" incident. More problematic for the Clinton narrative was that the *Arkansas Democrat-Gazette* could find no record of any black church being burned in Arkansas during that time. Retired state Supreme Court justice Jim Johnson spoke for many of his fellow Razorbacks when he defied Clinton to name at least "one black church which has been burned in the state of Arkansas or else apologize for the shame which you continue to bring to your native state!"[45]

In reality the epidemic of racist church burnings proved as fanciful as Clinton's memories. A month after Clinton's radio address, Fred Bayles of the Associated Press reported his agency's analysis of six years of federal, state, and local data. What Bayles and colleagues discovered was that there had been more fires at predominantly white churches in the South than black churches, that the totals for 1996 were within the normal range, that the numbers of fires had dropped off considerably since 1980, and that there was "no evidence . . . of a conspiracy or of a general climate of hatred."[46] The suspected arsonists included blacks and whites, insurance scammers, devil worshippers, drunken teenagers, and even bored firefighters.

Unfortunately, the media were not inclined to unspin the yarn they had been gleefully spinning all spring and summer. Reporter Michael Fumento, who helped expose the fraud in the *Wall Street Journal* and elsewhere, concluded that it was apparently "too much to expect any of the pundits and public figures who seized on the CDR's report as a vehicle for scoring points against their political opponents to register the fact that it was in essence a fabrication." The *Times*, for instance, mentioned the church burnings in more than one hundred stories but declined to mention the correctives introduced by the Associated Press, the *Wall Street Journal*, or any other responsible party.[47]

So the narrative stood through November. Racist church burners were still terrorizing black America. Church burners and conservative Republicans were cut from the same white sheets. And all that stood between the terrorized Southern blacks and the Republican night riders was a stalwart Democratic president. The strategy worked well enough. Bill Clinton got seven black votes for every one of Republican Bob Dole's, and the National Council of Churches raised a bundle of money. As to the Republicans, they were assigned the scarlet *R* for another four years—and counting.

## RACIST NEANDERTHALS

When it emerged out of nowhere in 2009, the tea party movement caught the left off guard. According to time-honored leftist lore, the Republican Party was the party of the rich. Everyday Americans naturally flocked to the various progressive banners. But that, very publicly, was not happening. Worse, the tea party people were not talking about social issues, let alone race. They were talking about the debt and health care and limited constitutional government. Democrats and their media allies knew they had to discredit the movement but, initially at least, were not quite sure how. They would figure it out soon enough.

In a thoughtful 2010 editorial for Politico, tea party activists Jenny Beth Martin and Mark Meckler summarized the shifting nature of the assault on their movement. "First, members of the tea party movement were called disgruntled voters," wrote the pair, "then House Speaker Nancy Pelosi (D-Calif.) said our movement was nothing more than 'astroturf' and laughed us off as a flash in the pan that would disappear overnight. Next the Democratic National Committee released an ad calling us an 'angry mob.' Now, we're being called racist."[48]

In an oddly candid moment during a 2010 Politico chat session, the leftist former chair of the US Commission on Civil Rights, Mary Frances Berry, confirmed Martin and Meckler's suspicions. After conceding there was "no evidence" the tea party was any more racist than any other group, Berry opined that it was an "effective strategy for Democrats" to taint the movement as racist nonetheless. "Having one's opponent rebut charges of racism is far better than discussing joblessness," said Berry.[49] As hard as progressives worked the race angle, they had little proof of the same. They had so little, in fact, that one member of the Congressional Black Caucus was reduced to citing—as his best evidence—a sign that showed "a Hitler-like mustache on President Obama."[50]

Frustrated, the Democrats in Congress decided to try a little hands-on agitprop of their own. In the way of background, the early Soviets coined the word *agitprop* as a blend between the Russian *agitatsiya* (agitation) and "propaganda." Russian intelligence kept the technique alive even after the collapse of the Soviet Union, but by this time the American left was fully capable of improvising on its own, nowhere more insidiously than at the nation's Capitol on March 20, 2010.

The occasion was a tea party–style rally protesting the impending congressional vote on the Affordable Care Act, better known as Obamacare. Although members of Congress almost always take the tunnel to get from the Cannon House Office Building to the Capitol and back, that afternoon a few members of the Black Caucus, including Rep. Andre Carson of Indiana and civil rights icon Rep. John Lewis, chose to walk through the gathered crowds. They left the Cannon House Building for the Capitol about two thirty. At the Capitol, Carson, one of only two Muslims in Congress and a member of the Progressive Caucus, told reporters what happened en route. Fortunately, the audio exists.

As Carson explained, he and Lewis were "walking down the steps" of the Cannon Office Building when they heard 'n-word, n-word,' at least fifteen times, hundreds of people." Eventually, said Carson, Capitol Police became aware of the slurs and offered the group protection. When questioned on specifics, Carson reduced the hundreds of people to "maybe fifteen," who were shouting "Kill the bill, then the n-word."[51] Added Carson for dramatic flair, "Yeah, I expected rocks to come."[52] On the return to the Cannon House Office Building from the Capitol at about 3:15 p.m., a larger contingent of the Black Caucus chose to avoid the tunnel, hoping to provoke anew Carson's racist, would-be rock throwers. They also carried at least three video cameras among them.

This was the "agitation" part. As the numerous videos of the walk showed, the Black Caucus members passed without violence, threats of violence, or even shouted profanity. In the group was Rep. Emanuel Cleaver (D-MO), the chair of the Black Caucus. He and his colleagues walked unmolested up the Cannon steps until an inattentive Cleaver, flanked by a white female police officer, passed right in front of a man shouting, "Kill the bill!" through cupped hands.

The shouter "allowed saliva to hit my face," Cleaver would later tell the *Washington Post*.[53] Visibly angry, he poked his finger in the man's face. About a minute after the incident, Cleaver returned to the scene of the presumed crime with a black male police officer. As the video made embarrassingly clear, Cleaver failed to recognize the man who was still shouting, "Kill the bill." Cleaver and the officer then headed back up the steps.[54]

At 4:51 p.m., fewer than ninety minutes after the group's return to the Cannon Building, William Douglas, a black reporter for the liberal McClatchy Company, a prominent newspaper publisher, posted a story that would have made Lenin proud. Its inflammatory headline read, "Tea party protesters scream 'nigger' at black congressman."[55] In those ninety minutes, Douglas—with an assist from James Rosen—had been able to interview Rep. Barney Frank, Cleaver, Lewis, and an unnamed colleague, write an eight-hundred-word article, and post it. That the headline was false in every detail would not deter an increasingly partisan media from spreading the libel and amplifying it. This was the propaganda part of agitprop.

When interviewed, Lewis told Douglas he heard protestors shouting, "Kill the bill! Kill the bill!" Lewis responded to the protestors, "I said, 'I'm for the bill, I support the bill, I'm voting for the bill.'" In his very next line, Douglas referred to Carson not by name but as "a colleague" who accompanied Lewis. Carson reportedly told Douglas that he heard

"Kill the bill, then the n-word." Douglas immediately followed the "colleague" quote with the following:

> It surprised me that people are so mean and we can't engage in a civil dialogue and debate," Lewis said.
>
> Rep. Emanuel Cleaver, D-Mo., said he was a few yards behind Lewis and distinctly heard "nigger."
>
> "It was a chorus," Cleaver said. "In a way, I feel sorry for those people who are doing this nasty stuff—they're being whipped up. I decided I wouldn't be angry with any of them."

Given the video and audio evidence, one can see Douglas's reporting for the agitprop it was. Lewis never heard the word "nigger." If he had, Douglas surely would have shared that quote with the reader. Curiously, Douglas quoted Carson on the most lethal of the slurs but attributed the quote only to "a colleague." Had he cited Carson by name, he would have entered into evidence Carson's preposterous audiotaped claim about crowds of screaming bigots. Instead, Douglas slid the accusatory burden onto Cleaver, who claimed to have heard one person say, "nigger" one time, a claim that would have been much harder to disprove. Douglas then took Cleaver's "chorus" quote and made it sound as though he heard a chorus of racial slurs when surely Cleaver said no such thing.

Douglas also implied that Cleaver was walking with Lewis from the Cannon Office Building to the Capitol when this happened, but he was not. Cleaver accompanied Lewis only on the way back, which suggests that there should be evidence of racial slurs both coming and going. Publisher Andrew Breitbart offered a one-hundred-thousand-dollar reward for such a video, but he got no takers.

At 5:41 p.m. on that Saturday, March 20, Brian Beutler of *Talking Points Memo* cranked up the agitprop meter with a story headlined, "Tea Partiers Call Lewis 'N****r.'" Beutler, a recent Berkeley grad and a leftist, named Carson as his source. Carson claimed to have been standing next to Lewis when they encountered a large crowd of protesters screaming,

"Kill the bill." Several times, added Carson, the protestors "punctuat[ed] their chants with the word 'nigger.'" Carson's charge so defied the reality of life in America circa 2010 that Beutler should have sought confirmation. He did not get it from Lewis. Lewis was only quoted as saying, "People have been just downright mean."[56]

At 7:21 p.m. that same evening, not to be bested in the propaganda sweepstakes, Douglas responded with a new posting, "Tea party protesters call Georgia's John Lewis 'nigger.'" Again, Lewis failed to confirm the slur. "They were shouting, sort of harassing," Lewis told Douglas. What they shouted, Douglas reported, was "Kill the bill! Kill the bill!"[57] The headline hinged on the accusations of the still unnamed "colleague" and on Cleaver, but Cleaver was showing himself to be almost comically unreliable.

That afternoon Cleaver's office had put out a press release saying that Cleaver had been spat upon. "The man who spat on the congressman was arrested, but the congressman has chosen not to press charges," read the release.[58] This was all inarguably false. "There were no elements of a crime, and the individual wasn't able to be positively identified," Sgt. Kimberly Schneider of the US Capitol Police would tell Fox News.[59] The video clearly supported the police. Although a Cleaver spokeswoman claimed Cleaver chose not to identify the man lest the police be "obligated" to arrest him, the video showed a clueless Cleaver unable to identify the same guy shouting through the same cupped hands he had seen a minute earlier.

None of this mattered to Cleaver's champions at the *Kansas City Star*, a McClatchy paper. On March 21, *Star* editorial page columnist Yael T. Abouhalkah made the toxic claim that "some tea party supporter spat on Cleaver Saturday on Capitol Hill *because* the U.S. congressman is black" (emphasis added). To gin up the racial tension a wee bit more, Abouhalkah repeated as fact the canard that "someone spat on [Cleaver], while the word 'nigger' was used to describe Cleaver and other black congressmen."[60]

Even after it became apparent to anyone who cared to know that

Carson and pals made the whole thing up, the media's heaviest hitters continued to pound away at the tea party. A few days after the incident, Cleaver himself spoke to *Washington Post* Metro columnist Courtland Milloy about the man "who allowed saliva to hit [his] face." Said Milloy of the protestors, "I want to spit on them, take one of their 'Obama Plan White Slavery' signs and knock every racist and homophobic tooth out of their Cro-Magnon heads."[61] And to think that just two years earlier dissent was patriotic.

Maureen Dowd of the *New York Times* preferred the term "racist Neanderthals" to "Cro-Magnon," both slurs being safe because they refer to long-dead white men. From Dowd's perch, three congressmen, including Andre Carson, whom she named, heard "a racial epithet."[62] Bob Herbert, also of the *Times*, did not name Carson but reported that two black congressmen endured the "vilest of epithets."[63] Both claimed Cleaver had been spit on despite the visual evidence to the contrary. Frank Rich of the *Times* made the same claim, although he preferred "goons" to "Neanderthals" and "venomous slurs" to Dowd's dainty "racial epithet." In an unhinged bit of hyperbole, Rich summed up the protest as "a small-scale mimicry of Kristallnacht."[64] Small-scale indeed: Kristallnacht was a Nazi-sanctioned rampage that saw a thousand synagogues burned, seven thousand businesses destroyed, and hundreds of Jews murdered. The unsanctioned protest on Capitol Hill saw one congressman sprayed unintentionally with saliva.

It was left to MSNBC's Keith Olbermann to pin the scarlet *R* on the tea party's chest. "If racism is not the whole of the tea party," pontificated Olbermann, "it is in its heart."[65]

## HUMAN STAIN

The former dean at the fictional Athena University in western Massachusetts was pleased to be back in the classroom. To acquaint himself with the names of his students, Prof. Coleman Silk took attendance at the beginning of each class. When, after several weeks, he had gotten no sign of recognition from two names on his list, he asked the students,

"Does anyone know these people? Do they exist or are they spooks?"

So wrote Pulitzer Prize–winning novelist Phillip Roth in his 1998 novel, *Human Stain*. As Silk would soon learn, he had uttered "the single self-incriminating word of the many millions spoken aloud in his years of teaching and administering at Athena." Unknown to Silk, the two absent students were black. When they got wind of what he had said in class, they immediately petitioned the dean for redress. Silk pled his innocence, "I was referring to their possibly ectoplasmic character. Isn't that obvious?"[66] Of course, it was obvious, but it did not matter. This fictional dean, like almost all figures of authority everywhere, wilted in the face of racial outrage and forced Silk's resignation.

Roth's story resonated in no small part because Coleman Silk, like so many real-life victims of neo-puritan rage, had done nothing to merit punishment. What made Silk's situation more intriguing was that he had been born into a black family and had been passing for Jewish since his transformative days in the Navy. Sometimes, Roth instructed the reader, one's race does not provide adequate protection against neo-puritan fervor. One's innocence almost never does. The "human stain" of racism, the nation's original sin, spares no American. For a career liberal like Roth, this was a stunning admission.

The litany of accusations against presumed racists in real universities makes the charge against the fictional Silk sound downright substantial. At UCLA, racial tensions were "inflamed" because a professor corrected the grammar in the papers of minority students. In November 2013, a group called "Call 2 Action: Graduate Students of Color" staged a sit-in to protest Prof. Val Rust's "micro aggression."[67]

There was more "micro aggression"—yes, by that name—at the UCLA Law School. Apparently, unthinking white students caused great offense that same stormy November by wearing T-shirts with the wording "Team Sander." Law professor Richard Sander, it seems, had written a book titled *Mismatch: How Affirmative Action Hurts Students It's Intended to Help*. For minority activists, to question racial preferences was to demand a scarlet *R*. "Can you imagine this happening in the reverse?" wrote one such student. "Can you imagine a law school saying, 'We're pleased to announce that Louis Farrakhan has joined our faculty.'?"[68] For the record, the law students wore the "Team Sander" T-shirts because they played on Sander's softball team. From the activists' perspective, they may as well have been wearing white hoods.

Meanwhile, up the coast, students had been petitioning Stanford University to can Hearst visiting professor Joel Brinkley. Brinkley's Pulitzer Prize and twenty-five years' experience as a *New York Times* foreign correspondent could not secure him immunity from the prick of campus pitchforks. His sin was writing an article for the *Chicago Tribune* in January 2013 on the esoteric and seemingly innocuous topic of Vietnamese dietary habits. "Animal trafficking explains the dearth of tigers, elephants and other big beasts. But what about birds and rats?" wrote Brinkley. "Yes, people eat those, too, like almost every animal that lives there."[69] Brinkley, who had recently visited Vietnam, traced the people's seeming aggression to their meat eating.

Brinkley had to be surprised by the reaction. His thesis may or may not have been correct, but compared to the professorial gibberish uttered every day on American campuses, it was a model of clear thinking. Students felt otherwise. They accused him of perpetuating "a post-colonial paternalistic attitude towards the Vietnamese people," whatever that meant. In a style so perfectly Maoist it would seem to justify whatever biases Brinkley had, the Vietnamese Student Association demanded he "publicly apologize, and in a highly-visible way, defer to actual experts on Viet Nam to correct his lies."[70] The Asian American Journalists Association supported the students. "Public outrage over the piece is certainly justified," its president wrote.[71] Although Brinkley refused to back down, Tribune Media Services kowtowed to the various pressure groups and issued the desired apology for their esteemed columnist. After seven years at Stanford, Brinkley left at the end of that turbulent year for the relative tranquility of a gig in Afghanistan. He died months later.

"Anger in the oppressed is a response to perceived opportunity, not to injustice," observed Shelby Steele.[72] And nowhere is the opportunity more abundant than at an American university. Liberal white guilt hovers over the campus like smog, and administrators reach the top only by acclimating. When racial issues arise in this environment, professors and students alike can be confident of only one thing: no one has their back. Although the examples above, real and fictional, may seem amusing from a distance, up close they can be terrifying, and no amount of good works can save the designated sinner.

If the faculty at Georgia Southern University had voted for the administrator least likely to earn a scarlet *R* it would have been their president, Dale Lick. His tenure there had been, in the words of one black scholar, "the most progressive period in the history of the college."[73] After nearly a decade at Georgia Southern, in 1986 the ambitious Lick was named president of the University of Maine. At Maine, Lick made some enemies, including history professor and future blogger Howard Segal. In a 2013 posting, Segal cited a laundry list of petty grievances against Lick that would have excited no one beyond the faculty lounge. Segal took particular exception to what he called Lick's "supreme self-confidence." This stemmed in part, said the disgruntled prof, from Lick's "strong religious beliefs as a lay preacher with a sense of divine approval."[74]

Lick's faith and self-confidence may have irritated Segal, but they did not diminish the demand for his services. He had, in fact, earned enough respect within the academic world to survive the offhanded comments he made in 1989 at a student senate meeting. When asked why black athletes seemed to dominate the university's football and basketball programs, Lick told the truth as he knew it. Citing research by a retired Georgia Southern physical education dean, Lick answered, "A black athlete can actually out-jump a white athlete on the average, so they're better at that game. The same is true for football. The muscle structure of the black athlete typically is more suited for certain positions in football and in basketball."[75]

Lick did well to qualify his answer with the phrases "on the average" and "typically," but there was no denying the real-world evidence. As a case in point, all fifty-six finalists in the last seven Olympic men's 100-meter races have been of West African descent. By the laws of chance, flipping a coin and getting "heads" fifty-six straight times would be far more likely. "Running is a natural laboratory for the science of sports," said Jon Entine, director of the Genetics Literacy Project at George Mason University. "It's empirically driven. There are winners and losers. No soft-headed sociological mumbo-jumbo allowed." The dominance of black athletes in sports that put a premium on running, like football and track, or running and jumping, like basketball, has almost nothing positive to do with the athletes' environment, their history, or their storied "lack of other opportunities." In fact, the realities of inner-city life have crushed the dreams of many a would-be star athlete. According to Entine, the dominance of black athletes has almost everything to do with the West African body type: their "generally" narrower hips, lighter calves, higher percentage of fast-twitch muscles, and other physiological factors.[76]

Almost never, however, do facts sway a neo-puritan from his prejudices. To judge from his students' generally dismal comments, Segal would seem to have the whiff of old New England about him. "Extremely liberal with ZERO courtesy to other people's views," said one student. Said another, "Segal is an absolutely awful professor. He spent so many hours brainwashing his students with his outlandish political views that have NO relevance to U.S. History." Said a third student, who actually liked Segal, "He is one of the most bitter men I've ever met. Completely disenchanted with the world and everything remotely associated with it."[77]

The bitterness bled through Segal's blog account on the Lick affair. According to Segal, one of his colleagues "largely denied the scientific veracity" of Lick's claim about black athletes, and Lick was forced to apologize for stating the obvious while still at Maine. As testament to Lick's perceived value, this incident did not derail his career. Soon afterwards, in fact, he accepted the presidency of Florida State University. In 1993, after two years at Florida State, Lick applied for the presidency of Michigan State University, his alma mater. "But FSU still wasn't good enough for Dale Lick," wrote Segal in 2013.[78] Twenty years after Lick's undoing, Segal continued to harbor an unhealthy contempt for his ambition.

If not Segal, some other ghost from Lick's past sabotaged his career. As Segal observed coyly, Lick "nearly got the job until someone at U. Maine apparently informed the MSU search committee of Lick's 1989 remarks." Once the story of Lick's presumed racism went national, Michigan State dropped Lick from atop its short list quicker than you could say, "Earl Butz." At the time, *Sports Illustrated* (*SI*) magazine had the clout to reverse the media momentum. This was, after all, the publication that had jokingly popularized the phrase "white man's disease."

*SI* may have had the clout, but it lacked the cojones. If there were a white man's disease in the sports media, it was the chronic unwillingness to speak honestly about race. If there were a patient zero, writer Jerry Kirshenbaum made for an excellent candidate. "Lick's simplistic remark feeds the stereotype of blacks as physical brutes and whites as thinking beings," huffed Kirshenbaum in an *SI* editorial. "As an educator, he should have known better."[79] Kirshenbaum insisted that "cultural and economic" factors accounted for the disproportionate success of blacks in sports. Strangely, he cited the relative success of whites in volleyball and soccer as proof of Caucasian athletic equality.

With no editorial pressure to keep Lick as president, Florida State decided to dump him as well. In fairness to Florida State, its board members had a legitimate gripe: Lick had discreetly applied for another job after only two years on campus. Still, in the progressive hothouse of academia, only a *New York Times* headline like "Racial Remark Stalls Job Seeker" could guarantee so quick an exit.[80] Likely to avoid litigation and short-circuit bad press, board members quietly agreed to keep Lick on campus as a professor. A chastened Lick had to be glad they did. With this scarlet *R* ablazing, he could forget about becoming president of anything and would have been lucky to get an adjunct gig at Tallahassee Community College.

## XENOPHOBIC CAVEMEN

A generation or two back, reporters were carved out of the same rough American stock as athletes. By century's end, however, most young sports reporters got their wisdom, such as it was, courtesy of America's increasingly liberal journalism schools, and it showed. Indeed, many seemed more eager to showcase their own piety than to talk about sports.

*Sports Illustrated* writer Jeff Pearlman's reporting on Tim Tebow is classic of the neo-puritan genre. When Tebow, then an all-American quarterback at the University of Florida, became eligible for the NFL draft, Pearlman let loose in his blog. "Tim Tebow scares me," he cautioned his readers, "and judging from his father's website and his upcoming Super Bowl ad and mounting knowledge of his way of life, he should scare you, too."[81] For the record, the father's website shows a photo of a smiling group of Philippine orphans and notes that Bob Tebow's goal is "to make the gospel of Jesus Christ available to every person in the world."[82] In the Super Bowl ad, Tebow's mom explains how Tim was a "miracle baby" whom they almost lost at birth. Tebow joins her and says, "Thanks, Mom. Love you too." The ad closed with an appeal to "celebrate family, celebrate life," and that was it. With the help of the fretting Cassandras who feared its "antichoice" message, countless millions watched the ad who might not have otherwise done so.[83]

What scared Pearlman about Tebow was that he did not play football "merely for the joy of the game"—as if anyone in the NFL actually did—but rather "to spread the word of Jesus Christ." The portrait that Pearlman painted of Tebow was that of a hectoring evangelist who, if he failed to convert his audience, would promise them they would "burn in hell." Pearlman concluded, "Some call this faith. I call it f***ing insanity." When he wrote this, Pearlman had access to hundreds of hours of Tebow interviews. A responsible journalist would have watched those interviews or read the transcripts and quoted Tebow fairly. Pearlman did not quote him at all. How could he have? The real Tim Tebow was relentlessly open, positive, and cheerful. He had an unkind word for no one. His teammates at the University of Florida loved him. Instead, Pearlman quoted at length from Bob Tebow's website.

A student of the book of Revelation, the apocalyptic final book of the New Testament, Bob Tebow believes in the end times, at the conclusion of which everyone is to be "judged according to his or her works." Although gender sensitive in his language, Tebow has an old-school belief in the Bible, and he obviously takes his faith seriously. He had dedicated the last thirty years of his life to working with orphans in the Philippines. That Bob Tebow believed in hell, as most Christians and many Jews do, was provocation enough for Pearlman to say of Tim Tebow, "Well, to hell with him."[84]

In 1999 Pearlman took his smug, secular brand of neo-puritanism to Georgia, to interview a rambunctious young Atlanta Braves pitcher whose life he would proceed to turn upside down. At the time, the twenty-five-year-old John Rocker was everything that Tebow was not: cocky, profane, and more than a little bit reckless. At twenty-seven, Pearlman was, in his own words, "an unknown, low-level baseball writer fighting to work my way up the *Sports Illustrated* masthead."[85] As events turned out, he would climb his way to the top on Rocker's back.

Rocker greeted Pearlman warmly when he arrived in Atlanta and took him for a ride in his Chevy Tahoe. "Jesus Christ," said Pearlman, writing about this incident fifteen years later. "The man was driving fast. *Really* fast." Rocker was not a guy to put on airs. He reportedly spit in a machine at a tollbooth that wouldn't take his money. He complained about Asian women drivers. He flipped off a fellow who was beeping at him. He called a second girlfriend after dropping a first girlfriend off. And he explained that the people dressed as cartoon characters at Disney World were all "faggots." In his article, dated April 4, 2014, Pearlman felt free to profane the name of Jesus Christ but felt obliged to render the gay slur as "f---s."

In 1999 neo-puritans had yet to take up the cause of gay rights in a serious way. Just three years earlier, two-thirds of the Democrats in Congress had voted for the Defense of Marriage Act, and a Democratic president had signed it into law. Athletes casually tossed the word *faggot* around the locker room, and sportswriters sloughed it off. The "faggot" remark about Disney World, for instance, did not make it into Pearlman's 1999 *Sports Illustrated* article on Rocker.

What did make it into the magazine would prove troublesome enough. As Rocker explained, he did not much like New Yorkers. "Nowhere else in the country do people spit at you, throw bottles at you, throw quarters at you, throw batteries at you and say, 'Hey, I did your mother last night—she's a whore,'" Rocker reported. Some New Yorkers he liked even less than others. "The biggest thing I don't like about New York are the foreigners. I'm not a very big fan of foreigners," Pearlman quoted Rocker as saying. He particularly did not like taking subways with New Yorkers. "Imagine having to take the [Number] 7 train to the ballpark," said Rocker, "looking like you're [riding through] Beirut next to some kid with purple hair next to some queer with AIDS right next to some dude who just got out of jail for the fourth time right next to some 20-year-old mom with four kids. It's depressing."[86]

In one no-holds-barred paragraph, Rocker insulted just about the entire multicultural pantheon. Although excoriated to this day for his "racist comments,"[87] his more careful critics branded him with the scarlet *X* for "xenophobia." Rocker himself insists he was speaking about illegal immigration and had done so at length with Pearlman. In a phone conversation with me, Rocker had only good things to say about the legal immigration process.[88] If so, Pearlman helped pioneer what would become a mainstay of progressive punditry, namely, calling anyone who protested illegal immigration "anti-immigrant."

Pearlman claimed to have struggled emotionally with whether he should report what he had captured on tape. As he saw it, Rocker was young, dumb, naïve, and quite possibly showing off for a reporter. Given his own worldview, Pearlman could not have struggled too hard. After all, he rationalized, Rocker "was a bigoted, xenophobic caveman, and I felt no need to protect a person with such beliefs."[89]

The interview made Pearlman's career and threw a major wrench into

Rocker's. Mets fans, many of whom surely harbored the same sentiments as Rocker, got a tantalizing taste of the elect's moral mojo and squawked to high heaven for retribution. Major League Baseball, for the first time ever, suspended a player for a speech issue. Jeff Pearlman got a career boost that he still brags about. And John Rocker got handed a scarlet *R*—or, more specifically, a scarlet *X* (the scarlet *H* for "homophobe" had not yet come into fashion)—that he would wear to the end of his days.

Those baseball days would end soon enough. Rocker was out of the league within three years. "Even though I told myself—repeatedly—that his downfall had nothing to do with my piece," wrote Pearlman, "well, I knew it was a lie." Pearlman has confessed to feeling guilty for what he did to Rocker, but, given his hit piece on Tebow, he apparently has not yet come to terms with the chilly narrowness of his neo-puritan heart.

For his part, Rocker laughs off the insinuation that Pearlman killed his career. He told me that he had two very good seasons following the *Sports Illustrated* article and that only a severe shoulder injury derailed him. Over time, that article has become an asset. Rocker started a foundation for homeless vets, and, thanks to Pearlman, the name "John Rocker" opens doors that would not open for players with comparable stats but lesser notoriety. Rocker's notoriety also got him a starring, if short-lived, role on the hit TV show *Survivor*. What continues to perplex Rocker about Pearlman and others like him is that "the cornerstone of liberalism is supposed to be tolerance and acceptance, but these guys practice anything but."

## KNUCKLE-SCRAPING BABOON-MAN

It was in the 1960s that sports reporters in the Pearlman mold began to make their presence felt in America's newsrooms. They introduced progressive concepts like "structural poverty" and "institutional racism" to change the way sports stories were reported. In the traditional hero saga, the individual was expected to overcome hardship and injustice. In the new grievance narrative, he nursed them like grudges.

Declaring those grudges openly and often was the athlete's way of aligning his interests with the media's and announcing his faith as a newly christened denier of the American dream. This shift in storytelling happened just in time to enable the hands-down ugliest instance of racial framing in sports history. Incredibly, the media were about to transform the twelfth child of a one-armed black South Carolina moonshiner into the public face of the Ku Klux Klan.

Although Muhammad Ali and his media acolytes would paint Smokin' Joe Frazier as "the great white hope" and worse, it is hard to imagine a more profoundly African experience in America than Frazier's. His family hailed from Gullah country, outside of Beaufort, South Carolina, the one part of the South most spiritually in touch with the African motherland. Born in 1944, two years after Ali, Joe was helping his father almost full-time by the age of six or seven. "I never had a little boy's life," he would say.[90] This background would count for nothing in the Ali myth.

In June 1957 thirteen-year-old Joe Frazier decided he had had enough education. "The fact is I didn't learn quick, and I didn't learn easy," recalled Frazier. So he quit school and went to work full-time on a series of backbreaking jobs that helped make him the hard man he became. Speaking of Beaufort, he said, "Its attitudes had me wanting to leave there from the time I was a boy." One day, without fanfare, Frazier packed his bags, headed to the Greyhound station, and bought a one-way ticket north on "the dog." "It was 1959," he remembered. "I was fifteen years old and on my own."[91]

In Philadelphia, Frazier laid the groundwork for his own Rocky-like career. In fact, Sylvester Stallone lifted elements of Frazier's story for his Oscar-winning movie, including the Philadelphia location, the morning runs through the streets, the culminating race up the steps of the Philadelphia Museum of Art, and even the carcass punching at the slaughterhouse where Frazier worked.

Compared to Beaufort, Ali's two-parent, two-child, middle-class boyhood in Louisville was pure *Leave It to Beaver*. If Ali never quite convinced himself of his badness or his blackness—two of his great-grandparents were white—he convinced the new generation of sports reporters. As they and their peers infiltrated America's newsrooms, and a less political generation of sportswriters faded away, these young critics increasingly seized control of the cultural apparatus and began to impose their tortured perspective on sports. "These were not boxing fans, they were seekers of the antihero," wrote sportswriter Mark Kram, the one notable exception to the cultural left's monopoly on the Ali story. "What mattered was Ali's style, his desecrating mouth, his beautiful irrationality so like their music."[92]

The one subject on which Ali and the audience truly connected was Vietnam. In refusing the draft—at the orders of the racist Nation of Islam—Ali gave what biographer Mike Marqusee called a "major boost to the anti-war movement." Ali's status as heavyweight champion removed some of the stigma attached to resisters as being unmanly or cowardly. Even more important, he helped dispel the "lily white image of the movement."[93] Here the Ali myth was born.

A rebel Joe Frazier was not. From the perspective of Howard Cosell, the broadcaster most responsible for shaping the Ali myth, Frazier was just "a white man's black man." As a proud Baptist, Frazier had no use for the Nation of Islam, the hateful cult to which Ali belonged. And as a proud American, Frazier thought this "a great country worth defending." Still, he generally liked Ali and kept his reservations to himself during Ali's forced exile from the ring. In fact, he helped Ali get back in. Ali returned the favor by attacking Frazier relentlessly and brutally.

Ali's ring doctor, Ferdie Pacheco, completely misunderstood the media dynamics. Like many of Ali's votaries, he saw Ali's attacks on Frazier as part of an "act," an attempt to build box office. "For one fight," Pacheco observed, "Joe Frazier became white, the public made him the good guy, the white guy."[94] What Frazier understood better than Pacheco, however, was that the "good guy" in this drama was no longer "the white guy." The white people that mattered, the ones who increasingly controlled America's newsrooms, colored Frazier white at

Ali's prodding, and they did this to insult Frazier.

In a divided nation, Ali had assigned an unlikely role to Frazier, that of traitor to his race and titular leader of the forces of racism and reaction, the unholy wearer of the scarlet *T*—for "Tom." With his greater rhetorical skills and his access to a friendly broadcast media, Ali painted Frazier into a corner. "Anybody black who thinks Frazier can whup me is an Uncle Tom," said Ali at the time. "Everybody who's black wants me to keep on winning."[95]

The black media joined in the taunting. *Jet* magazine described Frazier as an "unheralded white-created champion." Even more telling was the slight delivered by future *Today Show* host Bryant Gumbel, then writing for *Black Sport*. Gumbel asked in his headline, "Is Joe Frazier a White Champion in a Black Skin?" Gumbel would later concede that he and his peers saw themselves as "the chosen ones," but what he failed to see was just how intolerant and unmerciful the idea of their "chosenness" was making them.

Moved to anger by the media and Ali, the hard-core faithful threatened Frazier and his family by mail and phone. The police kept a watchful eye on Frazier, his wife, and his children. History had proven that Ali's Muslim colleagues were capable of killing. Even in Philadelphia, the black community turned against the imagined race-traitor. Schoolmates teased Frazier's son, Marvis, that his father was an Uncle Tom. "Young blacks bought the whole hog," wrote the hard-hitting Kram, "not knowing or caring that the Muslims had [Ali] in a choke collar and leash, taking no notice that he had betrayed another hero of large appeal, Malcolm X." The bullying of Frazier's children cut deepest of all. "[Ali] set out to cut me down, and hurt me," wrote Frazier in his autobiography, "the only way he knew how—with his lying, jiving mouth."[97]

The irony, of course, was that in almost every meaningful way, Joe Frazier led a "blacker" life than Ali. Most obviously, Frazier was conspicuously darker. He had proud Gullah roots, a black manager and trainer, and an integrated management team. "I grew up like the black man—he didn't," Frazier would tell *Sports Illustrated*. "I cooked the liquor. I cut the wood. I worked the farm. I lived in the ghetto. Yes, I tommed; when he asked me to help him get a license, I tommed for him. For him!"[98]

Ali and his supporters smeared the people who pulled for Joe Frazier much as they smeared Frazier himself. Fight manager and former sports editor Dave Wolf watched Ali on TV one night with Frazier. "The only people rooting for Joe Frazier," he remembered Ali saying, "are white people in suits, Alabama sheriffs, and members of the Ku Klux Klan." Enraged, Frazier smashed his fist mutely into his hand as he watched. Said Wolf, "It was cruel. That's all."[99]

When Joe Frazier left Philadelphia for New York a few days before "the fight," the first match between the pair in March 1971, five armed detectives escorted him. That was how seriously they took the threats on his life. He and manager Yank Durham had no sooner checked into their hotel than a bomb threat forced them out. When Ali made it to his dressing room before the fight, movie star Burt Lancaster was there to encourage him and shoot a documentary. Ali factotum Bundini Brown kept the atmosphere charged and celebratory. The mood in Frazier's dressing room was all business.

Ali entered the sold-out Madison Square Garden first. Frazier followed. "The roar was inhuman," said Pacheco. "It was a primal scream of anticipation. I've never heard such a sound." After fifteen savage rounds, the decision was unanimous. Frazier raised his hands in victory, thanked the Lord, and with a bloody mouth, sneered at Ali, "I kicked your ass." Referee Arthur Mercante thought it the most vicious fight he had ever seen. Kram called it the "most skillful." And by all accounts, it was the most dramatic. "I was twenty-seven years old, and there would never be another night like it in my life," remembered Frazier. He spent the next three weeks in the hospital.[100]

A more just world would have celebrated Frazier as the "Cinderella Man" of his era. From the beginning, however, careful observers knew the story wasn't going to play out that way. "Joe's such a decent guy," veteran black trainer Eddie Futch said of Frazier before the fight, "but when he beats [Ali], Joe is going to go down as one of the most unpopular black champions of all time." Futch was right as rain. The image of Frazier and his fans has not appreciated much over time. "The people who wanted [Frazier] to beat Ali," wrote self-declared "Marxist" Marqusee in 2005, "were the die-hard racists, the love-it-or-leave-it brigade, the people who resented everything Ali stood for."[101] A more reflective Bryant Gumbel would admit years later, "Joe Frazier became the symbol of our oppressors."[102]

After Frazier lost the title to George Foreman, and Ali won the title back from Foreman, Ali continued to taunt and humiliate Frazier. This persecution reached its nasty peak in the buildup to the pair's third and final fight, "the Thrilla in Manila." Even before arriving in Manila, Ali had determined how best to undermine Frazier's confidence. "He'd had me as a white man for the first two [fights]," recalled Frazier, "and now he was going to make me a cartoon of a nigger, a knuckle-scraping baboon-man. Gorilla. Frazier the gorilla." Or as Ali phrased it, "It will be a killer and a chiller and a thrilla when I get the gorilla in Manila."[103]

As *Sports Illustrated*'s main boxing reporter during Ali's career, Mark Kram got to see just how unfunny this ritual defamation had become. He recounted one chilling episode before the Manila fight in a gym packed with Ali fans. As Kram reported, after leading the frenzied crowd in chants of "The Greatest," Ali threw out the word "gorilla" and incited the audience to respond. "Joe Frazier," yelled one white guy. "Ape! Ape!" shouted a young blond woman. "Jist niggers," screamed a black guy. "Ain't that the truth," said Ali to the last comment, dropping to his haunches. "Gorilla," he howled now. "Ugly and smelly." As Ali lurched, apelike, around the ring, his fans jeered the mock Frazier much in the way the Parisian rabble might have jeered Quasimodo.[104]

For the one-fourth white Ali and his fans, Joe Frazier was both too black and not black enough. "A little old nigger boy from Philadelphia," said Ali, "who never had a thought in his dumb head 'cept for himself." Even if there were an appropriate response, Frazier had no microphone. By this stage in his career, Ali owned the media. The psychic blows from this relentless assault bruised Frazier more deeply than all the punches of all the fights he ever fought. "While the public found it amusing, I guess, and came to view [Ali] as a good guy," remembered Frazier, "I knew different."[105] Kram excepted, the media chose not to know at all. As time passed, they would elevate Ali to near sainthood. As for Joe Frazier, they would remember him, when they bothered, as roadkill along the way.

## RACIAL PORNOGRAPHY

"Intellectual fashion has dictated that all differences [between races] must be denied except the absolute undeniable differences in appearance."[106] So wrote authors Richard Herrnstein and Charles Murray in their controversial 1994 best seller, *The Bell Curve*. Within days of the book's publication, Murray would learn that on the left denial was more than just fashion. It was dogma.

Although they pride themselves on their openness to science and mock the right for being closed, progressives have made several fields of inquiry all but taboo. Herrnstein and Murray knew this to be so, but they proceeded on their book project in open defiance of the orthodoxy. "It is possible to face all the facts on ethnic and race differences in intelligence and not run screaming from the room," the authors had written hopefully.[107] It was possible. It just didn't happen.

Unlike Murray, Herrnstein had firsthand experience with the would-be taboo enforcers. As a psychology professor at Harvard in 1971, he dared to write an essay for the *Atlantic Monthly* asserting that intelligence was largely inherited. He followed that up with a book on the same theme in 1973, *I.Q. and Meritocracy*. "Because of his views," the *New York Times* would report matter-of-factly in his obituary, "Dr. Herrnstein was often harassed in the early 1970s and his classes at Harvard were disrupted by student protesters."[108]

Despite the occasional rough spot, Herrnstein enjoyed a fruitful thirty-six-year career at Harvard, where he would end his days as the Edgar Pierce Professor of Psychology. Try as they might, his foes never quite branded him with the scarlet *R*. His position at Harvard protected him. So did his background as the son of Jewish immigrants from Hungary, not the kind of stock from which the Klan typically recruits. Then too as one of his colleagues said upon Herrnstein's death, "He understood and honored data."[109] The *Times* headlined his September 1994 obituary, "Richard Herrnstein, 64, Dies; Backed Nature over Nurture." Had Herrnstein died just a month later, the *Times* might not have been so merciful.

October 1994 was the month *The Bell Curve* debuted. Herrnstein had been an equal partner in the book's creation. Had he lived, he would have had to share in the fury that followed the book's release. As it was, Murray had to face it alone. The abuse was worse than he anticipated, much worse. "I've never been punished like this before," Murray told Brian Lamb in a C-SPAN interview shortly after the book's release. "The rules are suspended for this book. I mean, what Dick Herrnstein and I have written is so awful in some people's opinion that anything goes in terms of what you can say."[110]

What made this eight-hundred-page book so popular was what made it so reviled, the clarity of the prose and the humility of the authors. Unlike so many scientists, social and otherwise, Murray and Herrnstein did not hide their thesis behind clouds of obfuscation. Nor did they overstate their claims. "It seems highly likely to us that both genes and the environment have something to do with racial differences," the authors argued, and they remained "resolutely agnostic" as to the nature of that mix.[111] Undeniable, however, was that genes played a large role in intelligence and that ethnic groups, writ large, consistently produced distinct test results. In fact, the fairer the test, the likelier the results were to confirm enduring group distinctions.

Black columnist Bob Herbert, new in his job at the *New York Times*, was among those who ran, as Murray feared, "screaming from the room." His review gave the impression that he ran from the room before finishing the book. Not one for subtlety, he called *The Bell Curve* "a scabrous piece of racial pornography masquerading as serious scholarship." Herrnstein's thirty-six years at Harvard apparently failed to impress him. "Mr. Murray can protest all he wants," Herbert raged, "his book is just a genteel way of calling somebody a nigger."[112]

If the authors' claim that whites outscored blacks on IQ tests offended Herbert, their claim that Asians outscored whites managed to offend at least a few Asian neo-puritans, law professor Margaret Chon among them. She saw this latter claim as something of a red herring designed to distract readers from the implicit racism in a work of, once again, "social science pornography." Wrote an indignant Chon, "If two white males admit that Asians are smarter than whites, then the rest of us might as well accept the inevitable: There are subhuman or 'bad' minorities."[113] Chon's use of the word "subhuman" suggests how comfortable neo-puritans had become with slander. Of course, the authors said or implied no such thing. "I mean, you've got lots and lots of blacks and whites in the same range," Murray told Lamb. "You also have tens of thousands of blacks at the very highest levels of IQ."[114]

Few on the left were listening. Minds had long since been made up. As Herrnstein and Murray had observed, "Taboos breed not only ignorance but misinformation."[115] Reviewers vied with each other to unearth new and sinister motives behind the creation of the book. Biologist Tim Beardsley suspected *The Bell Curve* to be "a calculated political move." Wrote Beardsley, "As the country lurches to the right, many people will be seduced by the text's academic trappings and scientific tone."[116] Sociologist David Kutzik marveled at the "triumph of packaging" that launched this piece of "scientific racism" into the marketplace, there to advance the cause of "a more openly racist ultraconservative agenda."[117]

So bold was the authors' heresy that the *New York Review of Books* chose to expose it in the most prominent spot. Assigned to the task was not a literary critic but journalist Charles Lane. In an unusual approach to book reviewing, Lane tracked down the funding behind virtually every source cited in the book. He discovered that some of the scholarly works the authors cited came from organizations with eugenicist roots.

In a curious turn of phrase, however, Lane described these scholars as "hardly less biased than those they are summoned to rebut." In other words, the "tainted" scholars were no more subjective than scholars of his own liking, perhaps even less so. That much conceded, Lane decided they were somehow "nastier," always a hard variable to falsify.[118]

Speaking of sources, a few years after he wrote this review, Lane took over as editor of the *New Republic*. There he inherited a wunderkind reporter named Stephen Glass. Before Glass tripped himself up a year into Lane's tenure, he had fabricated an admitted twenty-seven bylined pieces. "He got away with his mind games because of the remarkable industry he applied to the production of the false backup materials," wrote Buzz Bissinger in *Vanity Fair*.[119] But that was only part of the reason. Glass got away with this fraud because he was telling stories Washington's progressive elite wanted to hear.

In one of his breakthrough pieces, Glass concocted a tale about eight young Republicans who, hopped up on beer and marijuana, sought out the "ugliest and loneliest" woman at a conservative conference, lured her to their hotel room, and sexually humiliated her. The piece, "almost entirely an invention," observed Bissinger, "was spoken of with reverence." Had Glass submitted an article affirming the link between genetics and race, Lane would have nosed through it like a drug-sniffing dog at a crack house.

"No burden of proof at all is placed on commentators who claim that racial differences in intelligence are purely environmental," the authors wrote in *The Bell Curve*.[120] They overstated the case a little, but not much. By 1993, regardless of what IQ tests or Olympic time trials seemed to be saying, progressives had accepted racial equality as a matter of faith in all but superficial matters. Those who advanced the idea that ethnic or even gender differences had a substantial genetic component risked shunning or worse.

This had not always been so. In the not-too-distant past, the progressive elite not only embraced but also enforced a genetics regime that would have made Charles Lane shudder. Among its foremost champions was Planned Parenthood founder Margaret Sanger. True, Planned Parenthood does admit Sanger was "no saint," but to sustain the illusion that she "changed the world, forever and for the better," the keepers of the Planned Parenthood flame have airbrushed her sins out of the record.[121]

Sanger evangelized for birth control "to prevent the sexual and racial chaos into which the world has drifted." She cited one study claiming that nearly half of all American World War I draftees—47.3 percent, to be precise—"had the mentality of twelve-year-old children or less." In other words, wrote Sanger with her typical subtlety, "they are morons."[122] Sanger and her allies had enormous influence in their day. In 1927, five years after *The Pivot of Civilization* was published, the US Supreme Court accepted the state of Virginia's ruling that a woman named Carrie Buck was mentally defective and thus deserving of forced sterilization. "It is better for all the world," wrote famed progressive jurist Oliver Wendell Holmes Jr., "if instead of waiting to execute degenerate offspring for crime, or to let them starve for their imbecility, society can prevent those who are manifestly unfit from continuing their kind."[123] Sanger could not have said it better herself.

By the time Sanger died in 1966, the emerging neo-puritan priesthood had shoved her darker thoughts down the memory hole and transformed her into the Betsy Ross of birth control. "Eugenics" did not appear among the twenty-two hundred glowing words in the *New York Times* obituary. Nor did "sterilization," "*Buck v. Bell*," "racial chaos," "mentally defective," "abortion," "Nazi," or anything of the kind. The Margaret Sanger whom the *Times* reader was asked to remember was a "dynamic, titian-haired woman whose Irish ancestry also endowed her with unfailing charm and persuasive wit." Her perfectly progressive goal—"to create equality between the sexes by freeing women from what she saw as sexual servitude"—had seemingly cleansed her soul of all past sins, even her brutal and overt racism.[124]

The *Times* will give Charles Murray no such send-off. A sneak preview of what awaits him can be found in the listing for Murray on the "watch list" of the much too influential Southern Poverty Law Center (SPLC). The SPLC tells donors of its dedication "to fighting hate and bigotry and to seeking justice for the most vulnerable members of our society."[125] That mission may once have been real, but not in recent memory. "Today," observed Ken Silverstein in the left-of-center *Harper's* magazine, "the SPLC spends most of its time—and money—on a relentless fund-raising campaign, peddling memberships in the church of tolerance with all the zeal of a circuit rider passing the collection plate."[126] If the church of tolerance has a Torquemada, it is surely SPLC founder and director Morris Dees. Under his twisted guidance, the SPLC has done little over the years but slander conservatives and sow the seeds of racial and religious distrust.

Despite writing several best sellers after *The Bell Curve*, none of which were about race, all of which were with major publishers, Murray found himself on the SPLC "watch list" as a "white nationalist."[127] Although acknowledging Murray to be "one of the most influential social scientists in America," the SPLC slammed him for espousing a "racist pseudoscience." According to the SPLC, Murray had been busy preaching that white men were "intellectually, psychologically and morally superior." This, again, was all slanderous nonsense. Oddly, the SPLC also took Murray to task for warning that increasing inequality between classes was turning America into "something resembling a caste society." Twenty years later, progressives would repeat the word *inequality* like a mantra. Murray got no credit. He remains on the watch list.

## GENOCIDAL RACIST

"The disgraced detective from the O. J. Simpson case died today." So said former Los Angeles Police Department (LAPD) detective Mark Fuhrman when Oprah Winfrey asked how he would be remembered upon his death. "That will be the lead sentence."[128]

Fuhrman knew whereof he spoke. The year was 2010. He had been wearing a flaming scarlet *R* for the previous fifteen years. When Winfrey expressed surprise about his fatalism, Fuhrman assured her, "That's the way the media work. They always find the thing that's most reflective of how they feel." Although a self-described "blue collar" kind of guy, Fuhrman was savvy enough to sense the way neo-puritans rolled. Sin was "how they feel." And in their eyes, there could be no redemption for someone who once uttered a word that they, in their conspicuous piety, could no longer bring themselves to say out loud.

"My biggest regret," Fuhrman told Winfrey wistfully, "is that I ever answered the phone." That fateful call woke him from his sleep at 1:05 a.m. Pacific time on June 13, 1994. "We've got a double homicide," Ron Phillips, Fuhrman's boss at West L.A. Homicide, told him. "One of the victims might be the wife of O. J. Simpson."[129] His juices flowing, Fuhrman drove promptly to the West L.A. station, met Phillips, and together they headed to the crime scene at 875 South Bundy Drive in Brentwood. There they found a blood-soaked Nicole Brown Simpson crumpled up on her condo's front steps and her friend, Ron Goldman, sprawled faceup on the bloodstained walkway leading to the house. Among the items found on the scene—"You had to not step on evidence there was so much evidence"—was a single, left-handed glove.

Once Fuhrman's partner, Brad Roberts, arrived, the two deduced what had happened from the ample clues. As they saw it, the killer had lost the glove in a struggle at the front of the house. He then fled down the walkway, bleeding as he walked, and reached into his pocket for his car keys, spilling change. The pocket suggested he was male. The agitation suggested he was an amateur.

As Fuhrman was finishing up his notes, he learned that headquarters had assigned the case to Robbery/Homicide. Detectives Philip Vannater and Tom Lange arrived soon afterwards. Fuhrman briefed them on the case and showed them, at their request, the way to O. J. Simpson's estate on Rockingham Avenue. There the lead detectives planned to give Simpson the bad news about his ex-wife in person.[130]

When they arrived, Fuhrman noticed blood on the door of a hastily parked Ford Bronco. The detectives tried the doorbell at the front gate, and no one answered. Fuhrman raised the possibility that whoever killed

Nicole may have also come to the Rockingham address to continue killing. "I don't care whose house this is," he told the lead detectives, "there could be people injured or dying there right now." After a brief discussion, the detectives agreed to enter. As the youngest and the fittest of those on the scene, the forty-two-year-old Fuhrman scaled the wall of the estate and opened the gate from inside.[131]

On the grounds were three bungalows. In one of them Fuhrman found a groggy, disheveled Kato Kaelin, he of the lopsided grin and the soon-to-be-famous surfer-boy shag. "Kaelin was a little goofy," Fuhrman observed, "a little unorthodox, and actually pretty funny."[132] With Kaelin's permission, Fuhrman looked inside the house for possible evidence, then outside. It was behind the bungalow that Fuhrman found the right-handed glove.

At Vannatter's request, Fuhrman took the glove to the Bundy Drive crime scene. The gloves matched. The glove found at the Rockingham address had absorbed the blood of Simpson and the two victims. It also linked the crime scene at Bundy with the Simpson home on Rockingham. It was the single most incriminating piece of evidence in the entire case. Although Fuhrman had nothing to do with the case after the first day, the Rockingham glove ensured that he would have to testify at the trial. It also ensured that the defense attorneys, if they were to spring Simpson, would have to destroy Fuhrman.

Johnny Cochran, the unscrupulous black lead attorney, was the right man for that job. Knowing Simpson would have a largely black jury, he chose to frame Fuhrman as a racist cop envious of a successful black man. Initially, Cochran had no evidence to back up his intuition, but a month after the murder, he got lucky. A woman named Kathleen Bell came forward with the news that she had met Fuhrman nearly a decade earlier and remembered the meeting well enough to accuse him of racism.[133] Although Bell had no proof beyond her word, for Cochran that was proof enough. He began planting the seeds of Fuhrman's undoing in the media and in the minds of his opposition. Well before the trial, for instance, he approached Chris Darden, a member of the prosecution, and said, "My brother, I'm telling you, don't get involved with Fuhrman's testimony. You have a life after this trial. You're a black man. Don't do it."[134] Although Simpson was a nominal Republican with little interest in things black, this trial was going to be all about race.

In allowing Bell's testimony, Judge Lance Ito shocked many observers, among them former LA prosecutor and author Vincent Bugliosi, who called the ruling "egregiously erroneous."[135] On March 15, 1995, defense attorney F. Lee Bailey dropped this bombshell on Fuhrman: "Did you say while in the recruiting station at any time during those years that when you see a nigger driving with a white woman, you pull them over?" Fuhrman calmly answered, "No," but the damage was done with the question. Could it have mattered at this point how Fuhrman answered? Bailey continued maneuvering and boxed Fuhrman into a legal cul de sac. "Are you therefore saying that you have not used that word [*nigger*] in the last ten years, Detective Fuhrman?" he asked. "Yes," replied Fuhrman fatally, "that is what I'm saying."[136]

This whole line of questioning enraged Bugliosi. "Judge Lance Ito should never have allowed the defense to even ask Fuhrman whether he had used [the word]," he would write. As Bugliosi explained, the California Evidence Code states that if the relevance of that evidence is "substantially outweighed" by the prejudice it engenders, the evidence should be excluded. He argued that even if Fuhrman had used the word, there was no reason to believe he would go around framing black people for murder, let alone a much-loved celebrity like Simpson. The probability of prejudicing the case, however, was "monumental."[137]

Only after Fuhrman's original testimony did the defense attorneys get the tip that would ultimately free a double murderer. A North Carolina writer named Laura Hart McKinney told them she had tapes on which Fuhrman could be heard repeatedly using the word "nigger." Judge Lance Ito issued a subpoena, and Cochran flew to North Carolina to take possession of the tapes.[138] An aspiring writer, McKinney had met Fuhrman in 1985 and recruited him as a consultant on a project dealing with female

LAPD officers. In the course of the relationship, the two had a casual affair. Fuhrman would argue that he had been using the word only to provide context for McKinney's story and that he "got a charge out of shocking her,"[139] but it no longer mattered what Fuhrman said. The tapes included forty examples of Fuhrman using the word "nigger" in a disparaging way. His twelve sessions with McKinney had all taken place within the ten years preceding his original testimony. Whatever his intentions, Fuhrman had lied on the witness stand. During his final argument, Cochran savaged him mercilessly as a "lying, perjuring, genocidal, racist cop."[140]

The prosecution was not much kinder. "Is he a racist?" Marcia Clark asked rhetorically of Fuhrman in her closing statement. "Yes. Is he the worst LAPD has to offer? Yes. Should LAPD have ever hired him? No. Should such a person be a police officer? No." Clark, alas, was just warming up. "In fact, do we wish there were no such person on the planet?" she asked. "Yes."[141] If Clark thought she could win the jury's trust by flagellating her own witness, the jury quickly proved her wrong.

Until the moment the verdict was returned, most white Americans did not think the case racially charged. To them, the charming pitchman Simpson had long since transcended race. If any political perspective influenced reporting on the case, it was not race, but gender. This was the rare time, in fact, that feminists and ordinary justice-loving Americans found themselves on the same side of the cultural ramparts.

The videos of black crowds cheering the verdict shocked white America, left and right. Instinctively, the media shifted white disgust at the larger injustice away from Simpson and his black supporters and toward Fuhrman. "After his error on the witness stand, he was maligned and vilified perhaps more than any other person within recent memory, not even excluding O. J. Simpson," said Bugliosi.[142] Neo-puritans had to blame someone for this travesty, and Fuhrman's dishonesty played better with its base than did the corrupting influence of race. They found it much more satisfying to pin the scarlet R on Fuhrman than to probe the troubled soul of their angriest and most influential subcult.

Channeling the public fury, the state of California proceeded to indict Fuhrman for perjury. He pled "nolo contendere" in order to spare his family and stay out of jail. While Fuhrman was anguishing his way through the Southern California courts, Simpson was out hunting for killer Colombian drug dealers on the golf courses of Southern California. Bugliosi considered Fuhrman's victimization "a terrible, perhaps irrevocable injustice."[143]

Fuhrman was not the monster he was made out to be. He had finished second in his class at the police academy and had a good record in his nineteen years on the force. After Simpson was acquitted, the *Los Angeles Times* interviewed more than a half dozen of his minority colleagues and could find no one to say an unkind word about him.[144] "Mark is a complicated guy, like me," said celebrity author Dominick Dunne.[145] Two years after the Simpson trial, Dunne passed Fuhrman a copy of a private investigator's report on the 1975 murder of fifteen-year-old Martha Moxley in Greenwich, Connecticut, and got Fuhrman interested. Fuhrman's 1998 book, *Murder in Greenwich*, eventually led to the arrest of Kennedy cousin Michael Skakel, who had avoided justice for more than twenty years. With Skakel's conviction, Fuhrman told Oprah, "I think I did pay a debt." His *New York Times* obituary will prove, however, that Mark Fuhrman can never pay debt enough.

## CHILD KILLER

In the years since the Simpson trial, only one other person has experienced a comparable level of racial terror as Mark Fuhrman. That would be George Zimmerman, the neighborhood watch captain who shot and killed seventeen-year-old Trayvon Martin in Sanford, Florida. Officers Darren Wilson in Missouri and Daniel Pantaleo in New York would face angry mobs orchestrated much as Zimmerman's had been, but those two officers were never without institutional support. Zimmerman would face those mobs alone, and, unlike Fuhrman, he risked wearing his scarlet *R* not in the wilds of Idaho but in a Florida prison.

In March 2012 Zimmerman might well have felt the fear and

loneliness of an accused witch in Salem circa 1692. Al Sharpton and Jesse Jackson led a march in Sanford demanding his arrest. Film director Spike Lee retweeted Zimmerman's home address to his 250,000 followers. The New Black Panther Party openly offered a ten-thousand-dollar bounty for the capture of this "child killer" and passed out "Wanted Dead or Alive" posters. The New Black Liberation Militia promised to attempt a citizen's arrest. Latino activists condemned him as "a murderer and a racist." And President Barack Obama allied himself with Martin's family, saying for the ages, "If I had a son, he would look like Trayvon."[146]

To frame Zimmerman as a racist, neo-puritans in and out of the media embarked on a collective smear job unabated by the creeping awareness they'd picked the wrong guy. For the first week or so after the shooting, all reporters had to go on was Zimmerman's name, age, and status as neighborhood watch captain. Given the name "Zimmerman," they presumed he was what Obama might call "a typical white person," perhaps even Jewish.[147]

In fact, Zimmerman made about as unlikely a racist poster boy as America could produce. He learned to speak Spanish before he learned to speak English from his dark-skinned, Peruvian mother and grandmother. The pair largely raised him during his early years while his father, Bob Zimmerman, a career Army officer, moved from post to post, including two tours in Korea. Given his upbringing, Zimmerman had more claim to being "Hispanic" than the white-raised Obama had to being "black."[148]

Historically, the media have been as shy about highlighting Hispanic injustice toward blacks as they are keen on exploiting stories of white injustice toward blacks. Consider, for example, the August 2007 incident in a Newark playground that left New Jersey stunned. Jose Carranza and five friends were drinking and smoking marijuana that night when they spied four young, black students playing music. Like Zimmerman, Carranza was of Peruvian origin. Unlike Zimmerman, he was an outlaw. He and his gang pulled guns on the four, robbed them, forced them to lie facedown, and sexually assaulted the two girls in the group. When one of the girls summoned the will to push off her attacker and run, Carranza's crew opened fire, killing the girl's three friends with gunshots to the backs of their heads and wounding her.[149]

Yet for all the obvious horror, this story barely left New Jersey. The national media ignored it, and race hustlers like Sharpton kept their distance. The reason was simple enough: Hispanic-on-black crime has no political value for the Democratic Party and their neo-puritan enforcers, especially when the criminal is an illegal alien, as Carranza was. Almost assuredly, if a neighborhood watch captain named "Jose Carranza" had killed Trayvon Martin under the identical set of circumstances as Zimmerman did, no one outside of Florida would have heard of him or Martin.

It was not just Zimmerman's ethnicity that made him an unlikely white racist. He took a black date to his high school prom. He was mentoring two black teens at the time of the shooting. And most notably, the year before, he had involved himself in an incident in which a police lieutenant's son sucker-punched a black homeless man outside a bar. Upset at the lack of media attention the case was getting, Zimmerman and his wife, Shellie, printed fliers demanding justice. They then drove the fliers around to area churches and passed them out. Later, at a public meeting, Zimmerman took the floor and said, "I would just like to state that the law is written in black and white. It should not and cannot be enforced in the gray for those that are in the thin blue line."[150] As a result of the publicity, the police chief was forced to resign, and the lieutenant's son was arrested.

The media were too busy framing Zimmerman to share this side of his life with the public. In the first month after the shooting, ABC was caught doctoring a police surveillance video. NBC was caught doctoring the audio of George Zimmerman's initial call to the police. And CNN tried to convince the public that an indecipherable word on that call was the unlikely and archaic "coons."[151] In her book on the Zimmerman case, *Suspicion Nation*, NBC's legal analyst Lisa Bloom fully ignored the testimony of the most important eyewitness, said not a word about Zimmerman's work defending the homeless man, and, at her most Orwellian, failed to identify Zimmerman as Hispanic, not even as a "white Hispanic."[152] The uninitiated reader of the book would have thought him just another white racist in a jam.

In 2012 Zimmerman *was* just another white guy in a jam. It was a presidential election year. Florida was the ultimate of battleground states. And gun control was a potentially winning issue, but only to the degree that Martin's shooting was free of ambiguity. This gave neo-puritans the incentive to draw a stark distinction between the unarmed boy with Skittles and iced tea and the brooding vigilante George Zimmerman.

The media did an even more tortuous job framing Martin. Collectively, they violated all rules of journalistic ethics to picture him, literally, as a sweet little boy who loved football and wanted to become a pilot. In reality, Martin was a six-foot, 160-pound young man whose drug use went well beyond the THC found in his system. His cell phone exchanges showed his keen interest in mixed martial arts and handguns. His mother had recently kicked him out of the house for fighting. And he had been suspended from school three times in the past semester, once for drugs, another time for possessing stolen jewelry.

In the cruelest of ironies, a judge threw out George Zimmerman's libel suit against NBC because he had made himself a "public figure." Zimmerman did this not by shooting Trayvon Martin but by "voluntarily injecting his views into the public controversy surrounding race relations and public safety in Sanford." The judge was referring to the incident in which Zimmerman almost single-handedly secured justice for the black homeless man. Unfortunately, no one who watched NBC knew the first thing about this incident.

In July 2013 a Florida jury of six women acquitted Zimmerman of any crime in the shooting death of Martin. Neo-puritans, high and low, refused to accept the verdict. Said Martin family attorney Benjamin Crump, "Trayvon Martin will forever remain in the annals of history next to Medgar Evers and Emmett Till, as symbols for the fight for equal justice for all."[153] Till, a fourteen-year-old Chicago boy, was brutally lynched for allegedly flirting with a white woman in 1955 in Mississippi. Courageous civil rights leader Evers took a bullet in the back from a racist assassin in 1963 in Mississippi. Martin took a bullet to the chest while gratuitously bashing in the head of a Hispanic man he did not know in a multiethnic Florida community. That did not matter. Controlling the media as they did, neo-puritans did not need to vet their martyrs. Nor did they need to weigh the evidence before forcing an innocent man to mount a national scaffold and bear the scarlet *R*. They may have failed to send Zimmerman to the gulag, but it was not because they didn't try.

# 3

# THE SCARLET *D*: DENIER

American history is rich with movements, religious and quasi-religious, grounded in the belief that the end is nigh. Perhaps the most influential was the one inspired by William Miller, a New York State farmer who persuaded as many as one hundred thousand people the world would end in 1843. Although the apocalypse did not arrive for his followers in 1843—or 1844, after a hasty reset—it did for a gun-toting "branch" of his sect on the dusty plains of Waco almost exactly 150 years later.

The Branch Davidians were hardly unique in hastening the end times with, admittedly, more than a little help from the Clinton Justice Department. Charles Manson had his "Helter Skelter." Jim Jones had his "White Night." And Marshall Applewhite had a spaceship waiting for him and his Nike-wearing acolytes behind the Hale-Bopp comet. Joseph Bottum described the impulse as "the search for immediate application of the Book of Revelation."[1] To deny a believer his apocalypse is to challenge his very identity. That gesture often comes at a price.

## THE DENIER

On November 5, 2008, the very day Barack Obama was elected president, writer and producer Michael Crichton died at age sixty-five. The Harvard-trained MD had enjoyed a spectacular career. Several of his best-selling, science-rich novels had been turned into movies. These included hits such as the *The Andromeda Strain*, *Jurassic Park*, and *Lost World*. He had success as a screenwriter and a director and produced the megahit TV show *ER*, which he also conceived. Despite this résumé, or perhaps because of it, the progressive online journal *ThinkProgress* saw fit to headline his obituary, "Michael Crichton, world's most famous global warming denier, dies."[2] The neo-puritans buried him with the scarlet *D* for "denier" ablaze on his chest. To the hard core, he had no other meaningful credential.

The *ThinkProgress* headline would not have surprised Crichton. Some years earlier, he had taken it upon himself to question the prevailing scientific orthodoxy and did so most flamboyantly at the famed Commonwealth Club in San Francisco. The organizers of the September 2003 event had handed Crichton a weighty assignment, namely, to address the most important challenge facing mankind. The "challenge" he chose—"distinguishing reality from fantasy, truth from propaganda"[3]—surprised everyone. It seemed so lacking in gravitas. As Crichton explained, however, solving more tangible problems was futile if no one could discern which problems were real.

As an example of the challenge at hand, Crichton spoke about environmentalism, a bold move in a city that spawned the Sierra Club, Friends of the Earth, and a herd of other like-minded groups. If anyone had the chops to challenge eco-activists in their home court, it was Crichton. At this stage of his career, he did not need anyone's approval, and, in San Francisco, he wasn't about to get it. After reassuring the audience that, like all rational people, he understood man had a responsibility for his environment, he warned that civic leaders often failed to make the right decisions and, worse, refused to learn from their failures.

As a student of anthropology—he had taught the subject at Oxford—Crichton knew why this was so. "The best people, the most enlightened people," he argued, were making decisions based not on fact but on faith. They thought they had transcended religion, but they had not. For the West, said Crichton, "one of the most powerful religions" was environmentalism. He called it, in fact, "a perfect 21st century remapping of traditional Judeo-Christian beliefs and myths." This was the belief system that gave meaning to the life of the secular elite and shaped their sense of the world.

Crichton went on to explain how environmentalism mimicked Christianity. It started with the "initial Eden, a Paradise, a state of grace and unity with nature." Man then overreached. He plucked the technological fruit from the tree of knowledge, and this led to pollution. "There is a judgment day coming for us all," said Crichton. "We are all energy sinners, doomed to die, unless we seek salvation, which is now called sustainability." Not above a little humor, Crichton described communion in the church of Mother Earth as pesticide-free, organic food consumed by the elect, "the right people with the right beliefs." Bottum had come to the same conclusion. Environmentalism, he affirmed, "comes to us as Christianity without Christ."

Crichton had no argument with the Judeo-Christian tradition. Its adherents acknowledged many of their beliefs to be issues of faith. They did not pretend otherwise. Environmentalists had no such humility. They clung to their core beliefs as gospel even when confronted with new evidence. "Facts aren't necessary," Crichton taunted his audience. "It's about whether you are going to be a sinner, or saved. Whether you are going to be one of the people on the side of salvation, or on the side of doom. Whether you are going to be one of us, or one of them."

Crichton disabused the San Francisco audience of one core belief after another. There was no Eden. Life before the emergence of modern technology was rife with disease, appalling child mortality, and early death all around. The indigenous peoples no sooner crossed into America than they began wiping out hundreds of species of large animals. Well before Columbus, they lived in a state of constant warfare with each other. Human sacrifice and infanticide were common. Those tribes that could not compete simply vanished or hunkered down in hillside abodes. Similar conditions and worse prevailed throughout the world among indigenous peoples. "The noble savage is a fantasy, and it was never true," said Crichton. That anyone still believed in the concept, he said, was a testament to "the tenacity of religious myths."

Having dispensed with the notion of a godless Eden and fall

from grace, Crichton then questioned the rest of this ersatz theology, including the various apocalyptic scenarios. One that had not panned out, he observed, was the fear of rampant overpopulation. Although Crichton did not mention Paul Ehrlich by name, he did not have to. Ehrlich, the twentieth century's best-known neo-Malthusian, was foremost among the "preachers of environmentalism" to whom Crichton alluded. Indeed, he made the Millerites look like optimists. "The battle to feed all of humanity is already lost," Ehrlich lamented in the opening of his breakthrough 1968 best seller *Population Bomb*. The most "cheerful" scenario Ehrlich could envision for "the next decade or so" was one in which Americans assumed an unexpected "maturity of outlook," a new pope gave "his blessing to abortion," and only half a billion people died of famine.[4]

"Okay, so, the preachers made a mistake," said Crichton with a wee bit of irony. Not only did fertility rates fall everywhere and food surpluses grow, but also, he noted, twenty-first-century demographers were worrying about a shrinking, aging population throughout the Western world. The fact that Ehrlich got everything not just wrong but spectacularly wrong scarcely dimmed his star. He capped a lifetime of prestigious environmental awards in 1990—long after most of his predictions had proven absurd—with both a $345,000 MacArthur Foundation grant and the Craford Prize from the Swedish Academy of Sciences, the Nobel equivalent for environmentalists. This kind of acclaim made sense, said Crichton, if one thought of environmentalism as a religion, and a crackpot religion at that. "Remember, the nut on the sidewalk carrying the placard that predicts the end of the world doesn't quit when the world doesn't end on the day he expects," said Crichton. "He just changes his placard, sets a new doomsday date, and goes back to walking the streets."

Another article of faith that Crichton attacked that fateful night in San Francisco was the dogma that the miracle chemical DDT caused cancer and, worse, killed birds. One very determined woman, Rachel Carson by name, introduced this idea in her influential 1962 best seller,

*Silent Spring.* A Manichaean at heart, Carson envisioned a constant struggle between an evil, material world of darkness and the bearers of light like her. She pulled much of her literary power from this ominous vision. Her chapters have titles such as "Elixirs of Death," "Rivers of Death," and "Beyond the Dreams of the Borgias." The Borgias, it seems, were mere dabblers in the art of poison. America introduced the "age of poisons."[5] Carson used words such as "toxins," "contaminants," "hazards," "death-dealing materials," and the inevitable "poison" where others might use "chemical" or "insecticide." And she never let up.

As it happened, Carson proved to be the Elmer Gantry of environmental preachers. The esteemed entomologist Gordon Edwards, a Carson fan at the time, combed through the book page by page, noting literally scores of "deceptions, false statements, horrible innuendoes, and ridiculous allegations." At the end of the day, beyond all reasonable doubt, Edwards revealed Carson's claim that DDT is "deadly" to be "completely false."[6] Still, her careless, media-fanned hysteria contaminated the culture and politics of the day. In 1972 the newly formed Environmental Protection Agency issued an order ending the general use of DDT in the United States after nearly three successful decades of application. Worldwide bans would follow, and so would millions of needless deaths from diseases, most notably, malaria. "Banning DDT is one of the most disgraceful episodes in the twentieth century history of America," said Crichton. Eco-activists had no use for facts; he noted ruefully, "The tenets of environmentalism are all about belief."

## THE TERRIBLE COURSE

Before those millions could die, Rachel Carson's anxiety about pending catastrophe had to go global. Carson had many disciples, but if the movement had a Paul, it was veteran activist John McConnell. Born in 1915 to a traveling preacher and his wife, McConnell moved through progressive causes as his father moved through prairie towns. During World War II, he worked as a seaman on a merchant marine vessel. At sea, McConnell got it into his head that love had more potential power than bombs, and he conducted religious services accordingly. After the Soviets put *Sputnik 1* in orbit in 1957, McConnell launched initiatives to ensure peaceful cooperation between the United States and the Soviet Union—in space, no less. Throughout the 1960s, he organized a variety of wistful new peace initiatives, all global in scope, with an eye toward what he would call "world equality." In the late 1960s, like so many left-wing activists, McConnell turned his organizing attention to the environment.[7]

It was McConnell who conceived the first "Earth Day." He introduced the idea at the 1969 United Nations Educational, Scientific and Cultural Organization (UNESCO) conference in San Francisco. Later that same year, he proposed Earth Day to the San Francisco Board of Supervisors, and the supervisors signed on. Although McConnell's biographers like to talk about his Christian roots, by the time he emerged as an eco-activist he had largely abandoned life eternal in favor of "reverence and care for life on our planet." Indeed, his newly created rituals had a pagan element about them, testament to which was his choice of the vernal equinox for Earth Day. That was, after all, the time when "day and night are equal around the world and hearts and minds can join together with thoughts of harmony and Earth's rejuvenation."[8]

In the original "Earth Day Proclamation," McConnell fused equal bits of Marx and Jesus, added a dash of apocalypse, cloaked it all in Teddy Roosevelt–style environmental do-goodism, and drafted it in a flourishing seventeenth-century longhand to look and sound like the Declaration of Independence. "Whereas: In our shortsightedness we have failed to make provisions for the poor, as well as the rich, to inherit the Earth," he wrote, "and our new enlightenment requires that the disinherited be given a just stake in the Earth and its future—their enthusiastic cooperation is essential if we are to succeed in the great task of Earth renewal." An excellent salesman, McConnell recruited a sundry crew of dignitaries to sign the proclamation. These included presidential candidate Eugene McCarthy, all-purpose astronaut Buzz Aldrin, and UN secretary general U Thant. More than a decade before anyone worried about global warming, each pledged "to help change Man's terrible course toward catastrophe."[9]

Like Ehrlich, who would also claim to be a cofounder of Earth Day, McConnell was sowing the seeds for a worldview in which one either signed on to a global, covertly Marxist environmental program or ran the risk of being exiled from the zone of decency. The leaders of this movement had yet to fix the inflammatory word *denier* to those who resisted, but that would come soon enough.

Still another soi-disant cofounder of Earth Day changed his focus from Indochina to the earth in the late 1960s. Ira Einhorn attributed the shift to the "the accelerating destruction of the planetary interconnecting web." Not everyone was as tuned in as Einhorn, only the "few of us activists who took the trouble to read the then available ecological literature." Or so Einhorn explained in his book *Prelude to Intimacy.* "We intuitively sensed the need to open a new front in the 'movement' battle," he continued, "for Chicago '68 was already pointing towards Kent State and the violence of frustration that lead [*sic*] to the Weathermen and other similarly doomed and fragmented groups."[10]

Sen. Gaylord Nelson usually gets the credit for organizing that first Earth Day in 1970, but people like Einhorn were the ones recruiting and training the ground troops. Einhorn's terrain was Philadelphia. As he saw it, environmental protection required "a conscious restructuring of all we do."[11] To pull off so ambitious a program, Einhorn claimed to have enlisted a happy cabal of business, academic, and governmental factions. Together, they formed a broad popular front to deal with this unraveling of the planetary web.

Whether or not Einhorn played the role he claimed for himself, there is no denying how well he infiltrated the upper reaches of Philadelphia's decency zone. Ira had a "brilliant network," a local oil executive would later tell *Time* magazine. "He knew enough corporate people to get our projects funded simply by strolling into people's offices and asking for the money."[12] These connections would come in handy just nine years after that first Earth Day when police found the rotting and battered body of Einhorn's girlfriend, Holly Maddux, in a steamer trunk in Einhorn's apartment. She had been stashed there for eighteen months.

At his bail hearing, one after another of the city's liberal worthies took the stand to sing the accused murderer's praises. These included a minister, an economist, a corporate lawyer, a playwright, and many more in what *Time* called "an unlikely battalion of bluebloods, millionaires and corporate executives." Representing Einhorn was none other than future Republican *and* Democratic US senator Arlen Specter. The combined clout of those testifying swayed the judge to set bail at forty thousand dollars, only four thousand of which was required to put Einhorn back on the streets.

Fronting the money was Barbara Bronfman, a Montreal socialite who had married into the conspicuously liberal Bronfman family of Seagram's fame. After Einhorn jumped bail, Bronfman continued to funnel money to Einhorn for some seven years. French police did not catch up with the self-dubbed "Unicorn" until 1997, sixteen years into his subsidized European exile. In protesting extradition, Einhorn claimed to have been persecuted because he had given his life to "the cause of nonviolent social change." That boast did not overly impress the French, but in their eagerness to spite the United States on the human rights front, they kept Einhorn in country for another five years.

Justice finally felled the Unicorn twenty-five years after he killed would-be flower child Maddux. Einhorn's best line of defense at his 2002 trial in Philadelphia was that somebody—the CIA, most likely—stuffed Maddux's body into the trunk and secreted the trunk in his closet to frame him. The fact that he'd had prior altercations with females, had written about them in his diary, had engaged in a violent fight with Maddux about the time she disappeared, and repeatedly blocked the landlord from looking into his closet rendered his defense theory somewhat suspect. It took a jury all of two hours to convict him.[13]

Although the first full-scale Earth Day did have, as *Time* magazine conceded, "aspects of a secular, almost pagan holiday,"[14] it was not held on the vernal equinox, as McConnell had hoped. Rather, it took place on April 22, 1970, a Wednesday, one hundred years to the day after the birth of Vladimir Lenin. As historian Paul Kengor has observed, the selection of April 22 "didn't escape notice in 1970." One hundred thousand people marched in New York City that day, the city in which the communist presence was strongest. "Communists specialized in agitation and propaganda," said Kengor. "They had a campaign for everything. They excelled at suckering impressionable liberal/progressive dupes, especially youth." Kengor added that he "would be amazed if communists had not been involved in Earth Day from the outset."[15]

Whoever chose the date, chose wisely. The springtime pageantry gave students a pleasant reprieve from their strenuous antiwar activities and proved to be a huge success. In the years to come, Earth Day morphed into a messianic global institution, the commemoration of which was all but mandatory in many quarters. The 2014 San Francisco Earth Day, which was only slightly more exotic than most, provided attendees with all the ritualized back-patting an enthusiast could handle. In addition to the perfunctory speeches and symposia, celebrants were able to groove to the tunes of the New Monsoon and the Earth Day All-Star Band, watch Yaqui Indians dramatize a deer hunt, and ogle the Serpent Sirens as they spread "Gaia's Message" through belly dancing— Gaia, of course, being the primal Greek goddess of the earth and the reigning deity of the movement.[16]

San Francisco organizers, like those in other cities, used the pageantry to lure the young and fill their minds with eco-mush. "Let's put the political in Earth Day," read the program's formal "Call to Action." The political manifested itself in a march for "climate justice," a blanket term that covered a wealth of redistributionist schemes. The march culminated, appropriately enough, at San Francisco's UN Plaza. There, the politics got more intense when the day's featured speaker, Bill McKibben, the "nation's leading environmentalist," took the stage. Although he spoke for only eight minutes, McKibben had time enough to exorcise a roster of demons.[17] These included generic "oil company executives," civic leaders who refused to divest pension funds from the fossil fuel industry, and the very spawn of Satan, the Koch brothers. The sin for which McKibben chastised the Kochs was the Keystone Pipeline, a project favored at the time by three out of every four Americans.[18]

McKibben linked the movement of nearly a million barrels of oil a day through the pipeline to global warming and thus an impending apocalypse. "There is no more time for postponing," he warned his audience. California was drying up. The Solomon Islands were flooding. El Niño was threatening. There were "lots of dead people." What was the point, he asked, of saving for retirement if there were "no planet to retire on?" Scary as the talk might have sounded to the untrained ear, McKibben's jeremiad did not seem to trouble the audience. If anything, it reassured them they were among the chosen few who cared enough to listen.

## COLOSSAL BIGOT

It would be a decade after that first Earth Day before progressive environmentalists targeted their first widely recognized evildoer—the goggle-eyed, balding, and boldly Christian interior secretary, James Watt. A native of Wyoming, Watt came to office on the back of the Sagebrush Rebellion that had riled the West. Then as now, Westerners saw themselves as the real environmentalists. They had little use for what William Pendley, in his book on the rebellion, called "the high priesthood of environmental wisdom," the technocrats and progressives who flourished during Jimmy Carter's presidency.[19] The rebels rejected the imposition of an ecological conscience on America, particularly their slice thereof, and argued for the wisdom of the Tenth Amendment: "The powers not delegated to the United States by the Constitution, nor prohibited by it to the States, are reserved to the States respectively, or to the people."

Watt was their champion. He took President Reagan's "Good Neighbor" strategy to heart and immediately set about restoring the power over land and water management to the states, much to the delight of their governors, Democrat and Republican alike. Not surprisingly, progressives protested this devolution of federal power. Respectful of Reagan's emerging popularity, they chose to focus their discontent on the ungainly Watt.

During his confirmation hearing in 1981, Watt told the gathered senators, "I do not know how many future generations we can count on before the Lord returns; whatever it is we have to manage with a skill to leave the resources needed for future generations."[20] This was a straightforward reassertion of Christian stewardship principles, one that had guided American conservation policy since at least the age of Teddy Roosevelt. Even an innocuous mention of the Lord's return, however, proved to be a gift for the left. A year later, for instance, muckraker Jack Anderson would casually ridicule Watt for "thinking of ways to use up the nation's natural resources in time for the second coming."[21] Like a story passed around a campfire, Watt's comment grew increasingly absurd with each retelling. At the time, however, being Christian was not sin enough. Watt's enemies would need something more.

In April 1983 Watt met with a reporter from the *Washington Post* to discuss his support of the Holocaust Museum then under consideration. At the end of the discussion, Watt volunteered that he had instructed the National Park Service (NPS) to avoid a recurrence of the drug use and drinking that had marred the Fourth of July celebration on the mall the previous summer. In 1982 the vintage psychedelic rock band the Grass Roots had attracted vanloads of recreational pot users as well as a cohort of pro-pot activists who staged a smoke-in in support of marijuana legalization. Families with children complained, and Watt listened. He sent a memo to the NPS. It read in part, "Now on, July Fourth will be a [traditional ceremony] for the family and for solid, clean American lives." To headline the 1983 concert, Watt recruited Reagan supporter Wayne Newton, who was to be accompanied by the U.S. Army Blues Band.[22]

The week after his interview about the proposed Holocaust Museum, the *Post* ran a front-page story with a headline that had to surprise the interior secretary, "Watt Outlaws Rock Music on Mall for July 4."[23] Despite the punchy headline, this article was a more or less straightforward account of Watt's decision. In the course of the article, however, reporter Phil McComb quietly dropped a bombshell. The group that played in 1981 was the Beach Boys.

Few in Washington knew or cared about the Grass Roots, but they all knew about the Beach Boys, who had evolved into something of a national institution over the previous two decades. Watt never mentioned the Beach Boys in his memo and may not have known they played on the Mall in 1981, but the group's implied rejection sparked the controversy that followed. The next day, the *Post* printed another front-page story, "Watt Sets Off Uproar with Music Ban." When contacted, the Beach Boys told McComb that they had performed in Leningrad in 1978, and obviously the Russians "did not feel that the group attracted the wrong element."[24]

Sensing an opportunity to ally themselves both with America's eco-activists and its ageless youth, congressional members of both parties rushed to the microphones. To make their respective cases, they exaggerated Watt's *thought crime*. "Mr. Speaker," said Democratic representative Thomas J. Downey of New York, "I was deeply troubled, as I know other Members of Congress and people all across this country are, to learn that Secretary Watt has substituted Wayne Newton for the Beach Boys." In fact, the NPS had not scheduled the Beach Boys for the 1983 concert, but no matter, the disinformation spread quickly enough to "deeply trouble" even Republicans. "They're my friends, and I like their music," said Vice President Bush. Sen. Bob Dole, who was old enough to be Brian Wilson's father, offered the lads a charity concert in Kansas "now that the group seems to be available."[25]

The White House tried to ease the controversy by making a joke of it. On April 7, the day the second *Post* article ran, President Reagan awarded Watt a plaster trophy of a foot with a bullet hole in it. Apparently, Nancy Reagan was particularly fond of the Beach Boys. "She said that the Beach Boys are fans of hers," Watt told the *New York Times*, "and her children have grown up with them and they're fine, outstanding people."[26]

In truth, the Mall controversy was the best publicity the group had snagged since "Good Vibrations" went gold in 1967. Not much went well afterwards for these "fine, outstanding people." Drummer Dennis Wilson grew understandably paranoid after former housemate Charles Manson turned mass killer. Group leader Brian Wilson suffered a drug-fueled mental breakdown. Wilson cousin Mike Love burned through five wives. Dennis Wilson married one of Mike's nine children—his own fifth marriage—quickly abandoned his eighteen-year-old cousin and their child, and then drowned mysteriously in December 1983 after an all-day drinking binge.[27]

Wilson had lived just long enough, however, to see Watt's demise. Harassed relentlessly by the environmental lobby and bruised badly by the Beach Boy flap, Watt could not take another hit. As it turned out, the fatal one was self-inflicted. In September 1983, Watt said of a special commission reviewing his coal-leasing policies, "We have every kind of mix you can have. I have a black. I have a woman, two Jews and a cripple. And we have talent." For his part, Watt thought he "was extolling the very high qualifications of those citizens," but even if Watt had used the term "handicapped" instead of "cripple," his failure to take affirmative action with the requisite seriousness would likely have cost him his job. Republican senator Alfonse D'Amato, who had a moderate's keen sense of which Republicans could be safely abandoned, quickly denounced Watt as a "colossal bigot."[28] He never specified against whom Watt was bigoted. He didn't have to. The president accepted Watt's resignation before anyone asked.

In the way of postscript, more than twenty years after Watt left office, actress Meryl Streep presented neo-puritan scold and PBS savant Bill Moyers with an award from Harvard Medical School in recognition of "his commitment to the environment."[29] Streep had earned her place in the eco-movement sun twenty-five years earlier for helping spread panic, facts be damned, about the pesticide Alar, used on apples. As Berkeley biochemist Bruce Ames reported in *Science* magazine at the time, a schoolchild ran more risk of getting cancer from the natural carcinogens in a peanut butter sandwich than from the Alar residue in a glass of apple juice.[30] But Ames never won an Oscar.

Moyers had warmed himself to the Harvard elders with his prophetic warnings about the imaginary Christian belief that "environmental destruction is not only to be disregarded but hastened as a sign of the coming apocalypse." According to Moyers, "millions" of Christian fundamentalists believed this. Although eco-progressives had little or no use for a Judeo-Christian God, they did have use for ostensibly Christian shills like Moyers who could so craftily demonize Christian "deniers" like Watt. Moyers's Southwestern roots and seminary training gave him the church cred to be taken seriously, at least by people who did not know any better. With his neo-puritan gift for slander, Moyers singled out Watt in his Harvard speech as an icon of these environmentally wanton "rapture" believers:

> [James] Watt told the U.S. Congress that protecting natural resources was unimportant in light of the imminent return of Jesus Christ. In public testimony he said, "After the last tree is felled, Christ will come back."
>
> Beltway elites snickered. The press corps didn't know what he was talking about. But Watt was serious, as were his compatriots across the country. One-third of the American electorate, if a recent Gallup Poll is accurate, believes the Bible is literally true.[31]

In 2005 Moyers could have easily googled a quote this inflammatory, but he obviously did not feel the need. He sat atop the media pyramid, immune to anything Watt might say given the latter's deeply imprinted brand as an enemy of the environment, diversity, and rock music. To its credit, the *Washington Post* gave Watt the space to respond, and in May 2006, respond he did. As to the quote attributed to him, replied Watt, "I never said it. Never believed it. Never even thought it. I know no Christian who believes or preaches such error."[32] Watt explained that the Creator entrusted the land and resources to humans, and they, in turn, were expected to serve as careful stewards of that inheritance.

Watt acknowledged that Moyers had since apologized to him, but neither Moyer nor his allies apologized to the Christians they continued to smear. Watt cited a statement issued by the National Council of Churches (NCC) two months after Moyers's Harvard speech. In it, the NCC votaries condemned "teachings that suggest humans are 'called' to exploit the Earth without care for how our behavior impacts the rest of God's creation." According to the NCC, "This false gospel still finds its proud preachers and continues to capture its adherents among embold-ened political leaders and policymakers." When Watt contacted the chairman of the NCC task force and asked exactly who these preachers and policymakers were, the chairman could not name one. "Be alert," Watt warned in conclusion. "Never underestimate the political impact of the twisted charges by extreme environmentalists now advanced by the religious left to divide the people of faith." Added Watt, "I learned this lesson two decades ago—the hard way."[33]

## SCARY SCENARIOS

"Neo-Puritans never sleep," Christopher Buckley observed,[34] and on no subject have they been more wide-awake than that of climate. From the beginning of the twentieth century, if not before, scientists and their progressive allies have been warning the world about a climactic doomsday. The one obvious problem for those who might want to prepare is that the nature of the doomsday keeps changing. In 1912, a *New York Times* headline warned its readers of an "Encroaching Ice Age." In 1923, the *Washington Post* reaffirmed the "possible advent of a new ice age." By 1933, the *Times* had shifted its anxiety to a "25-year rise" in temperatures. The paper of record continued with the warming theme in a 1952 article that spoke of a "half-century" in which "the world has been getting warmer."[35]

By 1975 the science had shifted with the weather. "Scientists Ask Why World Climate Is Changing," read the May 21 *Times* headline. "Major Cooling May Be Ahead." As Walter Sullivan reported, a new ice age was on the way and may have already begun. Wrote Sullivan,

"The drop in mean temperatures in the Northern Hemisphere has been sufficient, for example, to shorten Britain's growing season for crops by two weeks."[36] The worry was, of course, that shortened growing seasons threatened worldwide food production.

What impresses the contemporary reader about the 1975 *Times* article was the humility of the climate scientists. Sullivan spoke of how they were "crippled by a lack of knowledge" and cited a report by the Academy of Sciences that confirmed as much. "Not only are the basic scientific questions left unanswered," wrote the Academy, "but in many cases we do not yet know enough to pose the key questions." Uncertain of the future and aware of their limitations, researchers refrained from attacking those who might disagree with their projections. This too would change with the weather.

In another of his combative 2003 speaking engagements, this one at Caltech in Pasadena, Michael Crichton explored the late twentieth-century corruption of the scientific method.[37] In what must have come as news to his audience, Crichton traced its source to the previously uncontroversial astrophysicist Frank Drake. Along with PBS icon Carl Sagan and others, Drake had pioneered the search for extraterrestrial signals (SETI). Crichton took particular issue with the equation Drake used to prove there was intelligent life elsewhere in the universe. As Crichton observed, every element of the equation was based on guess-work, and guesswork was nothing but a tricked-up bias. "The belief that there are other life forms in the universe is a matter of faith," said Crichton. "There is not a single shred of evidence for any other life forms, and in forty years of searching, none has been discovered."

The acceptance of the SETI experiments by the scientific community was "a crack in the door," said Crichton. It loosened the definition of what constituted sound scientific methodology. That loosening led in turn to the arbitrary and increasingly tyrannical reign of a climate science whose most popular theories were untested and unfalsifiable. These theories trended towards the alarmist, even the apocalyptic, none more so than the projected "nuclear winter." In 1983, a veritable supergroup of scientific rock stars, including the omnipresent Sagan, published a paper in *Science* called "Nuclear Winter: Global Consequences of Multiple Nuclear Explosions."[38] Like Drake, Sagan and his colleagues presented a complex equation to justify their thesis that even a limited nuclear exchange would cause global temperatures to drop by more than thirty-five degrees centigrade. As with Drake's equation, however, all of the variables in this equation were pure SWAG—scientific, wild-ass guesses.

In 1983 science was following the news. That year, with President Reagan's unswerving support, NATO was holding firm in its commitment to install US cruise missiles in Britain and Italy and Pershing II ballistic missiles in West Germany. To rattle the West's collective nerve, Soviet intelligence sparked a worldwide protest movement, most of whose participants had no idea who was doing the sparking.[39] One of the protestors that eventful year was an ambitious young leftist at Columbia University. In March 1983, the student journal *Sundial* published an essay of his on what he called "the flowering of the nuclear freeze movement." Although Barack Obama did not discuss nuclear winter, he focused on its presumed cause, the impending missile deployment in Europe. This subject did not trouble everyone, just the elect, or, as Obama put it, "the more sensitive among us."[40]

Sagan directed his message at receptive souls such as Obama. The shabby quality of his science did little to diminish his star among those attracted to his politics. And for Sagan, politics, like science, was pure theater. He rolled his thesis out in the popular Sunday supplement *Parade* and reinforced that the following day with a well-publicized conference in Washington, cochaired by all-purpose alarmist Paul Ehrlich. Between them, Ehrlich and Sagan would appear on the Johnny Carson show more than sixty times. "This is not the way science is done," said Crichton. "It is the way products are sold."[41]

If Sagan and crew were hoping to pressure Reagan to delay the missile deployment or scrap it, they confused the PBS audience with the real world. Their conference began in late October 1983. The Pershing II missiles went operational six weeks later. Once the missiles were in place, the nuclear winter hysteria dissipated almost as quickly as the nuclear freeze movement. The KGB lost interest in both. The Gulf War, however, offered Sagan the opportunity for a limited field test of his nuclear winter theories. He calculated that if Saddam Hussein were to set the Kuwaiti oil fields alight as promised, the result would be "serious, massive crop failures" throughout the known world.[42] In fact, Saddam did set the oil fields on fire as promised, but the "Saddam Autumn" did not materialize as projected. "The fires caused no long-term weather effects," reported meteorologist Joe Witte in the *New York Times*.[43]

Happily for Sagan, his failed projections largely escaped notice. By the time of the Gulf War, climate alarmists had found a new source of anxiety. In June 1988, just thirteen years after scientists fretted in the pages of the *New York Times* about global cooling, James Hansen introduced the idea of global warming to a US Senate committee. As director of the Goddard Institute for Space Studies, Hansen lent NASA's authority to his claim that global warming was "now large enough that we can ascribe with a high degree of confidence a cause and effect relationship to the greenhouse effect."[44] Although he conceded the "need for improving these global climate models," Hansen larded his presentation with enough official-looking graphs and charts to grab the media's attention and give the international left a new cause for moral indignation.

The following year, Stephen Schneider of the National Center for Atmospheric Research made the case for science as theater. As he saw it, although "ethically bound to the scientific method," scientists needed "to capture the public's imagination." To do this successfully, they needed to "offer up scary scenarios, make simplified, dramatic statements, and make little mention of any doubts [they] might have."[45] Schneider would spend the rest of his life complaining he had been quoted out of context, but it is hard to mistake his intentions.

The theater that emerged had all the subtlety of a medieval morality play. In its most common retelling, the narrative pitted a high-minded truth teller like former vice president and future Nobel Prize winner

Al Gore against what the Manichaeans called the "Demon of Greed." Activists initially cast industrial concerns in the role of Demon. In assigning parts, however, they could be remarkably careless, a phenomenon citizen journalist Russell Cook has documented well.[46]

For years, Cook observed, global warming activists fixated on the idea that industry—sometimes coal, sometimes oil, occasionally both—was bribing scientists to "reposition global warming as theory rather than fact." Cook traced the first use of that specific quote to a 1994 NPR interview with writer and global-warming activist Ross Gelbspan. The "reposition" quote had become a cliché by the time the 2006 movie *An Inconvenient Truth* scrolled it across the screen. At the time of the movie's release, film critic Roger Ebert asked Gore about the quote, and Gore cited 1998 as the year that "we found an internal memo."[47] This date, of course, was four years after global warming activist Ross Gelbspan started talking about how *he* had found the "secret" memo.

Said Cook, summarizing the history of the "reposition" quote, "This is the *only* accusation there is, and it spirals back in each case to one source. Ross Gelbspan. Nobody else independently confirms or corroborates it, they just repeat it. *Endlessly*."[48]

Equally difficult to trace is the semantic shift from "anthropogenic global warming" (AGW) to "climate change." If pressed, the media concede the phrasing has evolved but refuse to explain the evolution. In an all-too-typical 2009 article in the *Christian Science Monitor*—"Why are they calling it 'climate change' now?"—Eoin O'Carroll refused to answer the question posed in his title and attacked those who dared to ask it.[49] These were the same people, he implied, who insisted temperatures had been "falling" since 1998, a claim no serious critic has made. What skeptics have claimed is that global temperatures have defied the computer models, an argument conceded by all responsible observers. "Over the past 15 years," admitted the AGW-friendly *Economist* in 2013, "air temperatures at the Earth's surface have been flat while greenhouse-gas emissions have continued to soar."[50]

Having dashed the "completely bogus" claims of his denialist straw man, O'Carroll spent endless paragraphs showing that scientists had used the term "climate change" in one context or another for a century or more. This was all beside the point. Sometime in the previous decade, activists consciously changed the brand name of the crisis du jour from "global warming" to "climate change." Although admitting that environmentalists were "canny about messaging," O'Carroll never even dropped a hint as to why they had changed their message. No one else in the AGW camp did either.

If there were no obvious KGB fingerprints on the global warming narrative, they were about the only fingerprints missing. Progressives of all stripes got their mitts on this issue early on to push any number of pet causes, from promoting world government to punishing Texan oil company executives. The media, weather reporters included, signed on almost to a person. They insisted the debate was over and AGW was as undeniable a fact as gravity. Those who pulled their news exclusively from mainstream media had no reason to question the alleged "consensus" and every reason to doubt the sanity, even the morality, of those who got their news elsewhere.

In 2007 Pulitzer Prize–winning columnist Ellen Goodman nicely captured the moral hauteur of the AGW faithful. "I would like to say we're at a point where global warming is impossible to deny," she wrote. "Let's just say that global warming deniers are now on a par with Holocaust deniers, though one denies the past and the other denies the present and future."[51] If nothing else, Goodman at least acknowledged what many of her fellow alarmists would not: namely, the insidious roots of the word *denier*.

Rabbi Dennis Prager took advantage of Goodman's candor to highlight "one of the largest campaigns of vilification of decent people in history." As Prager explained, one earned a scarlet *D* not just by questioning whether the earth was warming or that humans caused the warming but also by doubting the scope of the catastrophe Gore and others had projected. Prager thought the odds good that European courts would start prosecuting global warming deniers much as they already did Holocaust deniers. "Just watch," said Prager cheekily. "That is far more likely than the oceans rising by 20 feet. Or even 10. Or even three."[52]

## THE HERETIC

Based on his personal profile, classmates might have voted Bjorn Lomborg least likely to be branded with a scarlet letter, let alone the scarlet *D*. On the face of things, Lomborg had all the credentials to be a progressive in good standing: as an openly gay Scandinavian he was a globalist, a vegetarian, a PhD in political science, and perhaps most important, a believer in man-made global warming. "The important question is not *whether* man-made $CO_2$ increases global temperature," Lomborg wrote in his provocative 2001 book, *The Skeptical Environmentalist*, "but *how much*."[53]

Skeptical Lomborg may have been, but there was nothing antagonistic about his language. Its matter-of-fact tone had to unsettle those who claimed ownership of the facts Lomborg disputed. In his book, he made the inarguable point that climate scientists have had to rely almost solely on computer models. Inarguable too was that computers were not yet able to manage the data needed to make reliable predictions for the next week, let alone the next century. Given the lack of reliable data, Lomborg concluded scientists and their political allies had likely "distorted the scenarios being presented to the public." They had also failed to do any serious cost-benefit analysis on the various fixes they were proposing. "The world as a whole," said Lomborg, "would benefit more from investing in tackling poverty in the developing world and in research and development of renewable energy than in policies focused on climate change."[54]

Lomborg made no friends with his italicized assessment that "*global warming is not anywhere near the most important problem facing the world.*"[55] For all that, his work was a model of restraint, free of hyperbole and ad hominem attacks. One would never guess this from the outcry of the scientific community, a response that Crichton described as "disgraceful." Lomborg's very progressivism seemed to work against him.

His critics could not dismiss him as some right-wing crank or a shill of the oil companies. So they attacked him, said Crichton, as "a heretic."[56]

At the head of the line to take a swing at the Lomborgian piñata were the editors of the magazine *Scientific American* (*SA*). They invited four "leading experts," including Stephen "scary scenarios" Schneider, to give Lomborg their best shot. As Lomborg pointed out in his one-page rebuttal, which *SA* initially begrudged him, *SA* did not choose the four experts randomly. In fact, Lomborg had criticized two of them directly in his book. He also took issue with the title of the collective attack, "Science defends itself against *The Skeptical Environmentalist*." Lomborg's book did not attack science, he argued. His book *was* science. He suggested a more precise title for the collection might have been "Alarmist environmentalism defends itself against the Skeptical Environmentalist."[57]

A statistician by training, Lomborg did a masterful job defending his thesis against critics in highly specialized fields. The technical errors he made were few, and his larger thesis was incontestable. That, of course, only provoked his critics to attack him, said Crichton, "in the most vicious personal terms." He may have looked, talked, dressed, dined, and even coupled like his critics, but on this issue he stood outside the magic circle, looking in. "Of course, any scientist can be charged as Galileo was charged," concluded Crichton. "I just never thought I'd see the *Scientific American* in the role of mother church."

## THE NEW LEPERS

"Nick Naylor had been called many things since becoming chief spokesman for the Academy of Tobacco Studies," wrote Christopher Buckley in the opening sentence of his satirical novel *Thank You for Smoking*, "but until now no one had actually compared him to Satan."[58] In fact, the pious had been discerning a satanic threat in smoking since one of Columbus's sailors, Rodrigo de Jerez, first introduced tobacco to Europe. As Iain Gately observed in his history of tobacco, the devil was often pictured blowing smoke out of his various orifices. So when Jerez returned to Spain doing the same, he was imprisoned by the Inquisition for three years, "presumably," wrote Gately, "the time it took to exorcize this novel form of possession."[59]

Despite appearances to the contrary, there is nothing Christian about the antismoking movement; nothing Marxist either. Indeed, this is the rare progressive cause that cannot be traced back to the Kremlin. Its roots, in fact, go not much deeper than a few do-gooder organizations and a handful of opportunistic trial lawyers. In 1961, the American Cancer Society and other like-minded groups sent a letter to President Kennedy requesting a study on the effects of cigarette smoking. The petitioners asked only for a "solution to this health problem that would interfere least with the freedom of industry or the happiness of individuals."

Kennedy turned the task over to his new surgeon general, Luther Terry, a small-town Alabama physician who had worked his way through the government health hierarchy. Terry took his charge seriously. He commissioned an exhaustive study that lasted nearly two years and resulted in a document titled *Smoking and Health: Report of the Advisory Committee to the Surgeon General*. The 1964 report "hit the country like a bombshell," Terry would reminisce two decades later. "It was front page news and a lead story on every radio and television station in the United States and many abroad."[60] He did not exaggerate its impact.

The trial lawyers took the lead from there. Foremost among them was George Washington University law professor John Banzhaf III. Although Banzhaf made the requisite noise about the public good, he had never been shy about making a buck. In one oft-told story, this aspiring gigolo claimed to have danced with older women on cruise ships to pay his way through law school. Upon graduation, he thought of taking on a new hustle—that of patent lawyer—for the simple reason that "they made more money than anyone else."[61]

Banzhaf switched his interest to antismoking on a whim: he wearied of all the smoking commercials on TV. "I'm not a crusader," he insisted. "I look for areas where I can put in the least and get the most—the biggest bang for my buck." Soon after graduating law school, he filed a petition with the Federal Communications Commission (FCC) demanding that radio and TV stations airing cigarette commercials give free time to antismoking messages. The FCC ruled in his favor, and Banzhaf successfully defended that decision when it went to court in 1968. In the interim, he founded a nonprofit known by the catchy acronym ASH, Action on Smoking and Health. Its self-described mission was "to use the tremendous but largely untapped power of legal action against a major social problem: smoking." Working from this base, Banzhaf succeeded in getting the FCC to ban all cigarette commercials—so much for "the freedom of industry"—and served as amicus curiae when the ban was challenged unsuccessfully on constitutional grounds.

What Banzhaf could not do through his efforts, at least not by himself, was demonize the individual smoker. The 1964 surgeon general report had treated smokers as victims. For nearly thirty years the media continued to treat smokers largely as victims, of their own folly perhaps but victims nonetheless. Even when the American Cancer Society and others began to refer to smoking as an "addiction," the implicit message was that addicts were to be pitied, not reviled.

Almost inevitably, however, "the Roundheads of neo-puritanism,"[62] as Buckley called them, turned the antismoking movement from a commonsense health campaign into a moral crusade. In 1992, five hundred years after Rodrigo de Jerez caught hell for breathing smoke, the Environmental Protection Agency (EPA) revived the spirit of the Inquisition when it produced a much-trumpeted study called *Respiratory Health Effects of Passive Smoking.*[63] In a stroke, the EPA turned the victims of smoking into victimizers, the disseminators of "secondhand smoke," more formally known as "environmental tobacco smoke" or ETS. According to the study, ETS caused three thousand cancer deaths a year in nonsmokers and as many as three hundred thousand respiratory tract infections in young children.

"I can tell you that second hand smoke is not a health hazard to anyone and never was," said Michael Crichton in his San Francisco speech. He had science on his side. In 2003, James Enstrom and

Geoffrey Kabat published in *BMJ* (formerly the *British Medical Journal*) an article detailing the most exhaustive study to date on the subject of ETS.[64] The database with which the researchers worked was vast, the 35,561 nonsmokers who participated in a longitudinal prevention study sponsored by the American Cancer Society. In that they were all married to smokers, the study participants would seem to have been at great risk from ETS, but they, in fact, were not. "The results do not support a causal relation between environmental tobacco smoke and tobacco related mortality," wrote the authors. "The association between exposure to environmental tobacco smoke and coronary heart disease and lung cancer may be considerably weaker than generally believed." As Crichton understood, appeals to the science would move few of the eco-faithful. "The beliefs of a religion are not dependent on facts," he told his audience, "but rather are matters of faith. Unshakeable belief."

The temperance movement took a century to develop and, even after being enshrined into the Constitution, it could not keep its hold on the public. The antismoking movement, by contrast, morphed from the wishful to the tyrannical in a historic eyeblink. Emily Badger's 2013 *Atlantic* headline summed up the situation with mathematical accuracy, "It Really Only Took about 20 Years for the U.S. to Turn Smokers into Pariahs."[65] Affirmed Art Caplan, director of the Center for Bioethics at the University of Pennsylvania, "The demonization of smokers is one of the most remarkable ethical changes in American society in the 20th century. It has transformed what was once a bad habit into an outright sin."[66]

By involving itself in what was ostensibly a public health issue, the EPA merged this newly dubbed "environmental blight" into the larger eco-consciousness. For the first twenty or so years of its existence, the environmental movement had limited targets: oil companies, industrial polluters, people who threw their McDonald's bags out of car windows. The antismoking movement proved to be a useful ally in that it created millions of sinners, millions of everyday Americans to whom the eco-elect could feel morally superior. Observed Jonathan Last, "Smokers are the new lepers, except that no one would look down on a leper as being morally repugnant."[67] To enjoy what Buckley called the "ecstasies of neo-puritanical fervor" all the nonsmokers had to do was not smoke. Redemption did not come much cheaper than that.

The hysteria quickly went global. Throughout the Western world, one community after another imposed bans on smoking, indoors and even outdoors. A column by British journalist Leo McKinstry nicely captured the moral energy of the movement. He detailed the case of a couple in the Essex town of Brentwood who hoped to bring a foster child into their home. When interviewed, the husband unthinkingly admitted to having smoked two cigars in the previous year. Although the demand for foster parents was pressing, the local social service agency rejected the couple's application. Apparently, foster parents had to be completely tobacco-free for at least the prior twelve months. "Wallowing in their pose of progressive wisdom," wrote McKinstry of Britain's civic leaders, "they sneer at the cruelties, prejudices and superstitions of the past. Yet when it comes to the issue of smoking they are as fanatically intolerant as any witch-finder of the 17th century."[68]

In Canada, meanwhile, a businessman in the town of Wiarton, named Jim Turner, was facing nine charges under the Smoke-Free Ontario Act for having allegedly lit a cigarette in his TV repair shop. The "smoking police" were extra vigilant in Turner's case, understandably so. Four year earlier he had been charged with having an ashtray in his shop. "So they came and watched me and watched me and watched me and watched me," said Turner of the smoking police. "And they saw me actually get up off my seat on the deck, they say with a cigarette in my hand, go inside, grab the phone and come back out. And for that, I got nine charges?"[69]

In New York City, Mayor Bloomberg's anticigarette crusade resulted in one of 2014's most controversial and tragic actions. During Bloomberg's tenure, smoking in public places was banned, and punitive taxes pushed the price of cigarettes up to fourteen dollars a pack. As a result, hustlers, like four-hundred-pound Eric Garner of Staten Island, took to selling individual, untaxed cigarettes—"loosies"—to people who wanted a quick fix.

In their attempt to arrest the chronically unhealthy African American, several NYPD officers took Garner to the ground, causing a fatal heart attack. Rather than examine the city's tax and tobacco policies, let alone the state of urban black culture, leftist mayor Bill de Blasio found it more morally satisfying to pin a scarlet *R* on the arresting officers, most of whom were white. To show their moral superiority to the New York cops, neo-puritans around the world indulged in a seemingly endless orgy of self-congratulatory protest.

To their humble credit, the "religious police" from the Islamic State in Iraq and Syria, or ISIS, have avoided the kind of petty bureaucratic harassment so common in the West. When they banned the public smoking of cigarettes and water pipes in war-torn Iraq, they banned just about everything else their citizens might enjoy as well. They did not bother with bogus studies and strained rationales. They didn't have to. Their authority came straight from Allah and right down the barrel of an AK-47. As the *New York Times* reported, Islamic authorities "have hunted down and killed those perceived as opposing their project."[70] Understandably, compliance has been high. Antismoking fundamentalists in the Western world lack the moral clarity of their Islamic brethren. The West's neo-puritans, like their seventeenth-century antecedents, dwell in that strange netherworld of uncertainty and anxiety, all too eager to punish those who make them question whether they have indeed chosen the approved path to salvation.

# 4

# THE SCARLET *S*: SEXIST

n no other subset of the neo-puritan coalition are the rules so maddeningly fickle as in the church of progressive feminism. Although feminism takes many forms, the women who speak for the more progressive varieties—"waves," in feminist patois—have a near monopoly on the distribution of the scarlet *S*, especially at the national level. The right target can turn even the libertines among them into neo-puritans. Similarly, the wrong target can make the most sensitive forget there ever was a feminist movement.

In an academic philosophy blog—and more on this later—a pretty young graduate student did the future historian a favor by cataloging the many emotional assaults that comprise the elusive rubric "sexism." She had apparently suffered them all. As an undergraduate, "Jender" had to endure a "sixty-something" professor who asked her to pose in the nude. As a grad student, she stared down a prof who, with his hand on her knee, waxed poetic about her beauty. On several occasions, she was "ignored, talked over, and talked down." She overheard male grad students mock their female colleagues and write off their presence in the department as due to affirmative action. And most cutting of all, she was told that women were unsuited for philosophy because they were "not as gifted in math and logic."[1] As slight as these abuses might seem, say, to an Afghani woman confined to her burka, or a Somalian girl deprived of her clitoris, there could be hell to pay for those accused of inflicting them in America.

## THE BOGEYMAN

"In Oleanna land is free," go the lyrics of the eponymous Norwegian folk song. "The wheat and corn just plant themselves / Then grow a good four feet a day / While on your bed you rest yourself." If America's leading novelist, Phillip Roth, felt the need to question the scarlet *R*, America's leading playwright, David Mamet, felt the need to question the scarlet *S*. He did so in his two-character, 1992 play, *Oleanna*, named after the folk song. The world of perfect sexual harmony, Mamet seemed to be saying, was as illusory as a land where wheat grows four feet a day.

In the course of *Oleanna*, John, a smug and self-righteous college professor, finds himself accused by his student Carol of an escalating series of offenses—sexism, sexual harassment, and, finally, rape. Carol locates her power in an imagined sisterhood. "I speak, yes, not for myself," she tells John, "but for the group; for those who suffer what I suffer." In the face of this collective punitive power, John can only protest that he is not a "bogeyman," that he does not represent some larger group, that he is just an individual. "I have rights too," he tells her. "Do you see? I have a house . . . part of the real world."[2] He *had* a house. By play's end, he has lost his house, his job, and his wife. He responds by resorting to his most primitive force and beats Carol savagely.

"It's a play about power," said Mamet in one of his rare interviews. "The person in power thinks he or she is right. And they use the power they have in ways that the other finds very objectionable and end up destroying each other."[3]

Women as a group do not have either the intrinsic moral authority that African Americans do or the same level of group cohesion. More important, they do not inspire anywhere near the same level of fear. There has never been a female "Ferguson," and there never will be. To punish an individual like John, to tag him with the scarlet *S*, women must do what Carol did—that is, enlist the power of sympathetic institutions and focus it. This is not easy. It takes a near-perfect alignment of forces. That is why so few individuals have had to wear a career-killing scarlet *S*, and those who clearly deserve to wear one often walk free.

Like John of *Oleanna*, University of Kansas law professor Emil Tonkovich was one of hundreds of American men, perhaps thousands, who innocently went to work one day only to discover he had become an enemy of the people. Although the case is not well-known beyond Kansas, it is worth recounting in that it speaks to the political subtext of so much of punitive neo-puritanism, even on the local level. On the national level, a parallel case was playing out at exactly the same time and for very much the same reason. Neither was an anomaly.

Tonkovich remembers the day of his undoing well.[4] It was June 1991, and he had just turned forty. His forty years had been eventful ones. The son of a Chicago truck driver, Tonkovich worked his way through college at the steel mills in nearby Gary, Indiana. Upon graduation, he became a Chicago District DEA task force officer. When he had saved enough, he enrolled in Notre Dame Law School, graduating summa cum laude. After graduation, he became a federal prosecutor and supervised, among other major investigations, the Chicago end of the "Strawman" case, the one that provided the grist for the movie *Casino*.

Tonkovich's fortieth birthday found him in a contemplative mood. He had served ten successful years as a prof at KU. His annual reviews had all been excellent. In fact, he had the best student evaluations on the faculty. And he had had no trouble getting tenure. To round out his life, he had become more active in politics. In founding the conservative Federalist Society chapter on campus, Tonkovich alerted his colleagues that he stood on an end of the political spectrum that most had only read about.

On the day in question, while Tonkovich mulled his future, Robert Jerry, the law school dean, popped into his office with a bit of news. He had just spoken with a recent law school graduate, who told Jerry that three years earlier Tonkovich had "made a pass" at her. Jerry thought the charge "frivolous," especially coming from a thirty-one-year-old divorcée.[5] He would not, however, provide Tonkovich with either the name of the accuser or the specifics of the charge. Jerry did, however, send a letter to the student that reflected his own lack of concern. "The first option available to you is to confront the faculty member directly," he wrote. "I encourage you to do so."[6] Tonkovich offered to meet with the student in Jerry's presence. The student refused.

Two months later, on the first day of the fall semester, the law student filed a formal complaint with the vice chancellor and upped the charges considerably. She was now accusing Tonkovich of having sex with her following a law student's party three years earlier. On that same day, a TV news crew from Kansas City came to Lawrence to investigate rumors of a sex scandal among the faculty of the KU Law School. Tonkovich was beginning to see where this was heading.

After the TV crew left, Tonkovich learned the name of the student and recalled very well the incident that provoked her allegation. According to Tonkovich's sworn hearing testimony, the student had followed him around at the party in question and pursued him outside when he went to leave. "She was very friendly and appeared to be following him around and flirting with him," confirmed Jean Younger, the party host, in a sworn affidavit. Younger told her future husband that the woman has "really got the hots for Tonk."[7]

According to Tonkovich, the law student claimed she was too drunk to drive and asked for a ride home. Wary of her intentions, Tonkovich drove her instead to the nearby campus police department parking lot and suggested they go for a walk to help her sober up. During the walk, the student tried to kiss him. When they got back to the car, she tried to sit on his lap. Tonkovich then drove this none-too-happy camper back to her car and dropped her off. There had been no sex. Days later, again according to Tonkovich, she apologized to him for her behavior. Shelley White, a fellow law student and friend of the accuser, would confirm Tonkovich's memory. "A few days after the party some students were talking about [the student's] conduct at Jean's party and that [the student] had apologized to Professor Tonkovich," White stated.[8] At the time of her affidavit, White was an assistant DA. That was the last personal encounter Tonkovich ever had with the student. White heard no more about it either. She confirmed, in fact, that she did not believe her friend's allegation.

At the time of this incident, the faculty code did not prohibit professors from dating students. Profs did so routinely and openly. The dean during Tonkovich's first eight years, Mike Davis, recalled at least four professors who dated students, and there were only six single faculty members. One female law professor married a student. Tonkovich, who was single in 1988, would eventually do the same. His future wife testified she was the one who initiated the relationship, having declined propositions from two other law professors. The other law student Tonkovich dated testified that she too had made the first move.

Wrote Davis, "No complaints concerning sexual harassment came to me or to anyone else in the law school administration during my service as Dean."[9] He never even heard a rumor of the same, and he was dean when the alleged incident took place. The law student would admit to having told no one about it for three years, but the story she finally decided to tell was a career-killer.

In the student's evolving version, Tonkovich convinced her to take a ride with him. During the ride, he allegedly commented, "Well, grades are important to you, aren't they?" and "What we're going to do tonight won't affect your grades." They parked and got out of the car. As they walked, Tonkovich put his arm around the woman and kissed her. Back at the car, according to the student, Tonkovich looked at her and said, "Why don't you do something for me?" He then unzipped his pants, and she performed oral sex on him.

When the university attorney later asked the woman why she had yielded so easily, she answered, "He talked about grades. I felt I was backed into a corner. I felt if I didn't do that, he would lower my grade."[10] As Tonkovich told this author, he gave multiple-choice exams, and law school exams were graded anonymously. She would eventually get a B+ in the course.

Based on her word alone, the vice chancellor recommended a one-year paid suspension for Tonkovich, and the chancellor approved it. It was about this time that Tonkovich began to feel like the John Proctor character in an updated version of Arthur Miller's play *The Crucible*. Set in seventeenth-century Salem, Massachusetts, the play speaks to the dark heart of human nature. It shows just how exciting and infectious it can be to accuse others, even the innocent, of evil. Although an imperfect human being, Proctor will not sign off on an accusation of which he and others are innocent. "It is my name!" he tells his prosecutors. "Because I cannot have another in my life. Because I am not worth the dust on the feet of them that hang! How may I live without my name?"[11] So saying, he condemns himself to the gallows.

Tonkovich did much the same. Unwilling to accept the paid suspension, he requested a public hearing, as was his right. The day after the offended student learned of Tonkovich's request, the Kansas City TV station ran another report on the law school, this one featuring a woman in the shadows talking about outrageous sexual behavior by unnamed law professors. The following week, six law school faculty members, with the blessing of the administration, signed a letter asking students to report anonymously any sexual misconduct by an unnamed law professor.[12] "In the interests of time," or so they said, they did not alert their colleagues to the letter in advance. Of the six, at least five, as Tonkovich saw it, were politically aggressive. The leader of the group had butted heads with Tonkovich in the past. On one occasion, Tonkovich had criticized him for trashing the Koch brothers' million-dollar donation to the law school. On another, perhaps more to the point, Tonkovich had opposed his bid to be dean. This same professor would later testify as the university's due process expert.

Before the letter, no student had spoken to any of the six profs about being harassed. The profs claimed only to have heard "second- and third-hand accounts" of the same. Nevertheless, activists walked the letter around the law school, soliciting complaints and telling students they needed their help to "bolster" a charge of "rape." The tone of the letter reflected that level of seriousness. Although the letter did not mention Tonkovich by name, the charges against him had been leaking into the ether since first brought. To this point, however, no student other than the accuser had ever complained formally or otherwise to anyone about Tonkovich's conduct.

As Tonkovich learned later, new allegations against him were surfacing, all solicited. In March 1992, two months before the premiere of *Oleanna*, KU chancellor Gene Budig moved to fire Tonkovich for a pattern of sexual harassment and moral turpitude. So "trivial" and "innocuous" were the new allegations, as the university eventually conceded, Budig could not identify any of them as faculty code violations. Tonkovich refused to resign quietly, but that only hardened his opponents' resolve.

The wheels of justice grind exceedingly slowly in academia. The hearing Tonkovich demanded did not begin until late August 1992, and the weekly sessions did not end until May 1993. For all the smoke surrounding Tonkovich, the only allegation that mattered was the one lobbed by the original complainant, the female law student who had met Tonkovich at a party in the summer of 1988. Initially, Tonkovich was charged with violating a "sex with a student" rule. When it became clear that there was no such rule, a sexual harassment/moral turpitude charge was substituted without benefit of any new evidence and in violation of the university's statute of limitation.

Nearly a year after the hearings started, a year fraught with the kind of rococo proceedings only a university could conceive, the hearing committee voted three to two to have Tonkovich fired. The three-person majority conceded that the woman "offered no indication that she was an unwilling partner" and that "all evidence point[ed] to Professor Tonkovich's integrity in assigning grades."[13] As to the two-person minority, they denounced the majority finding of sexual harassment/moral turpitude as "unjust and untenable."[14]

Three liberal law professors attended the hearings and reviewed the exhibits. In a public statement they admitted to being "appalled by the dishonesty" of the faculty and administrators in their attempt to "fabricate some wrongdoing." The professors concluded harshly, "The evidence did not establish a Faculty Code violation and the procedure was extremely unfair."[15] It did not matter what the law professors thought.

In Kansas, wheat grew no faster than it did in Oleanna. Not long after his termination, Tonkovich was diagnosed with leukemia. By choice, he has not worked since being fired. He told me, "I just checked out. I John Galted before John Galting was cool."

## SULLEN INTELLECTUAL LIGHTWEIGHT

In October 1991, at the front end of his own personal hell, Tonkovich watched a parallel inquisition unfold half a continent away. Its outlines were scarily similar: a suddenly revived memory of a heretofore untold abuse, a reluctant witness pushed forward by political foes of the accused, a media eager to see a man humbled, and uncorroborated charges that were impossible to disprove. What Tonkovich lacked was the extraordinary platform a nationally televised hearing afforded the man at the center of this distant ordeal, Clarence Thomas.

By any standard, the Hill–Thomas hearings that October were the most explosively divisive in Washington since Hiss–Chambers forty years earlier. Feminist contrarian Camille Paglia called them "an atrocious public spectacle, worthy of the show trials of a totalitarian regime." She did not overstate her case. She did not have to. They were that bad.[16] And yet for all the talk of sex and sexism, the hearings were never about either. What they were really about was abortion. "That," said Supreme Court Justice Thomas years later, "was the elephant in the room."[17]

On the hard edges of the feminist left, no "right" mattered more. University of Dallas scholar Bernadette Waterman Ward explained why. "Abortion in America is upheld not as medical or even political policy, but as, in fact, a religious sacrifice," Ward observed without approving. "Abortion appeases mysterious forces that threaten a woman not physically but spiritually, with the extinction of her being."[18] In 1992, a year after the Hill–Thomas hearings, feminist Ginette Paris published a book titled, without irony, *The Sacrament of Abortion*. In 1999, upon retiring from her career as the proprietor of an abortion clinic, Patricia Baird-Windle told *Florida Today*, "I now consider abortion to be a major blessing, and to be a sacrament in the hands of women."[19] Fifteen years later, feminists were still making this case, as activists did in Spain in February 2014 when they bared their breasts before a Spanish cardinal and screamed, "Abortion is sacred!"[20] To deny women this sacramental rite was heresy of the highest order.

On July 1, 1991, in Kennebunkport, Maine, President George H. W. Bush threatened to do just that when he introduced Clarence Thomas as his choice for the US Supreme Court. Those in the know had good cause to worry. For one, Thomas was only forty-three. He could serve on the court for another thirty or forty years. Worse, he was replacing the reliably proabortion Thurgood Marshall. A strict constructionist, Thomas was likely to see abortion not as a constitutional right—the Constitution was silent on the issue—but as a legislative matter for each individual state. "They knew one thing," Thomas would later say of the abortion activists. "They weren't in charge of me."[21]

Thomas worried the activists for another reason. As an African American, he could defuse the "states' rights" insinuation in ways a white constructionist could not. In 1987, Sen. Ted Kennedy branded prior Supreme Court nominee Robert Bork with half the letters in the neo-puritan alphabet in his protest of Bork's nomination. "Robert Bork's America," said Kennedy in a fact-free rant, "is a land in which women would be forced into back-alley abortions, blacks would sit at segregated lunch counters, rogue police could break down citizens' doors in midnight raids, schoolchildren could not be taught about evolution, writers and artists could be censored at the whim of government, and the doors of the federal courts would be shut on the fingers of millions of citizens for whom the judiciary is—and is often the only—protector of the individual rights that are the heart of our democracy." Twenty-five years later, every scurrilous word of the Kennedy quote made it into Bork's *New York Times* obituary.[22]

That shameless bit of slander was enough to kill Bork's nomination and solidify Kennedy's stature in progressive circles, but it would not work on Thomas. Kennedy and his allies would have to take another tack to stop him, and they were eager to try. Speaking to a National

Organization of Women (NOW) convention in July 1991, radical feminist Florynce Kennedy, no relation to Ted, proudly rolled out a newly minted verb in describing her plans for Thomas. "We're going to Bork him," she said. "We're going to kill him politically."[23]

The woman who would orchestrate the Thomas assassination watched the news of his nomination at her California home. "He's the one!" Susan Hoerchner screamed.[24] Thomas was the all-purpose hound dog, Hoerchner told her husband, who had harassed her Yale Law School pal Anita Hill back when she and Hill hung out together in Washington in 1981. At the time of this epiphany, Hoerchner was serving as a low-level judge in California, and Hill, despite her Yale credentials, was teaching at the backwater O. W. Coburn School of Law in her native Oklahoma.

Although no one would take public credit, it seems likely that the politically savvy Hoerchner put the harassment story in play. Before the month of July 1991 was out, well-wired media people like Tim Phelps of *Newsday* and Nina Totenberg of *National Public Radio* knew about the recycled Hill allegations. So too did abortion activists like Kate Michelman, the national director of the National Abortion Rights Action League. Since the more responsible media could not report mere rumors, it was the activists' job to turn those rumors into affidavits. If they could not burden Thomas with the scarlet *R*, as they had Bork, they knew he was as vulnerable as any man to the scarlet *S*, but only if Anita Hill would speak up.

Thomas expected the confirmation hearings in September to be rough, and they were. He expected the Democrats on the Senate Judiciary Committee to zero in on abortion, and they did. The Pharisees of the feminist left watched Thomas fend off the blows in a high state of alert. They knew their way around Congress well enough to know that, barring the unforeseen, the full Senate would confirm Thomas's nomination. To take him out, they would have to play the sex card, and who better to deal it than Hill? Her blackness would offset any advantage Thomas's race conferred upon him in the looming showdown.

Among those scheming to force Hill into the open was Ricki Seidman. The newly hired Kennedy staffer came to the task well-rehearsed. As research director of People for the American Way, Seidman had played a pivotal role in the borking of Robert Bork. On September 6, 1991, she called Hill about rumored misbehavior by Thomas at the Equal Opportunity Employment Commission (EEOC). Being coy, Seidman did not voice her suspicion that Hill was Thomas's victim. "At that point I told Ms. Seidman that I would neither confirm nor deny any knowledge of that,"[25] Hill would later testify. She did promise, however, that she would think about Seidman's request and get back to her.

A day or two later, Hill called back to ask Seidman, "If I were to discuss this matter, where should I go?" Seidman referred her to a staffer on the Senate Labor Committee, James Brudney. Reportedly it was Brudney who first told Hill the sexual harassment rumors centered on her, and that Thomas might withdraw his nomination if she were to come forward. "I did not want the committee to rely on rumors,"[26] she would later testify, as though she meant it.

In the following two weeks, Hill continued to vacillate. She did not want her name in play, and she certainly did not want to speak to the FBI, but Senate staffers continued to lean on her, as did her friend Hoerchner, as did the media. Finally, on September 23, Hill faxed a letter to the Senate Judiciary Committee, claiming Thomas had pressured her to date him and had talked graphically about sex in her presence. A staffer then persuaded her to speak to the FBI, and later that same evening, two FBI agents interviewed Hill in Oklahoma. She proved oddly evasive, telling the agents, as one of them testified, that she prepared her statement only after several phone conversations with Hoerchner. According to the agent, Hill "did not mention the telephone conversations that she had had with representatives of the Judiciary Committee."[27]

Two days later FBI agents went to Thomas's home to follow up on Hill's accusations. Upon hearing them Thomas confessed to being "shocked, surprised, hurt, and enormously saddened."[28] He had never before had an accusation like that leveled against him. In the days that followed, someone—likely a Senate staffer—leaked Hill's statement to the media, specifically to Phelps and Totenberg. In the meantime, Senate Democrats kept pressing for a delay in the confirmation vote. "Every effort was made to invoke the rules and to delay the matter," said Utah senator Orrin Hatch on the Senate floor. As a result, there would be an interim ten-day recess, which meant "a full two weeks where Judge Thomas could be smeared while all of us were out of town."[29]

The neo-puritans could not have been more pleased with the way events were unfolding. As Hill's story steamed into the headlines, the Senate called for a public session to air her grievances. With cameras rolling, Hill played the reluctant ingenue role as though she had been rehearsing it for weeks—which she probably had been. In response to a question from Sen. Joe Biden, Hill claimed she had gone public only because a reporter had called her and read "verbatim" the statement she had drafted. "Do you consider yourself part of some organized effort to determine whether or not Clarence Thomas should or should not sit on the bench?" Biden asked Hill. "No, I had no intention of being here today, none at all," she dodged. "I did not think that this would ever occur."[30] Likely for reasons both personal and political, she had handed her allies the means to derail Thomas's nomination. She just did not want to get caught with her hand on the switch.

In constructing her harassment narrative, Hill had some plot problems to explain away. The most obvious was her willingness to follow Thomas to the EEOC after being harassed at the Department of Education (DOE). She explained lamely that toward the end of their mutual tenure at the DOE, Thomas was behaving better. "It appeared that the sexual overtures, which had so troubled me, had ended," she testified with a straight face. Then, Hill testified, Thomas started misbehaving again at the EEOC. "He said that if I ever told anyone of his behavior that it would ruin his career," she claimed.[31] So she kept quiet throughout the four prior Senate confirmations that Thomas had undergone, maintained a friendly relationship with him over the years, used him as a reference for the law school job, and even helped recruit him to Tulsa for a conference on civil rights law.

In the most stunning part of her testimony, Hill listed the abuses to which Thomas had allegedly subjected her: he pointed out a pubic hair on top of a Coke can; he talked in detail about a porn star famously named "Long Dong Silver"; he bragged about his own sexual prowess; and he kept pressing her for dates that she continued to decline.[32] The very specificity of her claims lent them an aura of truthfulness. Following Hill's testimony, observers left and right thought Thomas's fate sealed. Had he heeded the advice of his supporters, it would have been. He might have mumbled some sort of apology, slumped away with his scarlet *S*, and humbly awaited his rejection from the full Senate.

In Hester Prynne's day, the town beadle represented "the whole dismal severity of the Puritanic code of law."[33] It was the beadle who officially chastened the offender. At the Hill–Thomas hearings, Biden attempted to play that role, but Thomas denied him. He trumped Biden's sex card with the inevitably more potent race card. Channeling a rage long suppressed, Thomas let the furies loose. "Senator," he said to a surprised Biden, "I would like to start by saying unequivocally, uncategorically, that I deny each and every single allegation against me today."[34] No one expected to hear this, certainly not with such ferocious conviction. Hill, after all, seemed so believable, and all Washington understood the risks of denying a woman's testimony.

"From my standpoint as a black American," Thomas thundered, "[the smear campaign] is a high-tech lynching for uppity blacks who in any way deign to think for themselves, to do for themselves, to have different ideas." For the first time in the post–civil rights era, an African American had called public attention to the oppressiveness of the left, and he was just warming up. "It is a message," Thomas continued, "that unless you kowtow to an old order, this is what will happen to you. You will be lynched, destroyed, caricatured by a committee of the U.S. Senate rather than hung from a tree."[35] As Thomas saw it, the "old order" was no longer Jim Crow. It was neo-puritanism.

"America is still burdened by its Puritan past, which erupts again and again in public scenarios of sexual inquisition, as in Hawthorne's *The Scarlet Letter*," wrote Camille Paglia of the hearings. As Paglia explained, the sexual revolutionaries of the sixties "broke the ancient codes of decorum" but were now insisting anew that women be treated like "delicate flowers." Even if telling the truth, said Paglia, Hill endured no real harassment, suffered no retribution, and deserved no legal redress. "If Anita Hill was thrown for a loop by sexual banter, that's her problem," said the straight-talking feminist.[36]

There is a real question, though, as to whether Hill was telling the truth. Only one individual testified that Hill had complained about Thomas in 1981. That was Hoerchner. In her deposition for the Judiciary Committee, Hoerchner told of how she and Hill spoke regularly throughout 1981 when both lived in Washington. It was during this time that Hill complained to her about Thomas's behavior. In September 1981 Hoerchner left for California, and the chats stopped. Hill, however, testified she began working with Thomas in "the early fall of 1981" and enjoyed a good working relationship "early on." Here is how this discrepancy played out in Hoerchner's deposition.[37]

Q. And, in an attempt to try to pin down the date a little bit more specifically as to your first phone conversation about the sexual harassment issue in 1981, the year you mentioned, you said the first time you moved out of Washington was September of 1981; is that correct?

A. Right.

Q. Okay. Were you living in Washington at the time you two had this phone conversation?

A. Yes.

Q. When she told you?

A. Yes.

Q. So it was prior to September of 1981?

A. Oh, I see what you're saying.

Hoerchner and her attorney, future Department of Homeland Security secretary Janet Napolitano, promptly asked for a recess. Hoerchner had just undercut the timeline on which the case against Thomas rested. By Hill's account, Thomas did not begin to pester her for roughly the first three months they worked together. At the earliest that would have been December 1981, three months after Hoerchner left for California, three months after she and Hill stopped talking on any kind of regular basis. Hoerchner, in fact, described her communication with Hill after September 1981 as "sporadic." In her deposition, she described only one post-Washington contact, that of meeting Hill at a professional seminar in 1984.

After conferring with Napolitano, Hoerchner had a convenient change of memory. Now it was time for the friendly Democratic counsel to ask, "When you had the initial phone conversation with Anita Hill and she spoke for the first time about sexual harassment, do you recall where you were living—what city?" Answered Hoerchner, "I don't know for sure."

The author who first reported the Hoerchner angle was none other than professional chameleon David Brock. Once the scourge of the left, he morphed into progressive scold extraordinaire as impresario of Media Matters for America. Although he has tried to distance himself from his reportorial past, his work on Hoerchner's testimony holds up. He explained why in a *New York Times* op-ed attacking Anthony Lewis's 1993 review of his book *The Real Anita Hill*.

The problem with Hoerchner, wrote Brock, went much deeper than "a harmless lapse of memory." Hoerchner, he explained, had been entirely clear on the regularity of her calls with Hill: when they took place, where they took place, and how they ended after Hoerchner moved. This all changed when a Senate lawyer pointed out the inconsistency in timing. When Hoerchner came back from a hasty recess, she "was suddenly unable to recall anything about the time or place of the call. But she was now adamant that Ms. Hill had named Judge Thomas as the perpetrator, a point on which she had previously been unsure."[38] The inference that Brock made here and in his book was that if Hill had been harassed as she charged, the harasser was not Thomas. The giddy momentum behind the accusation may have taken her to a place she did not really want to go.

In the years following the Hill–Thomas hearings, the *American Spectator* was the rare conservative journal to field boots-on-the-ground reporters, Brock among them. Fox News did not come online for another five years. Given their superior investigative resources, the major media took full control of the narrative. They dared not question the integrity of Hoerchner and Hill, but Thomas they felt free to doubt. Without necessarily endorsing this viewpoint, Steve Kroft of *60 Minutes* shared with Thomas his reputation in progressive circles more than fifteen years after the hearings: "A man of little accomplishment, an opportunistic black conservative who sold out his race, joined the Republican Party and was ultimately rewarded with an affirmative action appointment to the nation's highest court, a sullen, intellectual lightweight so insecure he rarely opens his mouth in oral arguments."[39]

As to Thomas's counterpart, "It's clear that Hill became, and remains, a heroine to many women," wrote the *Huffington Post*'s Jocelyn Noveck in discussing the debut of a flattering 2014 movie about her ordeal, tellingly titled, *Anita*.[40] Shortly after the movie debut, Barbara Walters welcomed Hill onto her show, *The View*, with the kind of reverence usually meted out to popes and presidents. "I would just like to say that I'm honored to be meeting you," gushed Walters. "I watched those hearings, as did so many other people. And to so many of us, you were our heroine."[41] The academic world took note as well. A few years after the hearings, Boston's Brandeis University rescued Hill from her forlorn outpost in Oklahoma.

Those who watched the hearings in real time were not quite so taken. A *New York Times*/CBS poll soon after the hearings found that

58 percent of Americans believed Thomas, and only 24 percent believed Hill.[42] "Make no mistake: it was not a White House conspiracy that saved this nomination," wrote Paglia. "It was Clarence Thomas himself. After eight hours of Hill's testimony, he was driven as low as any man could be. But step by step, with sober, measured phrases, he regained his position and turned the momentum against his accusers. It was one of the most powerful moments I have ever witnessed on television."[43] There was a lesson to be learned from Thomas, but too few future victims bothered to learn it.

## THE WAR ON WOMEN

On a personal note, the most trouble I ever got into in my five years hosting a daily talk radio show was stating a fact that was demonstrably true. The place was Kansas City, and the year was 1998. My guest that day was our female county executive. In attempting to explain the storied "gender gap," I observed that on average men know more about current events than women because on average they pay more attention.

Although I qualified my answer with "on average," the county executive looked shocked and hurt. When I offered to prove what should have been obvious, she exploded, the program director nearly expired, and the caller board lit up brighter than it had since O. J. walked free. The county executive wanted an apology, and now the station manager insisted I oblige her. "Do you really want me to apologize on air for telling the truth?" I asked. Thanks to the Internet, then a new tool in the studio, I was able to show him one survey after another. The data always and everywhere made my case, and he ultimately backed down.

If anything, the knowledge gap has only grown in the years since. In 2013, the UK's Economic and Social Research Council (ESRC) surveyed ten thousand citizens in ten countries, developed and developing. Researchers asked them questions based on hard and soft news reports, including recent international events. The results were consistent across the board. Men knew more. As good progressives, the researchers felt the need to explain away the results. The explanation could not be that men and women were simply different creatures with different interests. That made too much sense. The researchers preferred instead to blame the patriarchy. They imagined impediments like "the gender-bias of hard news content" or the "lack of visibility of women in TV and newspaper coverage," all of which could presumably be remedied with still more social engineering.[44]

What surprised the researchers—dismayed them, really—was that the political knowledge gap loomed largest in those countries that had done the most to assure gender equality. In the United States, the UK, and Canada, women scored 30 percent lower than men on average. The women in Greece, Italy, and Korea did not outscore their men but they did outscore women in the United States, the UK, and Canada. In no media account of the survey did anyone offer a halfway credible explanation as to why women with the best access to education and information did worse than their more repressed sisters.

Although they would never discuss these numbers publicly, Democratic strategists were well aware of them. They understood that to maintain the gender gap they needed to control the headlines. Many of their female constituents would dig no deeper. Conservatives could dominate certain long-form media all day long and into the night, but as long as Democrats and their allies ruled Google, AOL, and Yahoo! news services, women's magazines, the entertainment TV shows, and the daily newspapers, they could shape the political will of low-information female voters through the headlines alone. To precondition the low-information audience, Democratic strategists concocted the headline-grabbing "Republican war on women" theme. The more Republicans talked about women's issues, the more likely they were to offer up a choice sound bite or two for the Democrats to exploit.

The ultimate target, of course, was Republican presidential candidate Mitt Romney. A careful politician, Romney gave the Democrats little to excite the base. Their best opportunity came during the second debate with Obama in October 2012 when Romney told of the efforts he made as governor to diversify his cabinet. He had spoken to women's groups, he boasted, "and they brought us whole binders full of women."[45] So primed was the Democratic media complex for a takedown that when Romney said this, "Social media exploded."[46] So reported the *Washington Post*'s Suzi Parker.

What Parker could not explain, at least with any logic, was why exactly the social media did explode. Her best explanation was that Romney "went a bit patriarchal" in claiming he was able to recruit good .women because he offered flexible hours. "Do fathers not have to get home and cook dinner? Do they not want to be there for their children when school is out?" asked Parker peevishly. "The days of Donna Reed are long over, Mr. Romney." To frame an individual, conspirators need to fix on a kernel of truth and exaggerate it. In this case, the kernel was so tiny and tortured that the plot to frame Romney as sexist sputtered.

Radio commentator Rush Limbaugh was less cautious. To host a three-hour daily radio show with any kind of flair, he could not be both politic and entertaining. Although normally shrewd, Limbaugh walked himself into one very sophisticated trap. The trap was set after Republicans rejected a Democratic request to let a thirty-year-old Georgetown Law School student named Sandra Fluke testify at a congressional hearing on government rules. The subject at hand was whether religious organizations should be exempt from mandatory contraception coverage. The fact that Fluke attended a Jesuit law school did not, the Republicans figured, make her an authority on religious freedom. ABC News headlined this routine decision, "Rep. Darrell Issa Bars Minority Witness, a Woman, on Contraception."[47] The "minority" here meant "Democrat," but the Democratic strategy was all about headlines, and most headline readers likely thought "minority' meant black—a "twofer," black and female.

On February 23, Fluke, who sidelined as president of the Georgetown Law Students for Reproductive Justice, testified before a Potemkin hearing staged by congressional Democrats. She lamented that her Catholic law school did not provide contraceptive coverage and praised Obamacare for forcing it to do so. Fluke told of the many young women who "suffered financially and emotionally" because their employers would not cover their contraceptive cost. She then recited some hair-curling horror stories about women who contracted all kinds of awful afflictions for want of coverage. "In the media lately," said the indignant Fluke, "some conservative Catholic organizations have been asking what did we expect when we enroll in a Catholic school?" Fluke answered her own question, "We expected women to be treated equally." For the record, if Fluke meant equal to men, the university did not provide condom coverage either.[48]

The media dutifully covered Fluke's unchallenged testimony. NPR was the one of the few to note that employer mandates would not have affected Fluke because she was on a student plan. Then too, Georgetown already offered contraceptive coverage to its employees. "But none of that stopped [Fluke] from giving the handful of Democrats present, including former House Speaker Pelosi, a rousing lawyer-like defense of why failing to cover contraceptives is unfair to women," said NPR reporter Julie Rovner.[49] Nor did any of that prevent the media from giving Fluke's testimony much more attention that it deserved.

Fluke was too tempting a target for Limbaugh to resist. In an improvised comic monologue, he quoted Fluke to the effect that 40 percent of female Georgetown law students struggled to afford contraceptives. From that number he drew the inference that students were "having so much sex" they couldn't afford birth control. Riffing on the same theme, he interpreted Fluke's faux congressional testimony thus: "Essentially [she] says that she must be paid to have sex, what does that make her? It makes her a slut, right? It makes her a prostitute."[50]

Limbaugh made the mistake of taking Fluke at her word. He presumed that if she really wanted equal treatment, she could take the comic punch a man could. He misjudged Fluke and misread his Marquess of Queensberry 2.0. In a presidential election year, in the midst of the apocryphal Republican war on women, the Democrats and their media allies were rewriting the rules as the campaign progressed. Yes, major Obama donor Bill Maher called Sarah Palin a "c—," and, yes, Obama supporter David Letterman called Palin "slutty" and joked that her fourteen-year-old daughter had been "knocked up" at a Yankee game,[51] but both had the refs in their corner, and neither experienced anything like the prolonged assault Limbaugh endured.

In the two weeks that followed the Limbaugh riff on Fluke, the major networks—ABC, CBS, and NBC—aired thirty-two predictably indignant stories or interview segments.[52] ABC *World News* anchor Diane Sawyer could scarcely conceal her glee as she breathlessly recounted the "whirlwind he unleashed," the "big sponsors" he lost, and the Republican presidential candidates Limbaugh put on the hot seat. Lest they be given a scarlet *S* of their own, the candidates quickly distanced themselves from "Rush who?" Said Romney, "I'll just say this, which is, it's not the language I would have used." Added Rick Santorum, "[Rush is] being absurd, but that's, you know, an entertainer can be absurd." Neither explanation worked. Santorum's was "tepid." Romney's was "mealymouthed." The strategically aroused mob was never easily satisfied.[53]

## LEGITIMATE RAPE

Unlike his ideological ally Rush Limbaugh, six-term congressman Todd Akin had no great urge to provoke. On August 7, 2012, Akin won an upset victory in a tough three-way Republican primary in Missouri for a US Senate seat and was preparing to square off against incumbent Democrat Claire McCaskill in November. A serious Christian and constitutionalist, the straight arrow father of six—two of them girls—had passed the first sixty-five years of his life largely letter-free. That was about to change.

On Friday afternoon, August 17, Akin dutifully headed into the studios of Fox 2, KTVI, a St. Louis–area TV station. He had agreed to be interviewed for a local Sunday show hosted by Charles Jaco, an ill-humored liberal reporter on the downward end of his career curve. From the beginning it was obvious to Akin what Jaco hoped to do, namely, box Akin into a semantic trap and hoist him on his own principles. Jaco tried with questions on school lunches, student loans, the 1965 Voting Rights Act—nothing like a scarlet *R* for the homestretch—even the Seventeenth Amendment, the one that called for the direct election of US senators, as if anyone cared. Akin artfully dodged and weaved and sustained no more than the occasional glancing blow.

Inevitably, in this the year of the war on women, Jaco moved on to abortion. Knowing Akin to be consistently pro-life, Jaco hoped to use his very consistency against him, asking whether any set of circumstances justified abortion. Akin calmly explained that abortion was justifiable to save the mother's life. Not getting the sound bite he wanted, Jaco cut right to the chase. "What about in the case of rape?" he taunted. "Should it be legal or not?"

Akin chose not to duck this one. "If it's a legitimate rape," said the candidate, "the female body has ways to try to shut that whole thing down. But let's assume that maybe that didn't work or something. You know, I think there should be some punishment but the punishment ought to be on the rapist and not attacking the child." Jaco was nonplussed. "Let's go to the economy," he said in reply. Having heard Akin's answer in context, Jaco did not understand how nutty the neo-puritans would make the answer seem after picking it apart.

*The Jaco Report* aired two days later.[54] Not many people watched. Not many had to. All it took was one observant tracker from the McCaskill camp to spot the video online, post it on Twitter, and watch it go viral, Gangnam-style. The many, deep-pocketed, left-left-leaning blogs pushed it up the media chain, and well before the five o'clock news aired that Sunday, McCaskill was fitting Akin for his scarlet *S*. "I was stunned by what he said and how he said it," McCaskill fretted. "But it opened a window into his mind and showed his beliefs. And I'm very familiar with a long list of items where Congressman Akin is outside the mainstream."[55]

Outside the mainstream Akin may have been, but almost no one challenged him on his basic contention, namely, that if one believed in "life," he could not logically or morally condemn to death those innocents conceived in rape. Instead, his critics flogged Akin either for suggesting not all rapes were "legitimate" or implying that the act of rape made conception unlikely.

Obviously, not all claims of rape were legitimate. In his book *Firing Back*, Akin raised the case of Norma McCorvey, otherwise known as "Roe." Wanting an abortion, McCorvey told state authorities she had been raped. That was one of the few exceptions the state of Texas made to its abortion prohibition. When state authorities asked for a police or medical report to substantiate her claim, McCorvey could produce none and was turned down.

At the time, feminist attorneys Linda Coffee and Sarah Weddington were looking for a case to test Texas law and did not much care whether McCorvey's claim was legitimate. As McCorvey would later confess, it was not. "That one lie," Akin observed, "wrought the infamous *Roe v. Wade* decision, the Supreme Court's greatest assault on civil rights since Dred Scott, and a death sentence for some fifty-six million unborn babies."[56]

McCorvey was hardly unique. In a landmark study executed with cooperation of a small metropolitan police department, Purdue's E. J. Kanin found that over a nine-year period, 41 percent of reported rape allegations were shown to be false. Several false allegations have made the headlines in recent years.[57] Five years before the Akin blowup, rape charges against three Duke lacrosse players were famously revealed to be fabricated. Two years after Akin, *Rolling Stone* magazine caught enormous heat for running a steamy saga about a gang rape at the University of Virginia that never happened. At about that same time, pop icon Lena Dunham faced a potential lawsuit for her dubious claim that a young Republican raped her while she was a student at Oberlin.

More often than not, neo-puritans judged the legitimacy of a rape charge based on its political value. And no rape accusation had less value, and thus less legitimacy in their eyes, than the one brought by an Arkansas woman named Juanita Broaddrick against Bill Clinton. Unlike Akin, Clinton spoke concisely and authoritatively on the subject of rape.

He knew just what a woman who had been raped should do. As he told a weeping Broaddrick in a Little Rock hotel room in 1978 after he had allegedly bitten her lip to silence her, "You better get some ice on that."[58]

On the subject of lip biting, in 1999, after the Senate failed to convict Clinton on impeachment charges, NBC finally aired Lisa Meyers's interview with Broaddrick. "Then he tries to kiss me again. And the second time he tries to kiss me he starts biting my lip. Just a minute," said Broaddrick, pausing to regain her composure. "He starts to, um, bite on my top lip, and I tried to pull away from him. And then he forces me down on the bed. And I just was very frightened, and I tried to get away from him, and I told him 'No,' that I didn't want this to happen, but he wouldn't listen to me." At the time, Attorney General Clinton was the top law enforcer in the state of Arkansas.

Broaddrick was not the only woman who claimed to have been sexually abused by Clinton. Indeed, in the Ken Starr investigation, she emerged as "Jane Doe No. 5." She was likely not even unique in being raped by Clinton. In his book, *Uncovering Clinton: A Reporter's Story*, mainstream reporter Michael Isikoff related how Clinton, then Arkansas governor, had had sex with former Miss America Elizabeth Ward Gracen. "It was rough sex," Isikoff wrote, "Clinton got so carried away that he bit her lip, Gracen later told friends. But it was consensual."[59] Isikoff missed the lip-biting connection. He also failed to acknowledge that at least one of Gracen's friends, Judy Stokes, had told the legal team of Paula Jones—another Clinton accuser—that the sex was not consensual at all. "Do you believe Clinton raped her?" investigator Rick Lambert asked her. "Absolutely," Stokes replied. "He forced her to have sex. What do you call that?"[60]

It was Jones, an unsophisticated working class woman from Arkansas, who brought the initial civil suit against Clinton, the one that ultimately led him to commit perjury and get himself impeached. In dismissing her claim, Clinton adviser James Carville sneered, "Drag a hundred-dollar bill through a trailer park, you never know what you'll find."[61] Despite this showcase sample of both classism and sexism, Carville suffered not a whit. He later emerged as cohost of CNN's *Crossfire* and a high-level strategist in the farcical counterattack to protect America's women from hateful Republicans.

Akin caught the irony of the attack. He was about to be tagged point man for this imagined war because of a few awkward words on the subject of rape. Yet two weeks later, wrote Akin, the assembled delegates at the Democratic National Convention "would stand and cheer for Bill Clinton who was actually accused of sexual assault on multiple occasions."[62] That same convention would also honor the memory of the recently deceased Sen. Ted Kennedy. The nation's progressives, Sandra Fluke and Claire McCaskill among them, would cheer teary-eyed, forgetting for a moment the night the married Kennedy drove off a bridge and left the young woman in his car to drown lest his illicit tryst hurt his career.

The death at Chappaquiddick ended a decade that began with both John and Robert Kennedy seducing, then abandoning, doomed actress Marilyn Monroe, a New Frontier revival of droit du seigneur. Four years after Chappaquiddick, Ted's nephew Joe Kennedy, Bobby's oldest son, recklessly drove a jeep, with his girlfriend by his side, and flipped it. Joe temporarily lost his license. The girl permanently lost the use of her legs. That did not stop this young Democrat from serving six terms in the House of Representatives. Joe had planned to run for governor of Massachusetts, but as the *Washington Post* put it, the "messy publicity about the annulment of his first marriage" undid him. Joe was not helped, the *Post* added, by "the alleged affair of his brother Michael with a teenage babysitter."[63] The affair started when the girl was fourteen. Michael beat the rap by skiing fatally into a tree. In his defense, Michael did not kill the girl. The same could not be said for his cousin, Michael Skakel, who killed fifteen-year-old Martha Moxley and got away with it for nearly thirty years.

Another nephew, William Kennedy Smith, raped a young woman, or so she testified, while drunken Uncle Ted wandered half-naked around the premises. Three other women were willing to testify to earlier Smith assaults, but their testimony was excluded, and Smith walked. When he beat the rap—Kennedys inevitably did—his young Democrat friends and relatives cheered. In 2008, Democratic senator John Edwards ran a credible race for president only because the media refused to notice that a woman other than his cancer-stricken wife was carrying his child. In 2012, Robert Kennedy Jr.'s discarded second wife hanged herself out of despair. Later that year, but before the Akin scandal, Democratic New York governor Andrew Cuomo's discarded wife, Kerry Kennedy, nearly killed herself and others when she passed out on the highway from an overdose of sleeping pills.

What saved Ted Kennedy's career is what saved Clinton's is what saved Carville's: the impressively selective indignation of the neo-puritans. In July 1998, *Time* magazine scribe and fourth-generation atheist Nina Burleigh all but parodied that selectivity when she said of Clinton, "I would be happy to give him a blowjob just to thank him for keeping abortion legal. I think American women should be lining up with their presidential kneepads on to show their gratitude for keeping the theocracy off our backs."[64]

In August 2012 Republicans knew just how vulnerable Democrats were to the charge of sexism, let alone hypocrisy. But when reporters asked prominent Republicans to renounce Akin, they readily obliged. On the first day of the controversy, presidential nominee Mitt Romney told the media: "Congressman Akin's comments on rape are insulting, inexcusable and, frankly, wrong. Like millions of other Americans, we found them to be offensive." Akin wished Romney had said, "A credibly accused rapist is giving the keynote speech at the Democratic convention in two weeks, and you want me to denounce a decent, God-fearing man for his inelegant comments about rape? No, not happening, and if the truth hurts, get some ice on that."[65]

Having shamed the Republicans into silence, the Democrats noisily gathered for the public burning. And who better to read the charges against Akin than the suddenly famous Sandra Fluke? Without fear of contradiction, Fluke boldly lied in an e-mail blast sent to millions of Americans under the heading, "Legitimate Rape." Akin, she wrote, "thinks that victims of 'legitimate rape' don't get pregnant because 'the female body has ways to try to shut that whole thing down?'"[66] In fact, Akin implied no such thing. Aware of the role stress plays in conception, he claimed only that women *rarely* get pregnant because of rape. He knew better than to say "never." He had the children of rape victims working on his campaign. But with the Republicans cowering and her coreligionists clamoring for Akin's head, Fluke felt free to say whatever she pleased, and that is exactly what she did.

For all the forces aligned against him, Akin was running in a state that would give Romney a ten-point margin of victory. With just weeks left in the 2012 campaign, he had pulled to within a few percentage points of McCaskill. Then the McCaskill camp let fly with an ad, wrote Akin, "so lethal that it almost made me rethink who *I* was voting for."[67] The ad featured the words of the prominent Republicans who had trashed Akin—Romney, Ryan, McCain, and a trio of Missouri politicians—and concluded with Romney standing next to Paul Ryan and saying, "It was offensive. He should step out of the race." Akin did not have to. Romney's words did the job for him.

## GLOBAL JUSTICE

If progressives were half as protective of women's rights as they claimed to be, university philosophy departments would be all but immune to charges of sexism. On every major campus in America, these departments lean strongly to the left. One reputable survey, in fact, found that for every philosophy prof who identified as conservative, sixteen identified as liberal.[68] How then to explain the recent wave of reports about predatory philosophers? "A Star Philosopher Falls, and a Debate over Sexism Is Set Off," shouted a 2013 *New York Times* headline about philosopher heavyweight Colin McGinn.[69] "CU-Boulder reports pervasive sexual harassment within philosophy department," read a headline from the *Daily Camera*.[70] And from the self-pitying feminist blog *What Is It Like to Be a Woman in Philosophy?* came unending waves of headlines: "Not as women-friendly as it looks"; "Does your husband know you won't cook dinner every night?"; and, everyone's favorite, "Who's Ready for the Gang Bang?"[71]

In April 2014 an anonymous author of a *Thought Catalog* article told a story so wonderfully revealing it broke out of the academic ghetto. The article, saucily titled "I Had an Affair with My Hero, a Philosopher Who's Famous for Being 'Moral,'" reads like a postmodern *Scarlet Letter*.[72] For the reader's ease, let us call the anonymous heroine "Hester Prynne" and the prof "Arthur Dimmesdale," the name of the *Scarlet Letter*'s sanctimonious preacher/adulterer.

As Hester related in a second article, Dimmesdale singled her out at a conference and spoke to her about charity projects he had launched in her home country. The "starstruck" Hester doubted he would remember her, she being a lowly grad student. Instead, he initiated an e-mail exchange. "Lots of job openings cross my desk," he wrote, "so maybe I can help you find a place where you can be productive in the global justice universe."[73] Eventually, he visited her city, and she yielded readily to his charms. "He must be a good man, this moral philosopher," Hester mused bitterly after the fact. "He has, after all, devoted his life to global justice."[74]

The second time Dimmesdale visited Hester's city, she went to his hotel room and found him naked at the door. He claimed to have just woken, and since he lived alone, he had grown used to sleeping in the nude. Hester bought this line too, common sense obviously not being a criterion for high-powered graduate work.

On Dimmesdale's third visit, Hester "expressed astonishment" that her "global justice hero" would have no other woman in his life. Only then did Dimmesdale admit that, yes, he had been living with a certain woman since before Hester "was even born." He claimed his partner—a woman Hester dismissively called "the housewife"—would be happy he'd found true love. Hester bought this line too. At the time, she herself was involved in a "mutually consensual, non-monogamous partnership" with someone who, she imagined, would "bless" her affair with Dimmesdale.

As the relationship progressed, Dimmesdale's odd behavior finally alerted the comically obtuse Hester he was not quite the man his web page promised. Upon learning "his housewife" clung to him for fear of abandonment, she accused him of "patriarchy." He, in turn, accused Hester of "tyranny and conservatism," which to her must have seemed a redundancy. But only when she learned that he made a practice of deflowering idolatrous students of the "skinny Asian type"—like Hester but younger—did she finally rebel.

Fed up, Hester accused Dimmesdale of hypocrisy for devoting his life to human rights but treating women inhumanely. Unfazed, he "vehemently refused to subject the private sphere to assessments of justice." As he told Hester, "All's fair in love and war."[75] Without meaning to, and without comprehending what she had done, Hester had cut to the perverse core of neo-puritanism. Good works were irrelevant. Professing one's faith loudly and often was all that counted.

In her initial posting, our Hester, like her literary avatar, assumed responsibility for her own downfall. "I brought this upon myself," she conceded, "and I deserve to live with the consequences of my free, voluntary action."[76] She presumed nothing would come of her cri de coeur. Men like Dimmesdale, whose power derived from their place among the progressive elect, would continue to exploit "pretty young women" as long as those men stayed within the boundaries of the law.

Dimmesdale, however, may have strayed beyond the boundaries, if not of criminal law, at least of the academic mimicry of the same. Under President Obama, the US DOE's Office of Civil Rights (OCR) had been pressuring universities to set up draconian justice systems of their own to corral behavior as old as mankind. Anglo-Irish political philosopher Edmund Burke might have predicted this. "Society cannot exist unless a controlling power upon will and appetite be placed somewhere," said Burke more than two centuries ago, "and the less of it there is within, the more there is without."[77] The "within" part being off-limits on the left, the OCR was hell-bent on enforcing the "without."

The Dimmesdale case highlighted the increasingly obvious

schizophrenia of the progressive mind. This malady was nowhere more evident than on the American campus. One school of progressive thought, the OCR-oriented school, insisted that young women be protected from male predation at all costs. Another school mocked the OCR nannies who imagined young women as "the stereotypical Little Red Riding Hoods."[78] For a generation or more, the libertines prevailed on campus. They lobbied successfully for coed dorms, twenty-four-hour visitation, free condoms, easy abortions, and a Yale-originated phenomenon known as "Sex Week."

In his eye-opening book, *Sex and God at Yale*, recent graduate Nathan Harden described his own experiences with the biannual Sex Week. Although the university did not officially sponsor the event, the administration gave the organizers nearly free rein to promote it and to use campus facilities. According to Harden, they flooded the campus with Sex Week posters and banners, deluged students with e-mails, and staged as many as eleven days of "educational" offerings, such as a porn star look-alike contest, a lecture on the female orgasm, and a demonstration of sex toys featuring "product giveaways." Commenting on a session called "What a Girl Wants," Harden came to the conclusion that "what a girl really wants, if you were to believe the schedule of events, is to be a porn star."[79] It was in this randy environment that Dimmesdale, a Yale professor, flourished.

Although not a Yalie, Hester seemed comfortable with the school's values. She admitted to making the first move in her initial hotel room tryst with Dimmesdale. She engaged in at least two simultaneous "mutually consensual, non-monogamous" affairs,[80] and she had enough sexual experience to refer to herself, only half-ironically, as a "slut."[81] When her steamy saga was published, it caught the attention of another young woman, a Yale undergraduate. This second woman went by the codename "Lisbeth Mara" after the bisexual man killer (and the actress who played her) in the movie *The Girl with the Dragon Tattoo*. In a *Yale Daily News* expose, she would be identified as "Case 2."

Lisbeth claimed that in 2009–2010, Dimmesdale served as her

senior-essay adviser. During that school year, he kept trying, in her words, "to relax the terms of our relationship" by taking her to brunch and on bicycle rides. "I felt that he was treating me in a discriminatory way on the basis of my being female," she told Brenda Hughes Neghaiwi of the *Yale Daily News* in September 2011. Despite the discomfort Dimmesdale's behavior caused, Lisbeth agreed to serve as his translator/research assistant on a ten-day trip that summer. It did not take her long to suspect Dimmesdale of "ulterior motives." His booking of a single room for them both was clue enough for a Yalie— well, almost clue enough. When Dimmesdale claimed the funds saved "could be funneled towards charitable projects," Lisbeth had to weigh her "personal discomfort," reported Neghaiwi, "against her social and humanitarian values."[82]

Upon the publication of Hester's piece, a *Woman in Philosophy?* editor put Lisbeth and Hester together. They had been complaining about the same man. "When I found out that it was known to people that he has had previous sexual harassment cases, I was furious," Hester wrote in a follow-up piece on the *ProtectingLisbeth* blog.[83] This claim was more than a little disingenuous. Dimmesdale had admittedly bragged to her about how a student once performed oral sex on him, although in the retelling Hester used a sluttier phrase than "oral sex." But that was the old Hester. Out of the ashes of her relationship with Dimmesdale a new Hester was born.

"I am calling on all feminists and sympathizers to *give him war*," Hester thundered in italics from her newfound bully pulpit. She encouraged her allies to come forward with any dope they had on Dimmesdale. And as Hester made clear, Dimmesdale was just one old patriarch among many "powerful men." Progressive or not, these men mentored young women with no greater goal than to bed them. "This isn't just a one-off thing about my affair with my hero," she pled. "This is about our profession, culture, practices, and norms. This is about a rampant form of corruption in our discipline that thrives in a culture of silence."[84] Had Hester the wit to understand her world, she might have said, "This is about the failure of an indulgent, improvised ideology to override human nature."

The editors of the *Daily Nous*, an online newsletter for and about the philosophy profession, joined the posse. They openly identified Dimmesdale by his real name, Thomas Pogge. Scrawny, bearded, and bespectacled, Pogge did not look at all like the lothario he was accused of being. The spectacularly self-important website of "Thought Leader: Thomas Pogge" spoke to the real source of his sexual power. This was a guy, after all, who served as president of Academics Stand Against Poverty, president of Incentives for Global Health, the chair of at least three other high-powered panels, a member of the UNICEF Social and Economic Policy Advisory Board, and an advisor to no fewer than twenty-eight different journals.[85]

Unlike predators of a political stripe, Pogge did not have the power to protect his students from the right wing's war on women. This left him vulnerable to their wrath. Under the banner "Yale Seeks Information about Sexual Misconduct," the *Daily Nous* encouraged readers with dirt on Pogge, "even students in his areas at other universities," to contact Yale's Title IX coordinator.[86]

Writing in the *Weekly Standard*, Charlotte Allen called the outing of Pogge a "vendetta, actually one of a series of vendettas waged by feminists over the past few years against philosophy professors and philosophy departments."[87] The incidents around which these campaigns developed typically did not involve criminal behavior or even abuse enough to constitute a "hostile environment." They were successful, Allen observed, because universities were terrified of Obama's OCR. Philosophy departments have been particularly vulnerable as they are the last male bastions in the field of humanities. Only 17 percent of philosophy professors are female. The fact that female philosophers are cited in only 4 percent of scholarly citations suggests that those who compete at the highest level of the profession are even more disproportionately male.

No doubt, the profession's emphasis on mathematical thinking and its barroom brawl debating style have turned off females, but this is too easy an explanation for the neo-puritans in the profession, male and female. In explaining his donation to Lisbeth's fund, Ghent University's Eric Schliesser charged instead that there had indeed been "a systematic pattern of exclusion of women" in the profession. He traced that pattern not to any intrinsic gender differences but to "a culture of harassment, sexual predating [*sic*], and bullying to be reproduced from one generation to the next."[88]

To undo that culture, however, would require a systematic suppression of human nature and a sanctioning authority to assure it stayed suppressed. Keen on suppression, the neo-puritans were prepared to change the culture through a combination of litigation, prohibition, and bureaucratic pettifoggery. In fact, the American Philosophical Association's (APA) Committee on the Status of Women went so far as to recommend a ban on alcohol at departmental functions. How that committee planned to ensure the right mix of female philosophers in scholarly footnotes remains to be seen. Had these philosophers honored the Puritan values on which universities like Yale were founded, however, there would have been little need for a neo-puritan crackdown.

## THE PSYCHOLOGY OF TABOO

Lawrence Summers is one of only a handful of Americans whose *New York Times* obituary, he can be sure, will showcase his scarlet *S*. From a distance Summers seemed an unlikely candidate. Up to the moment his career imploded, he had lived his entire life within the zone of decency. A tenured economics prof at age twenty-eight, one of the youngest in Harvard's history, Summers coasted on the prevailing liberal currents to the Clinton White House, where he was designated secretary of Treasury before turning forty-five. Harvard took advantage of Summers's availability when Clinton left office in 2001 and named him president, the first Jewish president of that esteemed institution.

On January 14, 2005, he spoke at an invitation-only working luncheon on the subject of women and minorities in science and engineering. There, with just fifty scholars in attendance, he gave what may be remembered as the most honest discussion on diversity a university president would ever give.[89] Not wanting to waste anyone's time—especially his own—on meaningless boilerplate, Summers dove in and addressed the specific issue of female representation in tenured science and engineering positions at top universities and research institutions. He did not speak from a prepared text as this was to be candid conversation, or so he was promised. To begin, he laid out three broad hypotheses as to why so few females pursued degrees in these fields.

The first of the three Summers called the "high-powered job hypothesis." In certain fields professionals were expected to center their lives on their jobs. To achieve prominence in those fields, Summers explained, they had to. The evidence he saw suggested most women were unwilling to put in the sixty- to eighty-hour weeks those fields required. Those who did were likely unmarried or childless. Although Summers did not mention her by name, he cited the experience of his former chief of staff and future best-selling feminist author, Sheryl Sandberg. A 1994 graduate of Harvard Business School, Sandberg reported to Summers that only three of the twenty-two women in her first-year section at Harvard were still working full-time just ten years after graduation.

Had Summers stopped here, he would not have provoked the neo-puritans, at least not fatally, but he kept on going. He argued, as Charles Murray had, that on average women tested for intelligence as well as men, but men were overrepresented at the extremes, both high and low. On subjects like math and science, Summers continued, there was "relatively clear evidence" that men dominated the extreme high end of the intelligence curve for reasons that had little to do with environment or expectations. The "unfortunate truth," as he called it, was that "the combination of the high-powered job hypothesis and the differing variances [hypothesis] probably explains a fair amount of the problem."

What this meant—and here Summers was putting a whole industry at risk—was that he did not buy the idea that a biased system somehow denied capable young women the opportunity to succeed. He called systemic discrimination, generously, a "lesser factor." In fact,

Summers thought it wise to start testing the "remedies" already in place. Universities ought to know whether they represented progress or, as "right-wing critics" presumed, "clear abandonments of quality standards."

Summers did not have to say any more. By this time, the neo-puritans in the audience were in a swoon, literally. Sitting just ten feet from Summers, MIT biologist Nancy Hopkins, a 1964 Harvard graduate and renowned cancer researcher, closed her laptop, put on her coat, and conspicuously walked out. "I would've either blacked out or thrown up," Hopkins told the *Boston Globe*.[90] Five other attendees the *Globe* contacted would admit to being "deeply offended." Four were not. "For him to say that 'aptitude' is the second most important reason that women don't get to the top when he leads an institution that is 50 percent women students—that's profoundly disturbing to me," said Hopkins. "He shouldn't admit women to Harvard if he's going to announce when they come that, hey, we don't feel that you can make it to the top."[91]

The luncheon was on Friday. The *Globe* reported the story on Monday based on a Hopkins e-mail, and it quickly went viral. By the end of that day, the producers of ABC's *Good Morning America* and several other television shows asked Hopkins to talk about Summers on the air. For major media execs the branding of a public figure with a scarlet letter was more fun than a pay raise. Certainly, they would have preferred to roast a Republican, but at this stage, Summers was of little value to the Democratic Party. His standing among America's elite money managers and his position at Harvard left him exposed as a class villain as well as a sexist. The serfs would have their day.

For about twenty-four hours after the story exploded, Summers held his ground. "I'm sorry for any misunderstanding but believe that raising questions, discussing multiple factors that may explain a difficult problem, and seeking to understand how they interrelate is vitally important," he told the *New York Times*.[92] But just a day later, Summers made the mistake virtually all the newly lettered do. He apologized. "I was wrong to have spoken in a way that has resulted in an unintended signal of discouragement to talented girls and women," he wrote in an open letter to the Harvard community. "As a university president, I consider nothing more important than helping to create an environment, at Harvard and beyond, in which every one of us can pursue our intellectual passions and realize our aspirations to the fullest possible extent."[93]

Neo-puritans from coast to coast could smell the weakness. NOW moved quickly to get in its licks before the field got too crowded. "Apologies are not enough," said NOW president Kim Gandy the following day. "Summers must go, and Harvard must start with a clean slate." The NOW press release thrashed Summers for his "public demonstration of sexism and ignorance" and threatened ominously, "NOW will be watching Harvard University."[94]

For the next several months, the Massachusetts Bay State simmered with a righteous fury unseen since about 1693. The chattering classes chattered. One hundred Harvard profs denounced Summers in a signed letter. And on February 15, a month after his talk, the full faculty called him in for what early Harvard dons might have called a come-to-Jesus meeting. It was not pleasant. To this point, Summers had refused to release the transcript of his luncheon remarks. Although not scripted, the talk had been recorded. The faculty wanted to see it. Sociology professor Theda Skocpol accused Summers of "wrapping [himself] in the mantle of academic freedom" and added, "We do not fear open give-and-take about anything you might have said."[95]

If Skocpol meant what she said, not many others did. Two days later Summers caved and produced the transcript along with a further apology, "Though my NBER remarks were explicitly speculative, and noted that 'I may be all wrong,' I should have left such speculation to those more expert in the relevant fields."[96] That concession only fueled the neo-puritan fervor. Female faculty members demanded their own meeting, at which Summers reportedly disowned his observation that "intrinsic aptitude" may account for the lack of females in science and engineering.[97] By now, the tumbrels were rolling.

Among the few scholars who came to his defense was one Summers probably wished had not. In a *New York Times* op-ed, academic bad boy Charles Murray marveled at "the wholesale denial that certain bodies of scientific knowledge exist."[98] From the outraged response, he argued, one would have thought that Summers had advanced a radical idea. In fact, said Murray, the opposite was true. Were the scientists in this field to be surveyed, "all but a fringe would accept that the sexes are different, and that genes are clearly implicated." Murray noted that scientific research on this subject had been trending in Summers's direction and had "the vibrancy and excitement of an important new field gaining momentum." The one factor stifling scholarship, as Murray well knew, was fear of the results.

Summers could not expect much help on a campus of cowards and conformists, but psychology professor Steven Pinker had the clout to brave the mob. A year earlier, *Time* magazine had named him one of the hundred most influential scientists and thinkers in the world. He was not easily intimidated or ignored. In a February 2005 op-ed in the *New Republic*, Pinker described the analysis done by Summers as "unexceptional."[99] That men had on average a higher level of interest in science and engineering was obvious to everyone who cared to reflect on the issue. To what degree those interests and aptitudes originated in biology, wrote Pinker, "must be determined by research, not fatwa."

Pinker went well beyond Summers in listing the consequences of progressive illogic: well-meaning people are charged with sexism; young women are cajoled into academic fields they don't enjoy; the demands of childbearing are slighted; and compensatory quotas put even the deserving under a cloud of suspicion. He traced these self-inflicted wounds to what he called "the psychology of taboo," the eagerness to share fears and beliefs even when unfounded.

In defending Summers, Pinker shrewdly dissected the psychological origins of neo-puritanism. He argued that at some recent moment in academic history, "the belief that men and women are psychologically indistinguishable became sacred." This belief was, of course, one of many irrational fixations in the progressive credo. These shared beliefs, added Pinker, "work as membership badges in coalitions. To believe something with a perfect faith, to be incapable of apostasy, is a sign of fidelity to the group and loyalty to the cause." Unfortunately, this groupthink had a major downside, Pinker argued, namely, that it was "incompatible with the ideal of scholarship." Fortunately, the Harvard of 2005 had less interest in scholarship than it did in diversity, and groupthink made diversity at least seem to make sense.

For all his clout on campus, Pinker made few converts. A year after the fatal conference, Summers resigned his Harvard post under pressure, making his the shortest tenure for a Harvard president since the Civil War. Embarrassed perhaps by conservative criticism of liberal squeamishness, many in the major media soft-pedaled the role Summers's comments on gender differences played in his forced departure. The *New York Times* did not even mention the sex-and-science controversy until the sixteenth paragraph of its article on the subject. Nine paragraphs later, the *Times* added some specifics, "His remarks about women in the sciences led to last year's 218-to-185 no-confidence vote, and, several professors said, that anger never dissipated."[100] The *Boston Globe* waited until the twenty-eighth and twenty-ninth paragraphs to remind its audience that "Summers sparked international outrage" just a year earlier with his comments on gender differences, and that in turn led to a no-confidence vote.[101]

If Summers thought the controversy would dim when he left Harvard, he underestimated the wattage of the scarlet *S* ablaze on his chest. In July 2013 Washington scuttlebutt had it that President Obama would choose Summers to succeed Ben Bernanke as head of the Federal Reserve. Knowing how craven its own allies were, the feminist group UltraViolet threatened, "Women will not soon forget if President Obama picks Mr. Summers." The *National Journal* headlined that story, "What Potential Fed Front-Runner Larry Summers Said About Women."[102] And *Salon* ran the headlined story, "Sexist Larry Summers Will Destroy the Economy."[103]

Thinking one public burning per lifetime was plenty, Summers withdrew his name from contention. In explaining his decision to Obama, he understated the obvious in his prediction of an "acrimonious" confirmation process.[104] Obama did not protest. Given that the Fed's number two person was a woman, pundits had been charging the White House with sexism for even considering the toxic Summers. NOW president Terry O'Neill called the very thought of choosing any man over Janet Yellen "pure sexist."[105] The Democrats had spent too much energy framing Republicans as antiwoman. Not wanting to squander all that ill will, Obama chose Yellen to be the first woman to head up the Fed in its history. For the moment at least, the tinderboxes were put away.

## BÊTE NOIRE

If it is possible for a woman to wear the scarlet *S*, a top candidate would be Camille Paglia, a high-profile author and university professor whom *Time* magazine once famously dubbed the "bete noire of feminism."[106] Not at all afraid of going mano a mano with her progressive sisters, Paglia weighed in to the Harvard brawl with her customary brio. "The feminist pressure groups rose en masse from their lavishly feathered nests and set up a furious cackle," wrote Paglia in a sentence so unblushingly sexist it would have cost a male professor his job at any university anywhere, Bob Jones included. Paglia said this, by the way, not in some obscure blog, but in a *New York Times* op-ed.[107]

Paglia faulted Summers for failing to understand "the tribal creeds and customs" of Harvard's entrenched professoriate. As she observed, campus feminists would not satisfy themselves with his numerous apologies or even his post-imbroglio offer to spend fifty million dollars recruiting more women and minorities to Harvard. "That one desperate act of profligate appeasement," wrote Paglia, "tells volumes about the climate of persecution and extortion around gender issues at too many American universities."

Paglia has never let the threat of persecution shut her up or even slow her down. Her very femaleness has protected her, but so too has her self-designation as a proabortion, propornography, lesbian Democrat. Thus armored, Paglia first put the neo-puritans on defense in 1990 with her dazzling best seller *Sexual Personae*, a sweeping seven hundred–plus page assessment of the roots of Western art and culture. Although the book had something to offend nearly everyone, many of the targets, Christians most notably, had long since grown used to the abuse. Progressive feminists had not. For the previous twenty or so years, the media and academe had treated them as tenderly as motherless puppies. Paglia was not quite so nurturing. Not only did she subvert feminist delusions, but she also celebrated male achievement. "One of feminism's irritating reflexes is its fashionable disdain for 'patriarchal society,' to which nothing good is ever attributed," wrote Paglia. "But it is patriarchal society that has freed me as a woman." That freedom came as a result of what Paglia called "one of the greatest male accomplishments in the history of culture."[108] She referred specifically here to the capitalist distribution network.

Fully aware of the effect she would have on her socialist sisters, Paglia gave her full-throated endorsement to that "epic catalog of male achievements"—paved roads, indoor plumbing, washing machines, eyeglasses, antibiotics, safe milk, tropical fruits, disposable diapers. "Let us stop being small-minded about men," Paglia insisted. "If civilization had been left in female hands, we would still be living in grass huts."[109]

Over the years, Paglia has refused to yield to what weak-kneed males dread, namely, "feminist bullies sermonizing from every news show." In a much discussed *Time* magazine piece in 2013, provocatively titled "It's a Man's World, and It Always Will Be," Paglia took on those bullies and their "carelessly fact-free theories alleging that gender is an arbitrary, oppressive fiction with no basis in biology."[110]

Something of an optimist, Paglia argued that these "Stalinist feminists" had lost their power. Certainly, they have lost some visibility as their big stage pioneers aged or died, but their collective power may be more formidable than ever. In the same year that Paglia wrote the *Time* column, for instance, feminist fellow travelers had little trouble overriding President Obama's plan to appoint Summers Fed chief. One underestimated them at his peril.

In 2013, with their president reelected and Summers benched, the neo-puritans had no need to stay on war footing. The protection they offered to women had always been selective in any case. Former vice presidential candidate Sarah Palin understood this well. In 2013, MSNBC host Martin Bashir said on air that if anyone deserved "a dose of discipline from Thomas Thistlewood," it was Palin. Bashir had just spent an unseemly amount of time relating how Thistlewood, a Jamaican plantation owner, would punish unruly slaves by forcing other slaves to defecate or urinate in their mouths.[111] The following year CNN anchor Carol Costello laughingly called a police tape of Bristol Palin, Sarah's daughter, hysterically describing how a man beat and dragged her "quite possibly the best minute and a half of audio we've ever come across."[112]

Akin had awkwardly linked the words "legitimate" and "rape." Limbaugh called Fluke a "slut." Bashir had recommended the vilest of punishments for a mother of five. Costello joked about an assault on her daughter. The conservatives got handed their scarlet *S*'s. The progressive did not. The networks ran no stories on Bashir's truly pioneering bit of on-air perversity or Costello's callousness. NOW remained silent. And the media failed to ask President Obama or any other Democrat to denounce him or her. Costello went unpunished, and although Bashir resigned, he can be confident the *New York Times* will make no mention of this incident anywhere near the top of his obituary. Todd Akin will not be so lucky.

## INSENSITIVE BIGOTS

If Hollywood were casting the "Battle for Augusta National," its agents would have chosen someone who looked—and especially sounded—just like William Woodward "Hootie" Johnson. Born in South Carolina in 1931, Johnson took over his daddy's small-town bank as a young man, transformed it into a regional power, and emerged ultimately as the chairman of the executive committee of the Bank of America. From this perch, in 1998, he was named chairman of the Augusta National Golf Club, host of the celebrated Masters Tournament.[113] On the way to the top, the stocky, bespectacled Johnson lost not a drop of his Southern charm or his accent.

In 1999 Johnson oversaw the Masters for the first time. For the first time too, veteran sportswriter Christine Brennan, reporting for *USA Today*, posed the question that would soon enough come to consume, if not the nation exactly, at least the *New York Times*. "If you wouldn't mind telling us," asked Brennan, "how many African Americans there are at Augusta National and how many woman members?" Always gracious, Johnson answered, "Well, that's a club matter, ma'am, and all club matters are private." In fact, the club had three black members. Black golfers had been playing in the tournament for twenty-five years, and the multiracial Tiger Woods had won the tournament two years earlier. Johnson himself was, in the words of black congressman Jim Clyburn (D-SC), "the biggest supporter of African Americans in the history of the state of South Carolina."[114] He was also the first white Southerner to serve on the national board of the Urban League. That much said, he was white, Southern, no longer a Democrat, and thus fair game.

"I made a right turn off the main drag in Augusta the other day and ended up in 1975," wrote Brennan in the lead sentence of her April 8, 1999, column. "Or perhaps it was 1940. It was hard to tell." Although largely benign, the column concluded with a gratuitous racial jab at the "white men of Augusta National." Brennan argued that since the Masters was played in their "luscious backyard" and was seen as a "national treasure"—Johnson himself said so—the club's membership policies should be "the nation's business."[115] This was the kind of power-grabbing non sequitur only a progressive could write.

Johnson took the column in stride. The next day Brennan approached him and asked, "So why don't you have a woman member?" He kindly responded, "We will, in due time." Brennan persisted, "Why not do it now or sometime soon, if only to quiet people like me who will keep bringing it up."[116] Johnson politely blew her off. He and his fellow heavyweights at Augusta were not about to cut their collective conscience to appease Brennan or anyone else. Brennan returned to the Masters in 2000 and 2001, persisted in asking the same question, and made no more progress than she had in 1999.

In 2002 Brennan had an assignment that took her off the Masters beat. On Monday of Masters week, however, she was thumbing through a magazine and came across an article about Augusta National titled "Ladies Need Not Apply." That the article appeared in a magazine called *Golf for Women* did not strike Brennan as ironic. In the course of the article, golf journalist Marcia Chambers named—"outed," more precisely—the club's three black members. On the lookout for a fresh angle, Brennan called the one black member she knew, Lloyd Ward, the new CEO of the US Olympic Committee (USOC). In exposing his membership, she presumed he would have to quit either Augusta or his USOC job.[117]

Ward finessed his way through the conundrum. Claiming he preferred to work from the inside, he bought Brennan off with a useful quote, "Inclusion does not just mean people of color. It should be extended to that broader base that includes women." That quote and his very membership gave *USA Today* the edge it needed to break the club's historic gender exclusivity as a news story. Brennan followed up with a column. "In golf," she wrote, "there are two kinds of discrimination: There is acceptable discrimination and then there is unacceptable discrimination."[118] The war was joined.

Among its first casualties was Tiger Woods, the son of a black father and Asian mother and, at the time, the best golfer in the world. In time-honored progressive tradition, the media tried to coerce Woods into echoing the party line. When he refused to play along—"[The members] are entitled to set up their own rules the way they want them," said Woods—he lost his political value as a black man. "Columnists, pundits, talk shows," wrote Brennan gleefully, "they all came down on Tiger."[119] Tiger eventually buckled, but Hootie Johnson did not. And Hootie was who mattered.

Martha Burk, a committed feminist and chair of the National

Council of Women's Organizations (NCWO), read Brennan's 2002 article and decided it was time to take Hootie down. Burk, whose nickname as a child also happened to be "Hootie," did not shy from conflict. As president of the Wichita chapter of NOW, she led the charge to defeat abortion restrictions in Kansas and preserve that red state's unlikely status as late-term abortion capital of the world. By comparison, Augusta National must have seemed a soft target. "Hootie Johnson," she told her colleagues while mocking Johnson's drawl, "ah'm a-gonna wraaaht yew uh letter." That she did. It ran just nine sentences and concluded threateningly, "We urge you to review your policies and practices in this regard, and open your membership to women now, so that this is not an issue when the tournament is staged next year."[120]

Johnson responded on his own schedule. After due deliberation and a little strategic stalling, he decided to take the battle to the enemy. To Burk, he sent a short letter. To the news media, he sent a press release so forceful it negated the news value of anything Burk might say in response. "We will not be bullied, threatened, or intimidated," Johnson wrote in the release. "We do not intend to become a trophy in their display case. There may well come a day when women will be invited to join our club but that timetable will be ours and not at the point of a bayonet." Lest Burk think him naïve, Johnson described NCWO's likely strategy and let her know Augusta National was fully prepared to deflect it. "We expect such a campaign would attempt to depict the members of our club as insensitive bigots and coerce the sponsors of the Masters to disassociate themselves under threat, real or implied, of boycotts and other economic pressures," said Johnson.[121]

The letter shocked Burk, who had grown used to getting her way. "He went ballistic," she told the *Times*. "He has ended any possibility of direct communication. My choice is to communicate with others, and that may include sponsors of the Masters and individual members of the club."[122] Even Burk was impressed that Johnson had anticipated her strategy before she had a chance to formulate it. "He's certainly given us a good blueprint," she mused.[123]

Before the 2002 golf season ended, Johnson thwarted Burk's best line of attack by dropping the contracted television sponsors of the 2003 tournament—IBM, Coca-Cola, and Citigroup—as a way of protecting them from harassment. The sponsors liked the move because it saved them from a no-win decision. Fans liked it because there would be no TV commercials during the Masters, the highest rated of all golf tournaments. In making the gesture, Johnson signaled the club's willingness—and ability—to pay for its principles.

When Johnson announced the decision to shield his sponsors, Burk went after the broadcaster. "We expect to have a conversation with CBS," she told the Associated Press. "It will be about whether they want to broadcast an event, held in a venue that discriminates against half the population, and what kind of statement that makes about CBS as a network." CBS gave that notion no time to fester. A network spokeswoman shot back, "CBS will broadcast the Masters next year."[124] Undaunted, Burk predicted that if Johnson did not yield on the issue, the Masters would "fade as a major tournament." Hootie was not about to yield. In fact, he seemed to enjoy taunting Burk with her movement's own rhetoric. After allowing that the club might very well admit a woman in some distant future, Johnson added slyly, "In the meantime, we hold dear our tradition and our constitutional right to choose."[125]

Burk had one major ally in the fight, the *Times*. Before the battle was through, the *Times* would run more than one hundred articles or columns on the subject. In virtually every one of them, typically within the first sentence or two and often in the headline, the reporter established Burk as the Joan of Arc in this holy war, to wit: "Burk Applies for Protest Permit," "Burk to Appear at City Hall," and, a *Times* classic, "Citing Role of Women in War, Burk Raises Pressure on Augusta." The "war" in the third of those headlines was the Iraq War. It had begun just a few weeks before the 2003 Masters. Burk thought it would make a good hook to advance her cause. The *Times* editors agreed. "It's appalling that the women who are willing to lay down their lives for democratic ideals should be shut out of this club," said Burk, who, to her humble credit, allowed that the war in Iraq was a more serious concern.[126]

There was no faulting Burk's energy. Undistracted by the showdown in the Mideast, she was pressuring the Augusta City Council, organizing demonstrations, collaborating with the American Civil Liberties Union (ACLU), enlisting Jesse Jackson, hectoring members, browbeating sponsors, and demanding that CBS not televise the tournament. On the eve of the 2003 Masters, however, she had gained precious little ground. The one "clear victory" she could cite nearly a year into the battle was the resignation from the club of John W. Snow. Nominated by George W. Bush to be secretary of the treasury, Snow, Burk figured, "couldn't aspire to the job if he's associated with this club."[127]

As the tournament approached, the *Times* ran articles on the Burk jihad very nearly every day, often two a day. They did no good. An April 14 headline summed up the outcome, "She Did Not Prevail This Year, but Burk Has Time on Her Side." It should have read, "But Burk Has the *Times* on Her Side." Two days later, in a piece thick with class envy, *Times* columnist George Vecsey conceded short-term defeat but claimed a long-term victory. Crowed Vecsey, "Burk has put a mark on Hootie and his playmates." That mark, of course, would be the scarlet *S*. Vecsey imagined Citigroup CEO Sandy Weill sitting through an eternity of dinner parties at which some guest would inevitably scold him for his company's sponsorship of the Masters. And when that happened, Vecsey said piously, "Weill can thank Martha Burk."[128]

Burk and the *Times* kept beating the drum, but Hootie chose not to march. After two years, he reopened the tournament to sponsors and had no trouble finding all he needed. In 2006, when Johnson retired as chairman, Burk expressed her hope that "a change in leadership would bring a change in attitude." The new chairman, Billy Payne, would seem to have had that potential. He had been the CEO of the Atlanta Committee for the 1996 Olympics, a model of "inclusion," and was a winner of a distinguished service award from the Martin Luther King Jr. Center for Nonviolent Social Change. But Payne had no interest in obliging Burk and her teeny crusade. "I'm very much aware of her position on all issues as they relate to Augusta National," he said on assuming the club chair, "and I don't see at this time that any dialogue would be meaningful or helpful."[129]

One women who had no issue with Augusta's policies was former secretary of state Condoleezza Rice. An avid golfer, Rice was asked by *Golf Digest* in 2011 whether she thought Augusta had an obligation to open its membership to women. "No. I actually don't," said Rice. "These are issues for the membership. I've got a lot of good friends at Augusta who are really good people. And it's really up to them."[130] A year later, apparently appreciative of her attitude, Augusta National asked Rice to join the club. She was delighted to accept. So was Darla Moore, a South Carolina financier, philanthropist, and friend of Hootie's.

Ten years after Burk had given Hootie Johnson a one-year deadline, Augusta National opened its doors to two women, both wealthy, both Republican, one black, one white. Although Burk was quick to take credit for their admission, feminist groups did not exactly celebrate these pioneers for breaking the notorious "grass ceiling." In fact, there wasn't much love forthcoming from progressives anywhere. Two years later, the faculty council at Rutgers University made enough of a stink over Rice's scheduled appearance as commencement speaker that she felt compelled to back out.[131] That was okay. It was May. The Azaleas were in bloom, and the good old boys at Augusta were much more welcoming.

# 5

# THE SCARLET *I*: ISLAMOPHOBE

I f Neo-Puritanville were to elect a town beadle, talk show host Bill Maher would be a prime candidate. Smug, godless, and self-righteous, he has taken the whip to many a sinner, and I have, indirectly at least, felt the lash. In May 2011, on his HBO show *Real Time*, Maher grilled the late Andrew Breitbart on my thesis that terrorist emeritus Bill Ayers had helped Obama write his memoir, *Dreams from My Father*.

"Let's get on to the racism of today," Maher said to Breitbart in introducing this subject. "You do not believe Obama wrote his own book." To provoke Maher's insinuation, Breitbart had simply tweeted that my evidence for Ayers's involvement was "compelling." For Maher, in 2011, that one tweet provided grist enough to pose a question with no safe answer, "Do you think you can be a racist and not know it?"[1]

In an October 2014 edition of the same show, Maher and his guest, Sam Harris, a neuroscientist and fellow atheist, got a taste of Maher's own venom. Harris was trying to explain how liberals abandon their principles when faced with the issue of Islamic theocracy. "We have been sold this meme of Islamophobia," said Harris, "where every criticism of the doctrine of Islam gets conflated with bigotry toward Muslims as people."[2] Maher agreed. Fellow panelist Ben Affleck decidedly did not. The actor/director burst in rudely, "You're saying Islamophobia is not a real thing."

Without a trace of irony Maher reminded Affleck of the impunity the elect enjoy. "It's not a real thing when we do it," protested Maher. "It really isn't." Affleck was not convinced. He called the comments by

Maher and Harris "gross," "racist," and "ugly." Not to be out-offended, panelist Nicholas Kristof of the *New York Times* added that the criticism of Islam leveled by Maher and Harris had "the tinge, a little bit, of how white racists talk about African Americans."

Harris tried to explain he was not attacking Muslims as people but rather their applied theology, specifically the illiberal practices of stifling speech, suppressing women, stoning homosexuals, and separating infidels from their heads. "We have to be able to criticize bad ideas," said Harris, "and Islam is the mother lode of bad ideas." He lamented that Affleck refused to understand the point he was making. "I don't understand it?" shouted Affleck. "Your argument is 'You know, black people, we know they shoot each other, they're blacks!'"

As Harris wrote after the fact, "What did he expect me to say to this—I stand corrected?" For Harris, perhaps even for Maher, the show was a learning experience. "One of the most depressing things in the aftermath of this exchange is the way Affleck is now being lauded for having exposed my and Maher's 'racism,' 'bigotry,' and 'hatred of Muslims,'" wrote a dispirited Harris, already weary of the scarlet *I* Affleck had slapped him with. "This is yet another sign that simply accusing someone of these sins, however illogically, is sufficient to establish them as facts in the minds of many viewers."[3] Bingo!

The presumption that runs through Harris's 2004 best seller, *The End of Faith*, is that people like him can shuck the oppressive dogma of traditional religion and create "moral communities" based on logic and reason.[4] If there were such a community on air, it had to be Maher's *Real Time*. Yet there Harris sat, accused of freshly minted "sins" by neopuritans purer in their faith than he. Whether Harris learned any larger lessons from his pillorying remains to be seen.

## AMERICA CULPA

Today, every thinking person who ventures into the public square runs the risk of leaving with a scarlet letter or two on his or her letter sweater. I have been awarded a few, but only one letter surprised me.

That was my scarlet *I*. The year was 2002. The place was the venerable Chautauqua Institution in western New York. In the way of background, a Methodist minister started a campground meeting for summer school teachers on Chautauqua Lake in 1874, and the idea proved popular enough to imitate. By century's end, traveling "chautauquas" were educating and enlightening people all across the country, and the lakeside original grew and flourished.

The climactic scene of my one and only novel, the then futuristic *2006: The Chautauqua Rising*, unfolded at the Institution. Set, as the reader might surmise, in 2006, this political action thriller tells the tale of a grassroots insurrection that in many ways anticipated the tea party insurgency of 2009–2010. As an aside, those thinking of writing a book should be sure to give it a title that people can pronounce. The Institution is pronounced *sha-TAWK-wa*.

At the time of the book's publication, the year 2000, I was unaware of any political turmoil at Chautauqua. In the book, I described the Institution as "a perfectly preserved wish dream of late 19th century Americana." My gripe was that it was "too quiet, too calm, too relentlessly civilized."[5] A casual visitor, I did not sense that Chautauqua had long been drifting leftward both politically and theologically. Nor did I know that in 1985, an informal group, now incorporated as Chautauqua Christian Fellowship (CCF), had sprung up to correct the drift. In the previous decade or two, much of the tension between progressives and conservatives at the Institution revolved around the former's embrace of Chautauqua's growing gay population. The neo-puritan fondness for imputing bigotry to others, however, was about to find a new focus.

The same year my novel was published, the Institution chose the former "general secretary" of the National Council of Churches, the Reverend Joan Brown Campbell, to be its director of religion, a more powerful position than its title might suggest. Four years earlier, Campbell had helped orchestrate the black church-burning hoax of 1996. The year before her appointment to Chautauqua, Campbell did her Christian best to deliver child refugee Elián González back to the godless purgatory of Communist Cuba.

A longtime apologist for Fidel Castro, Campbell hewed faithfully to the party line. Her dogmatism became frighteningly obvious to a liberal nun who worked with her on the Elián case, Sister Jeanne O'Laughlin. In meeting Elián's visiting grandmothers, O'Laughlin saw how intimidated the women were, not just by their Cuban handlers but by their chaperone, Reverend Campbell. Shocked by what she saw, O'Laughlin had a public change of heart about Elián's fate. Campbell was none too pleased with O'Laughlin's apostasy. She had the NCC issue a press release condemning O'Laughlin for fueling "the fire of controversy" and promptly removed her from her role as facilitator.[6] In the years to come, the progressives running Chautauqua would remember this power play fondly. At Campbell's 2013 retirement roast, an admirer recounted how when attorney general Janet Reno went "looking for someone really tough" to handle the Elián affair, she turned to Campbell. "You have some sense of whom we are dealing with here," he joked. "Don't Mess with Joan."[7]

Upon her arrival at Chautauqua, Campbell embarked on two contradictory missions, one public, one private. Publicly, she championed "interfaith dialogue," specifically, an outreach to Muslims, known as the "Abrahamic Initiative." A gay-friendly Christian community with a bathing beach, an active theater scene, and a substantial Jewish population might not seem a natural draw for Muslims, but Brown was insistent. "We didn't have a Muslim presence," she told a reporter for a local newspaper, "but we knew if we wanted to talk about the Abraham link, we needed to have all three legs of the stool." She expected resistance. "There is among the Jewish groups, and some conservative Christian groups as well, an objection to Islam," Campbell lamented.[8] It would, of course, take some persuasion to build a three-legged stool when two of the legs objected, but as Chautauqua was learning, "Don't Mess with Joan."

Privately, for all her talk of "inclusivity," Campbell began to crack down on the CCF. The group once ran its own programs freely and without interference, but Campbell now limited the CCF to three speakers a year. She would vet the speakers in advance and monitor them as they spoke. In the summer of 2002, the CCF invited me. Since I had never spoken or written about Islam, I apparently passed muster. That same summer Campbell had invited imam Feisal Abdul Rauf to lay the groundwork for a Muslim cultural center at Chautauqua. This was the same New Jersey slumlord who called the United States "an accessory to the crime" of September 11, the same one who demanded George W. Bush give an "America Culpa" speech to apologize for the damage America had inflicted on the Islamic world, and yes, the same one who threatened to build a mosque and community center at the site of Ground Zero.[9]

When the CCF invited me to speak, I was not aware Campbell had seized control or had started her Abrahamic stool-building. Addressing what I called the "illiberal orthodoxy" of the media, I dedicated most of my talk to the media's crude stereotyping of the religious right. Toward the end, I pointed out the one notable exception to the media's bias. "Islamic extremists in America," I argued, "have proven to be exactly the bogeyman that the media have long imagined the Christian right to be—patriarchal, theocratic, sexist, homophobic, anti-choice, and openly anti-Semitic."

I then mentioned a "particularly honorable and brave" Muslim moderate named Shaykh Muhammad Kabani. I cited his testimony that 80 percent of the mosques in America were in the hands of extremists, some of whom, I added, were not above encouraging murder. Kabani, the chairman of the Islamic Supreme Council of America, had made this claim at a State Department event in 1999. His numbers came from his own eight-year study of 114 American mosques.[10]

Campbell had one of her minions monitor my talk and record it without my permission. She apparently did not like what she heard. Her reaction as headlined in the *Chautauquan Daily*—"Brown comments on Cashill statement"—was a minor masterpiece of do-gooder doubletalk.[11] Campbell began with progressive boilerplate about the Institution's commitment to a free exchange of ideas. She then quickly segued into the inevitable caveats. One was that speakers be "respectful of the views of all." The second was that their information be "factual." Campbell was to be the judge of both, and an unforgiving judge she proved to be.

"Jack Cashill stepped outside the boundaries of civil discourse," she ruled. "Several of his comments were not only provocative, but potentially harmful." The only evidence of potential harm Campbell mentioned was my reference to Kabani. She did not claim I had misquoted him, but rather that I had taken the quote "out of the context of Kabani's own struggle with Saudi Arabia." In a historically Christian summer community of ten thousand with no known Muslims in residence, Campbell censored me for failing to acknowledge the intramural nuances of Muslim politics. This was nuts. "The Kabani statement feeds fear and prejudice," Campbell claimed. "Pandering to fear through innuendo can hardly be defined as civil discourse." I was coming to grasp what the CCF already knew: tolerance was not exactly in the neo-puritan wheelhouse. With her editorial, Campbell planted a scarlet *I* on my Google feed and exiled me for the foreseeable future from the Chautauquan zone of decency. On the plus side, I escaped without a fatwa on my head. Not everyone who offended the "prophet" Muhammad has been so fortunate.

In the spring of 2015, before this book was published, the CCF invited me once more to come speak. I offered to talk about progressive neo-puritanism, but wary of the Institution's politics, I made no reference at all to either Islamophobia or homophobia in my proposal. It did not much matter what I proposed. "The Department of Religion said that since you had previously spoken at Chautauqua, they wanted me to consider recommending a new and different speaker," wrote my disappointed host. As we both understood, Chautauqua favorites like Karen Armstrong return to Chautauqua as faithfully as the swallows do to Capistrano. In 2014, Chautauqua proudly featured Armstrong, "the 'runaway nun,' the rebellious ex-Catholic with outspoken opinions about religion—comparing, for example, Pope John Paul II to a Muslim fundamentalist." She came to speak about her twelfth book, *Islam, a Short*

*History.* Discourse, apparently, is much more "civil" when everyone agrees with everyone else.

## THE NEW GAY

For all their internal disagreements—should gays, for instance, be celebrated or stoned to death?—the various subcults of the larger neo-puritan ecclesia have studied each other's strategies and absorbed each other's tactics. The more political among American Muslims have proved particularly creative in their adaptations. Borrowing from their African American allies, they coined the term "Muslim American." This gave their ethnically diverse followers the patina of racial oneness. So designated, they could posture as oppressed, plumb the fruits of liberal guilt, and accuse critics of "racism."

"Black Muslim leadership has foisted an ideology of victimization on immigrant Muslims," explained Abdur-Rahman Muhammad, an African American convert to Islam who watched this happen, "and it has stuck."[12] When Muhammad converted to Islam in about 1985, he joined a radical wing of that faith. The events of September 11 made him rethink his allegiances, and at the risk of never getting invited to Chautauqua, he committed himself to exposing "the stealth elements of radicalism" that permeated Islam in America. Among those he has exposed was Chautauqua golden boy Feisal Abdul Rauf. He rejected as "absurd" Rauf's contention that building the Ground Zero mosque would benefit moderate Muslims. "That mosque is going to be seen as a triumph for bin Laden," he told a congressional panel at the height of the controversy in 2010. The message Islamists would pull from its construction, said Muhammad, was this: "We could take down the symbol of their power and their economic dominance and their cultural hegemony. We can take it down, and Allah will give us a mosque in its place. Let's do it again."[13]

Although 70 percent of Americans opposed the mosque,[14] the furor around its construction gave the other 30 percent an opportunity to reinforce their standing among the elect. To make others aware of their worthiness, neo-puritans took to calling the non-elect by a word relatively new to the lexicon of defamation, "Islamophobe." Muhammad knew something about that word. He was there at the creation. He traced its origin to a group meeting at the International Institute for Islamic Thought (IIIT) in northern Virginia.

"Muslim is the new gay,"[15] said Canadian writer Mark Steyn only half-jokingly, and he was more right than he knew. According to Muhammad, the IIIT Islamists consciously decided to mimic homosexual activists who had been successfully using the "phobia" trope to defame opponents of their political agenda. Muslim activists saw the same potential in the concept of "Islamophobia." With just this one word, they could tie their struggle to those of other marginalized groups and "beat up their critics." The word—and the charge behind it—offended Abdur-Rahman Muhammad. The suffix "phobia" means irrational fear. As he saw it, there was nothing irrational about America's reaction to September 11.

"You had Muslims saying, 'She looked at me at the airport, they looked funny at me. I was oppressed,'" Muhammad told Congress. "No, this country just got hit by our people—by Muslims. And they're acting like all of this anxiety over Islam and Muslims is happening in some type of vacuum, like 9/11 didn't happen, like Fort Hood didn't happen, like Abdulmutallab trying to put a bomb on a plane didn't happen—like none of this is happening." Muslims tell each other that Americans and other Westerners "are just evil, rotten people that hate Muslims," said Muhammad. "That's the narrative."[16] It was certainly the narrative at Chautauqua and in much of the Western world, Canada included, Canada especially.

In 1977 prime minister Pierre Trudeau and his Liberal Party passed into law an open-ended piece of legislation known as the Canadian Human Rights Act. As drafted, the act gave authorities the power to ensure "all individuals should have an opportunity equal with other individuals to make for themselves the lives that they are able and wish to have." Specifically, it forbade discrimination in the provision of goods and services and protected a wide range of potential victims. A glowing written history of the human rights movement in Canada, authorized by the Human Rights Commission itself, praised the legislation as "among the most comprehensive in the world."[17] In handing authorities jurisdiction over the private sector, the act gave aspiring neo-puritans all the levers of control needed to suppress genuine civil rights, including freedom of speech and religion.

The most diabolical of these controls was encoded in Section 13 of the act. As modified over time, Section 13 gave the Canadian Human Rights Commission (CHRC) the power to sanction editors and producers in virtually all media, including the Internet. Any creative effort that might expose members of a protected group to "hatred or contempt" fell within the purview of the CHRC inquisitors. At least three-quarters of all Canadians belonged to at least one protected group. Scarier still, the CHRC would bypass the protections afforded Canadian citizens by about eight centuries of English common law and apply sanctions through its own adjudication process.[18]

In December 2007, as was almost inevitable, a Canadian citizen named Mohamed Elmasry of the Canadian Islamic Congress filed a complaint against Canada's leading weekly magazine, *Maclean's*. He filed it not only with the CHRC but also with its regional clones, the British Columbia Human Rights Tribunal and the Ontario Human Rights Commission. The charge was Islamophobia. Among the individuals accused along with *Maclean's* was Mark Steyn, a chapter of whose 2006 book, *America Alone*, *Maclean's* had excerpted.

Elmasry picked the wrong targets. Had he gone after someone without the resources of *Maclean's* or the wit of Steyn, that individual would have had little choice but to accept the public dunking from one or more of these soi-disant "Human Rights" tribunals. Steyn, thanks to his role as Rush Limbaugh's premier replacement host, is as well known in the United States as he is in Canada. In choosing to resist his inquisitors, he used the one weapon against which they were defenseless—ridicule.

"I don't want to get off the hook," Steyn said of a recommended exit strategy. "I want to take the hook and stick it up the collective butt of these thought police." Steyn would not abide what he called "the arbitrary criminalisation of dissent from state orthodoxy"[19] and was prepared to take his dissent public. His goal was to so embarrass Canadian authorities that they would have to repeal the law under which he was accused. Fortunately, he had the media platforms from which to do it.

Elmasry and his youthful media representatives—the "sock puppets" as Steyn called them—did not welcome debate. With the complicity of the Canadian media, they expected to own the narrative. Steyn was not about to let them. For starters, he denied the validity of the neologism "Islamophobia." Steyn too saw nothing "irrational" about fearing people who routinely parade down the streets of Western capitals, holding signs that read, "Behead the Enemies of Islam." By classifying opposition to Islam as a disease, said Steyn, Islamists expected "to end the argument by denying it [was] an argument at all." Even were Islamophobia a legitimate charge, Steyn refused to accept that his writings were "hateful."[20]

As I learned at Chautauqua, the surest way to be accused of hate is to quote prominent Muslims. Steyn's offense was to quote the late Iranian despot Ayatollah Khomeini. In his authoritative "Blue Book," Khomeini laid down any number of behavioral dicta. These were not, as Dr. Peter Venkman might say, "guidelines." These were *rules*. Among them was this: "A man who has had sexual relations with an animal, such as sheep, may not eat its meat." This, of course, inspired a Steyn riff or two on sheep shagging, which, in turn, prompted the accusation he had misrepresented Islam. As Steyn retorted, if Khomeini did not speak for Islam, who did? Who was more influential than the man who launched the Islamist revolution and presided over it for decades? Steyn refused to apologize for ridiculing a man "who issues rulings on when it's appropriate to eat one's ovine concubine."[21]

It took years and cost vast sums of money and time, but Steyn and *Maclean's* prevailed. The CHRC eventually dismissed the charges. The Ontario HRC dropped the case over a technicality. Steyn was willing to waive the technicality and fight to the death, but the HRC apparatchiks knew when to go to ground. Finally, in a decision with no precedent, the British Columbia Human Rights Tribunal (BCHRT) acquitted Steyn and *Maclean's* of "flagrant Islamophobia."

So out of character was the BCHRT's decision that Steyn offered to chip in a thousand bucks if the Canadian Islamic Congress chose to appeal it.[22] This burlesque culminated in June 2012 when the Canadian Parliament scrapped Section 13 altogether.[23] Steyn and his allies had done so thorough a job of discrediting the statute that it had no serious public defenders. To be sure, progressive MPs cast their votes to retain Section 13, but on this occasion they knew better than to put up a public fuss. In their storied march through the institutions, they were playing the long game.

## GOING GHOST

Although a Canadian citizen, Mark Steyn lives in New Hampshire. Among the features he finds attractive about America is the free speech protection the First Amendment affords political pundits. Few countries anywhere provide a comparable guarantee. Likewise, few countries have libel laws that give writers the kind of leeway American laws give.

What Canada and the United States do have in common is a quiescent media. As the various star chambers moved to strip Steyn of his ability to speak freely, he marveled at a Canadian media "generally indifferent to the outrage."[24] The American media, alas, have been as indifferent as their Canadian peers to the outrages inflicted on their fellow citizens. Wrote Christopher Hitchens of the United States in 2006, "Within a short while—this is a warning—the shady term 'Islamophobia' is going to be smuggled through our customs."[25] Hitchens did not have to wait long.

In 2001 Trey Parker and Matt Stone created an animated Muhammad on their profanely irreverent cartoon show *South Park*. At the time, no one protested their Muhammad. Neo-puritans had not yet fully embraced Islam and all its sensitivities. When Parker and Stone brought Muhammad back for a guest slot to celebrate *South Park*'s two hundredth episode in April 2010, they knew full well the worm had turned. Neo-puritans had transparently different standards for Islam than for, say, Mormonism, which Parker and Stone would mock in their soon-to-be hit Broadway show, *The Book of Mormon*. So, the pair parodied the left's dhimmi-like appeasement of Muslim sensitivities by putting Muhammad in a bear suit.

When even this gentle ribbing resulted in a death threat from an obscure Muslim blog, the network that airs *South Park*, the boldly progressive Comedy Central, blocked the image of the bear, bleeped out all references to Muhammad in the episode's sequel, and refused to post the episodes online. "In the 14 years we've been doing 'South Park' we have never done a show that we couldn't stand behind," said Parker and Stone. "We delivered our version of the show to Comedy Central, and they made a determination to alter the episode." The creators had written the episode to end with a speech "about intimidation and fear." Although the speech did not mention Muhammad, said the pair, "it got bleeped too."[26]

Industry peers did not exactly rush to their defense. Blogger and former Comedy Central employee Lindsay Robertson spoke for many in her scolding of Parker and Stone. "They owe an apology to every Comedy Central employee they've put in danger in pursuit of their own glory and publicity," said Robertson. "If god forbid something does [happen], it is on Trey Parker and Matt Stone's shoulders."[27]

Not everyone in the media turned dhimmi. To support the *South Park* creators, *Seattle Weekly* cartoonist Molly Norris conceived the nicely mischievous new holiday, "Everybody Draw Muhammad Day." On April 20, 2010, Norris created a poster to announce the new holiday. On it, she drew humanized images of a coffee cup, a cherry, a box of pasta, and other objects each claiming to be the likeness of Muhammad. "Do your part to both water down the pool of targets," wrote Norris bravely, "*and*, oh yeah, defend a little something our country is famous for (but maybe not for long? Comedy Central cooperated with terrorists and pulled the episode) the first amendment."[28]

The cartoon quickly went viral, and Norris attracted a small army of sunshine patriots eager to defend the cause, at least on Facebook. Just as quickly, some Islamic firebrands went postal. Norris came under increasing pressure and quickly backed off. On April 29, Norris suggested the new holiday be deep-sixed. "Let's call off 'Everybody Draw Muhammad Day' by changing it to 'Everybody Draw Al Gore Day' instead," Norris wrote. Challenging global warming was edgy, she must have realized, but not deadly. "Enough Muhammad drawings have already been made to get the point across," a frightened Norris pled. "At this juncture, such drawings are only hurtful to more liberal and moderate Muslims who have not done anything to endanger our first amendment rights."[29] Not satisfied with Norris's groveling, Yemeni American cleric Anwar al-Awlaki insisted she be made "a prime target of assassination."[30]

The FBI took the threat seriously enough to recommend Norris "go ghost." In other words, Norris had to scrub her identity and disappear. She may have anticipated a "Spartacus" moment, when her colleagues at this predictably self-satisfied, left-of-center rag would stand up and say, "I am Molly Norris." That did not happen. To justify the staff's timidity, one *Seattle Weekly* colleague informed the readers, "Depictions of the prophet are considered sacrilege by many Muslims."[31] He and the other staff watched her vanish as passively as the Eloi watched their pals vanish into the Morlock underground in H. G. Wells's *The Time Machine*. Norris disappeared in July 2010 and has not been seen in Seattle since. A US drone strike dispatched Anwar al-Awlaki to a rendezvous with his seventy-two virgins a year later, but Norris remains a ghost.

In 2010 the Obama administration did nothing more active in the Norris case than to suggest the poor girl hide. In 2012, when confronted with a new offense to Muhammad, Obama officials took the unprecedented step of silencing the offender. Although they found a more legally viable charge than Islamophobia to hang on Nakoula Basseley Nakoula, they clearly punished him for his impolitic take on that benighted cult.

Nakoula's future took a southward turn when Islamic militants stormed the US consulate in Benghazi on September 11, 2012. Before the night was through, these Muslims would kill four Americans, including popular ambassador Chris Stevens. Needing to blame something for the attack other than the administration's fatally befuddled foreign policy, Secretary of State Clinton released a memo that very evening indicting "inflammatory material posted on the Internet."[32] Although unmentioned in the memo by name, the Internet sensation that allegedly did the inflaming was the trailer for an amateurish video called *Innocence of Muslims.*

"The United States deplores any intentional effort to denigrate the religious beliefs of others," said Clinton. "Our commitment to religious tolerance goes back to the very beginning of our nation. But let me be clear: There is never any justification for violent acts of this kind." In truth, Clinton could be pretty flexible when it came to blasphemy. A year earlier, the Associated Press reported that she had been among those celebrities giving "standing ovations" to the *Book of Mormon.* Parker and Stone's scandalously potty-mouthed lyrics, like "F*** you, God, in the a**, mouth, and c***," apparently did not conflict with Ms. Clinton's "commitment to religious tolerance."[33] But then again, Mormons rarely attack US consulates.

The Smoking Gun, a website that posts legal documents, somehow managed to secure and publish Nakoula's sealed sentencing transcript from 2009. He had been arrested in June of that year for his role in a check-kiting ring. He chose to cooperate in the fed's pursuit of the ring's mastermind in return for a lesser sentence. Someone in the federal government released this document fewer than forty-eight hours after Secretary Clinton first blamed the Benghazi attack on Nakoula's video. "Why did the government release the deal?" Nakoula asked me. "Why did they put my life in danger?"[34]

It seems likely that the Obama administration was also leaking its Nakoula strategy to the *New York Times.* According to the *Times,* "Earlier in the week, federal officials appeared to be investigating whether

Mr. Nakoula had been the person who uploaded the video to YouTube." The *Times* reported that if Nakoula had uploaded the video—thus using the Internet without permission—he would have violated the terms of his sentencing from the check-kiting conviction. What stands out here is the phrase "earlier in the week." Someone in the Department of Justice had to have shared this information with the *Times* almost immediately. This article appeared on September 15, just three days after the smoke had cleared in Benghazi, and it put a life-size target on Nakoula's back.[35]

A week after the attack, despite ample evidence to the contrary, Barack Obama was still blaming the video. Inexplicably, he chose the occasion of the *Late Show with David Letterman* to finger the perpetrator. "Here's what happened," Obama told Letterman. "You had a video that was released by somebody who lives here, sort of a shadowy character who—who made an extremely offensive video directed at Muhammad and Islam." The usually irreverent Letterman seemed taken aback. "Making fun of the Prophet Muhammad!" he said solemnly. "Making fun of the Prophet Muhammad," confirmed Obama.[36] This was the same David Letterman who, a year later, would use the occasion of Pope Francis's World Youth Day appearance to say, "And I'm telling you if there's anything the kids can't get enough of, it's a 76-year-old virgin. Come on! World Youth Day. Or, as the Vatican calls it, salute to altar boys."[37]

That "shadowy character" of Obama's imagination was, of course, Nakoula, a Coptic Christian. Nakoula did not just "live here." He was an American citizen, but no matter. In characterizing Nakoula, Obama pulled his adjectives straight from the pages of the *New York Times*. Its reporters described him as "a shadowy gas station owner." More troubling for the reporters was that Nakoula had reportedly "expressed anti-Muslim sentiments as he pushed for the making of the film."[38] The *Times* and the other media camped out in front of Nakoula's California house, not to protect him, but to join in the manhunt. As a courtesy to their readers and a guide to would-be assassins, the *Times* showed the similarities between Nakoula's front door and the front door used in the infamous movie trailer.

For the most part, progressive First Amendment champions chose not to interfere. The ACLU, for instance, barely stirred itself to protest either Nakoula's arrest on a trumped-up "parole violation" or the White House pressure on Google to pull Nakoula's video from YouTube. When Politico asked the ACLU's Ben Wizner for a comment, he offered lamely, "There's no indication that the government is questioning the right of these idiots to make that repellent film. On the other hand, it does make us nervous when the government throws its weight behind any requests for censorship."[39] Wizner served as the ACLU's director of the Speech, Privacy & Technology Project. In that role for that organization Nakoula's plight should have horrified him. It obviously did not. Wizner's passivity provided further evidence, if any were needed, of the ACLU's mission-defying endorsement of the neo-puritan assault on civil liberties.

At the time, given the White House's widely echoed blame-the-video narrative, Nakoula believed himself responsible for the death of the four Americans in Benghazi. "I felt I had blood on my hands," Nakoula told me. "I felt like I deserved my punishment."[40] That punishment was swift in coming. Less than two weeks after the Smoking Gun article, a federal judge ordered Nakoula to be detained without bail. Although the authorities were still holding Nakoula's US passport, federal judge Suzanne Segal deemed him a flight risk who posed "some danger to the community." The only "danger" that Nakoula posed was if his potential assassins shot carelessly when they took him out.

Among the very real death threats that Nakoula faced was one from a Pakistani cabinet minister who put a ten-thousand-dollar bounty on Nakoula's head. The Egyptian courts meanwhile sentenced Nakoula to death. The Department of Justice responded to these foreign threats by recommending a two-year prison term for the American. Nakoula did, after all, use the Internet without authorization. Without allies or resources, he felt he had little choice but to plead guilty to four of the eight charges against him. His video-making netted him one year in prison and four years of supervised release.

Imprisoning Nakoula served two purposes for the Obama administration. The first was to signal to the Muslim world Obama's willingness to suppress any anti-Muslim sentiment. The second was to silence
Nakoula—not that the media needed much prompting to deny him his
voice. Their giddy quest to reelect Obama took easy precedence over
the rights of an accused Islamophobe.

Some months after his arrest, I tracked Nakoula down to La Tuna,
a federal prison in the westernmost tip of Texas. I was the first person
in the media to contact him. When I called him in May 2014, he was
still confined to a halfway house in Orange County, California, nearly
six months after he was supposed to have been freed. "Why did [they]
punish me again?" Nakoula asked angrily of the Justice Department.
"Why? It was not in original judgment."[41] In the age of Obama, though,
with all due apology to Alfred Lord Tennyson, Nakoula's role was not
to reason why. His role was to do and die or, at the very least, keep his
mouth shut until someone shut it for him.

To get some sense of how times had changed, one need only consider
the international outcry in 1989 when Iran's supreme leader Ayatollah
Ruhollah Khomeini urged the murder of the India-born writer Salman
Rushdie for his blasphemous novel, *Satanic Verses*. Although Rushdie
was not even an American, then president George H. W. Bush called
the death decree "deeply offensive to the norms of civilized behavior"
and warned Tehran that it would be "held accountable" for any reprisals
against American interests. By the time Bush responded, the sixty-five-
hundred-member Authors Guild and the ACLU, among other interest
groups, had publicly demanded the president fire back, and the *New
York Times* applauded their demands.[42]

It was not the artistic quality of Nakoula's work that inspired the
contempt of the media and the left. Nor, as *The Book of Mormon* proved,
had a generalized intolerance of blasphemy swept the West. No, Nakoula
owed his imprisonment and his scarlet *I* to the unholy alliance formed
by Islamic and progressive neo-puritans. As early as 1989, at the time
of the Rushdie incident, Christopher Hitchens was shocked to find the

"postmodern Left in league with political Islam."[43] Most of his political allies refused to shelter Rushdie, and some even scolded Rushdie for disturbing the status quo. That alliance, however, was still in its embryonic stage. In the years to come, these unlikely allies would invent the concept of "Islamophobia" and elevate it to the level of sin. In North America that sin was still venial. In Europe it had long since turned mortal.

## FILTHY THING

Like Trey Parker and Matt Stone, filmmaker Theo Van Gogh was fully ecumenical in his satirical assaults. He once referred to Jesus Christ as "that rotten fish of Nazareth" and was not above ridiculing the Holocaust. In the language of the artistic left, this great grandnephew of artist Vincent Van Gogh was admirably "transgressive." Dutch novelist Leon de Winter described him as an "artiste provocateur—troublesome, offensive and hyperbolic but, it should be said, within the wide boundaries of Dutch culture."[44]

Van Gogh, however, had grown concerned that those boundaries were constricting, and it was not Christians or Jews applying the pressure. Rather, a vocal Muslim minority was transforming "the most tolerant country in Europe" into something considerably less. Van Gogh was not the first to register his concern publicly. That honor belonged to the fearless and flamboyant politico Pim Fortuyn. An openly gay professor and former leftist, Fortuyn attacked multiculturalism, the welfare state, and the "backward culture" of Islam. This did not sit well in certain quarters, Islamic and progressive. In May 2002, for instance, the editors of the *Arab News* denounced Fortuyn as a "bigot" and "an unashamed Islamophobe."[45] They did so on the occasion of Fortuyn's assassination at the hands of Volkert van der Graaf, a Dutch animal rights activist who shared their opinion. According to van der Graaf, he shot Fortuyn to "prevent much harm to vulnerable groups such as Muslims and illegal aliens."[46]

A friend of Fortuyn's, Van Gogh set out to make a fictionalized film version of his pal's life and death, called *May 6th*. While that project was wrapping, Van Gogh teamed up with a Somali immigrant named Ayaan Hirsi Ali to make *Submission*, a short film about the plight of Muslim women. Hirsi Ali wrote the script. She knew her subject well. As a five-year-old in Somalia, she had been made "pure" by having her genitals cut out, a practice that was "always justified in the name of Islam." Also justified in the name of Islam were forced marriages and the abject submission of women to the will of their husbands. "I could never become an adult," Hirsi Ali said of her life as a Muslim.[47] She would attribute the seeds of her liberation to an early exposure to Western literature, romance novels included. To avoid a forced marriage, she fled to Germany and then to the Netherlands, where she settled in as a refugee in 1992.

"My heart was on the left," wrote Hirsi Ali about her early days in the Netherlands. As she saw it, that was the camp to which free-thinking, open-minded people gravitated. She loved her new country and cherished its freedoms. What troubled her was that she was among the very few Muslim refugees who felt that way. Too many of them had retreated into enclaves of their own creation, refusing to integrate and, in many cases, refusing to work. Even more troubling, most of the women remained as trapped and as terrorized as they had been in their home countries.

Immigrant men and women tended to blame their plight on the Dutch. As Hirsi Ali saw it, the accusation of racism was a "strategic" gambit designed "to externalize the cause of their unhappiness." Her friends on the left, however, did not want to hear her concerns. As in America, they were "blinded by multiculturalism."[48] Like multicultural-ists everywhere, they had no pride in their own extraordinary heritage and no stomach for imposing their values on oppressed people of color.

The events of September 11, 2001, failed to shake Hirsi Ali's friends from their perverse faith. They found reasons to excuse the Muslims celebrating the attack in Dutch streets and refused to see that celebra-tion as intrinsic to Islam. Hirsi Ali knew better. "This is based in belief," she warned them. "This is Islam." In the ensuing days, Dutch talking heads insisted Islam was a religion of peace, no more violent than any other. The real threat facing the Dutch people, progressives insisted, was the "terrible wave of Islamophobia" unleashed on September 11. Their studied ignorance stunned Hirsi Ali. "These were fairy tales," she thought. "I have to wake these people up."[49] Going forward, she would dedicate her life to doing just that, an effort that came with a price tag.

The more Hirsi Ali spoke about Islam, especially its ritualized abuse of women, the more threats she received from her coreligionists and the less support she got from her friends on the left. "You're not a socialist," a female politico on the Dutch right told her one day. "You're one of us." Hirsi Ali had to concede the woman was right and switched to the VVD, the Dutch center-right party. In 2003, she surprised herself by winning a seat in the Dutch parliament. Shortly before she took her seat, a Dutch publication ran an earlier interview with Hirsi Ali in which she had said, "By our Western standards, Muhammad is a perverse man and a tyrant." The interview ran under the unhelpful headline, "Hirsi Ali Calls Prophet Muhammad a Pervert."[50]

Following publication, hundreds of people headed for Dutch police stations, demanding Hirsi Ali be punished, calling her an "Uncle Tom" and much worse. Others simply threatened to kill her. In parliament, even her political allies attacked her. "Why did you say that?" asked one. "Because it's true," she replied. "I'm not going to apologize for the truth."[51] She now needed police protection. She would soon need more protection than the police could provide.

In making *Submission: Part I* with Hirsi Ali, Van Gogh muted his urge to shock and stuck to the sobering script Hirsi Ali provided. In the artfully shot, ten-minute video, a young female narrator, with only her eyes showing, speaks directly to Allah. She tells the story of four young women, one flogged for committing adultery, another forced into a marriage with a loathsome man, a third beaten regularly by her husband, a fourth shunned by her family after her uncle rapes her—all of them abused according to the dictates of the Koran. "The verdict that has killed my faith and love is in your holy book," the narrator despairs as the sound of a whip is heard in the background. "Faith in you, submission to you, feels like self-betrayal."[52]

There would be no *Submission: Part II.* As Van Gogh bicycled to work on a November 2004 morning in Amsterdam, a Dutch Muslim of Moroccan origin named Mohammed Bouyeri shot him. Van Gogh fell off his bike and collapsed on the roadway. "Can't we talk about this?" he feebly asked his assassin. He asked in vain. Bouyeri shot him four more times. He then took out a butcher's knife and slashed Van Gogh's throat. With a separate knife, he spiked a five-page letter addressed to Hirsi Ali into Van Gogh's chest. In the letter, Bouyeri lamented the Jewish control of the Netherlands and demanded jihad against the nation's infidels. At the top of his list for elimination was Hirsi Ali. In a separate letter he called for the destruction of that "filthy thing," Dutch politician Geert Wilders. The private lives of both Wilders and Hirsi Ali were days away from being over.

A member of parliament, the outspoken Wilders had been challenging "the dogma" of multiculturalism for years.[53] His bold defiance earned him any number of death threats from without and increasing hostility from within his own party, the VVD. Just months before Van Gogh's murder largely because of its support for Turkey's entry into the European Union, he quit the party. That news prompted even more death threats than usual and inspired an Internet video demanding his head. When Bouyeri very nearly beheaded Van Gogh in full view of the Amsterdam citizenry, Dutch police started taking those threats seriously.

As angry as Wilders was at the slaughter of Van Gogh "simply for criticizing Islam," he was angrier still at the neo-puritan reaction. Within hours of Van Gogh's murder, neo-puritan talking heads were "spouting their usual apologetics," namely, that Islam was a religion of peace and that Bouyeri had somehow committed an "anti-Islamic act." Worse, instead of cracking down on Islamic terror, Dutch officials were proposing to penalize "insults and blasphemy."[54] Two days after the murder, Dutch police intercepted an active plot to kill both Wilders and Hirsi Ali and whisked them away into full, permanent lockdown.

Neither has been able to walk the streets of Amsterdam since.

In the years after Van Gogh's murder, Islam made Europe considerably more dangerous for creative truth-tellers. The watershed event occurred in September 2005 when a local Danish newspaper, the *Jutland Post*, asked several artists to draw a cartoon image of Muhammad. The editors intended to confront the trend towards self-censorship by European media. It was a confrontation they lost.

Of the twelve entrants, seventy-year-old Kurt Westergaard drew the most provocative cartoon—an image of a fierce terrorist with a bomb tucked in his turban. Once alerted to the cartoon, the Muslim world exploded, literally. Rioters attacked Danish properties where they could find them and left more than 130 people dead worldwide. Sympathetic or fearful, or both, most Western media refused to show the cartoon that provoked the riots. Yale University Press, which commissioned a book on the incident, would not even allow the image to be used in the book. In Canada, Ezra Levant, the publisher of the *Western Standard*, reproduced the cartoons and was dragged in front of the various human rights councils for his efforts. Perversely, observed Christopher Hitchens, the violence resulted in "not opprobrium for the religion that perpetrates and excuses it, but increased respectability."[55]

Still, Wilders would not be silenced. In 2008, he made a fifteen-minute movie called *Fitna*, the Arabic word for "a test of faith in times of trial." As Hirsi Ali did with *Submission*, Wilders used actual Koranic verses to show the book's sacralized incitement to violence. He juxtaposed those words with real-life images of Muslims at war. "I did not make the movie," said Wilders. "Islam made it for me."[56]

Wilders's enemies weren't buying. The neo-puritan clerisy howled. The Dutch Muslim Council denounced Wilders as "a racist, fascist, and authoritarian." Less subtle Muslim groups threatened to kill him. Dutch businessmen raged openly about potential boycotts of Dutch products. The trade unions showed no sympathy. Said one prominent union leader, "Geert Wilders is evil, and evil must be stopped." YouTube did its best to oblige the critics by refusing to host the video. A Labor Party leader demanded Wilders's prosecution. The Dutch prime minister deplored the film—"We don't see what purpose the movie serves but to offend the feelings of others"—and denounced Wilders. The NATO secretary general warned of its negative consequences. United Nations secretary general Ban Ki-moon condemned *Fitna* "in the strongest terms." The British home secretary banned Wilders from entering that country. And finally, the Dutch Court of Appeal in Amsterdam ordered that Wilders be tried for "insulting Muslims,"[57] a case, like the one against Steyn in Canada, that would collapse under its own absurd weight.

At the time of this writing, Wilders was facing prosecution anew for "having insulted a population group with respect to their race and of incitement to discrimination and hatred." The group in question was the Moroccans living in the Netherlands. "I have yet to meet the Dutchman who wants more Moroccans in the Netherlands," said Wilders during his interrogation by the Dutch state police. "In my fight for freedom and against the Islamization of the Netherlands," he continued, "I will never let anyone silence me. No matter the cost, no matter by whom, whatever the consequences may be."[58]

As far down the road to dhimmitude the United States may have traveled, it was the one nation in the Western world, said Wilders, which "behaved as befits a free country."[59] Sensing the potential and weary of living in safe houses, Hirsi Ali moved to America in 2006. In 2007, her autobiography, *Infidel*, was published in English to great acclaim and excellent sales. If Hirsi Ali thought this country above the multicultural mania that has thrown Europe into chaos, an incident in early April 2014 instructed her otherwise.

A week earlier administrators at Boston's Brandeis University had announced their intention to award Hirsi Ali with an honorary degree. When the word got out, the neo-puritans, both Muslim and progressive, went to work. Ibrahim Hooper, a spokesman for the Council on American-Islamic Relations, sent a letter to Brandeis president Frederick Lawrence, calling Hirsi Ali a "notorious Islamophobe." Said Hooper, "She is one of the worst of the worst of the Islam haters in America, not only in America but worldwide." Not surprisingly, Lawrence folded like a cheap suit. "We cannot overlook that certain of her past statements are inconsistent with Brandeis University's core values," said the university in a cringe-worthy apologia.[60]

"What was initially intended as an honor has now devolved into a moment of shaming," said Hirsi Ali in response. The university had been talking with her for months about her commencement speech. Its claim that administrators had been unaware of her past statements, said Hirsi Ali, was "scarcely credible." Nor did the university consult with her before dropping her. Even worse than her personal rejection, Hirsi Ali continued, was "that an institution set up on the basis of religious freedom should today so deeply betray its own founding principles."[61] If feminist groups protested Hirsi Ali's public shaming in the same city that shamed the fictional Hester Prynne, no one reported those protests.

For all her travails, Hirsi Ali has fared better than the cartoonist Westergaard. In 2008, Danish police intercepted a Muslim plot to kill the unlucky prizewinner. In 2010, a Somali Muslim attacked Westergaard's Danish home. Only a well-fortified panic room allowed the then seventy-five-year-old to survive the attack. The police shot the axe-wielding terrorist as he tried to slice his way through the panic room door. "There is no better way to illustrate the difference between Western values and 'the true faith of Islam,'" said Wilders, "than the difference between a pen and an axe. We settle our differences with the former; Islam uses the latter."[62]

# 6

# THE SCARLET *C*: CLASSIST

On February 19, 2009, surrounded by brokers on the floor of the Chicago Board of Trade, CNBC's Rick Santelli let loose with an inspired tirade against President Obama's plan to keep millions of Americans in houses they could not afford. "This is America!" shouted Santelli to the working traders nearby. "How many of you people want to pay for your neighbor's mortgage that has an extra bathroom and can't pay their bills? Raise their hand?" The trading floor erupted in boos. After some additional jousting with the broadcasters back at CNBC and the brokers nearby, Santelli made the comment that would launch the most significant grassroots movement of his lifetime. "We're thinking of having a Chicago tea party in July," he said. "All you capitalists that want to show up to Lake Michigan, I'm gonna start organizing." This prompted a good deal of whistling and cheering. Asked what he proposed to dump, Santelli answered, "We're going to be dumping in some derivative securities. What do you think about that?"[1]

Filmmaker Michael Moore did not think much of that plan at all. Three weeks later, he appeared on Brian Lehrer's radio show in New York City. High among his beefs was Santelli's rousing call to arms. "Ah, the sound of angry white guys wafting its way through the airwaves," said Moore, himself an angry white guy.[2] He accused Santelli of blaming the whole mortgage crisis on "the little guy." Like most leftists, Moore preferred to lay the blame for the 2008 meltdown on the banks and lending institutions. Although financiers surely deserved their share of criticism, Moore slighted the role of the home purchaser and ignored altogether the crucial role of Democratic initiatives that recklessly goosed the housing market.

According to Moore, Santelli was employing Depression-era dema-goguery to divide people on the basis of class. "The way Santelli pre-sented it," said Moore ineloquently, "was a classist, bigotist way of presenting it." In fact, Santelli was protesting new government policies, not old personal habits. Then too, he chose "derivative securities" as his first item for dumping. These were not exactly the playthings of the little guy. But Moore never did care much for the facts.

The charge of classism was both new and old. In America, despite Moore's best efforts in the twenty years after his breakout movie *Roger and Me* exposed GM chairman Roger Smith and those "damn fat cats" at General Motors,[3] class warfare had gained little traction. By the 1990s, thanks in no small part to the digital revolution, the word *capitalist* had yielded to *entrepreneur*, and entrepreneurs were cool. Steve Jobs was rarely confused with J. P. Morgan. As a result, the word *classist* lacked the sting of either *racist* or *sexist*. It was for this reason that Moore added the neologism "bigotist" and lumped Santelli in with the presumed rac-ists who complained about "*those* people in the inner city." In March 2009, however, momentum favored Santelli.

A month later, on tax day, activists staged more than 750 tea parties across America. The *New York Times* did its best to deny the spontaneity of the events, its reporters preferring the critics' alibi that the move-ment was "largely created by the clamor of cable news and fueled by the financial and political support of current and former Republican leaders."[4] Those on the ground knew better, but the editors in the suites strove to identify the right-wing plutocrats who, they insisted, had to be pulling the strings.

The hunt for class enemies has long been a favorite pastime of the world's progressives. The Soviets had a particularly gruesome fondness for the practice. In December 1929, Stalin made the hunt a policy of state when he demanded "the eradication of all kulak tendencies and the elimination of all kulaks as a class." By definition, a kulak was a wealthy, land-owning peasant, "wealthy" meaning anyone who produced more than his family consumed. In time, the Soviets defined the term down to just about anyone who resisted the collectivization of the nation's farms. By stripping the countryside of its more productive citizens and reducing the rest to penury, Soviet officialdom had set the stage for the horror show that was to follow.

Stalin and his cohorts began by shaking down those left on the land for a bigger slice of the action. When the people resisted, Stalin sent in his shock troops. They had come to enforce the infamous 1932 "ear law," so dubbed because an individual could and would be arrested for withholding any "socialist property" right down to an ear of corn. By late summer 1932, when even hard-liners began to plea for Stalin to ease up on the kulaks—more than five million would be slain or starved to death—Moscow turned the petitioners down cold. "We Bolsheviks cannot afford to put the needs of the state—needs that have been carefully defined by Party resolutions—in second place, let alone discount them as priorities at all," wrote Stalin's minister, Vyacheslav Molotov. This hard-heartedness gave birth to the adage, "Moscow does not believe in tears."[5] As they would prove over and over, neo-puritans did not believe much in tears either.

## FARM ANIMALS

If there was one liberal innovation embraced by America's generally illiberal frat boys, it was the sexual revolution. Few resisted its perks, and very few of those who did resist enrolled at Duke University in Durham, North Carolina. In March 2006, in the spirit of the age, a group of bored Duke undergraduates combed through the Internet listings, looking for strippers. Doctors may not have made house calls in Durham, but strippers still did.

The students, all lacrosse players, had no trouble finding some at a place euphemistically called "Allure Escort Services." Given the relaxed moral standards of the American university, this was not an unusual request.[6] More than twenty times that school year, students groups at

Duke, male and female, had hired strippers. Sensitive to the nuances of race, a lacrosse player asked for white girls, and Allure promised the same, four hundred dollars each for two hours of performance at an off-campus house rented by a couple of the players.

Kim Roberts, part Asian, part black, arrived on time and talked amiably with the students while they awaited the second stripper. Crystal Mangum, a troubled black prostitute with a criminal record, showed up forty minutes late. Although the strippers were not what was promised, the players decided to proceed in any case. The performance did not exactly go well. Mangum, who arrived drunk, stumbled around the improvised stage, tripping over Roberts and irritating her audience. When Roberts asked if any of the players would be willing to expose his penis so the strippers could "play with it," she got no takers. A player proposed instead that the strippers use sex toys. Roberts offered instead to "use [the player's] dick but it would be too small." This same player grabbed a broom and offered it as a potential substitute. Apparently, even strippers have their standards. This proposal enraged Roberts, who stormed offstage, with Mangum staggering behind her. The performance was over in four minutes, but the nightmare was just beginning.[7]

While some of the players apologized, others demanded their money back, and others still simply quit the party. The two women locked themselves in the bathroom for five or ten minutes and finally left the house together, half-dressed. Mangum, however, went back inside to find a shoe she had left behind, failed to find it, and passed out on the back steps of the house. A player then picked her up and carried her to Roberts's car. Before they drove away, a player complained to Roberts about being scammed. "I called him a little dick white boy," she would tell Ed Bradley on *60 Minutes* with a laugh. "We wanted white girls, not niggers," said the player in response, and that one taunt by one player helped trigger a national furor.[8]

After driving away, Roberts found herself with an incoherent passenger. Uncertain what to do with Mangum, Roberts drove past a police station and dropped her off at a twenty-four-hour supermarket "passed-out drunk." The police were called, and they took Mangum to a facility for drugged and/or mentally ill patients. There, a nurse leadingly asked Mangum if she had been raped. Fearing arrest for her behavior, Mangum answered that, yes, indeed, she had been raped by three white men. In the previous ninety minutes, Mangum had made no such claim to Roberts, the supermarket security guard, or the police.[9]

When informed of Mangum's accusation, the players initially blew it off. They knew she was lying. All forty-six white lacrosse players were soon summoned to the Durham police station. There, they stripped down to their boxers to allow Durham police to look for the scratches that Mangum claimed to have administered. They submitted DNA samples as well. None of the samples would match any of the DNA found on Mangum.[10]

In her first several rounds of interviews, Mangum had difficulty identifying or even describing her alleged rapists. Finally, she settled on three players seemingly at random, and that was good enough for Mike Nifong, an unscrupulous Durham County district attorney then in a desperate fight for his political life. Without any evidence beyond Mangum's wildly inconsistent testimony, and despite the lack of a DNA match, Nifong charged the three players with first-degree rape, first-degree sex offense, and kidnapping. The gist of the charge, however, was "white privilege," a popular accusation in academic circles, "structurally identical," observed Joseph Bottum, "to the Christian idea of original sin."[11]

What was missing at Duke, however, was any hope of redemption. For the previous decade, dean of faculty William Chafe had been consciously hiring left-leaning professors to counter Duke's image "as a place of wealth, whiteness, and privilege." Chafe may not have changed the university's image, but he did change the political bent of the faculty. Even before the students were arrested, the Duke profs were busily fashioning the most venerable scarlet letter of them all, the scarlet *C*. As Stuart Taylor and KC Johnson argued in their definitive account of the incident, *Until Proven Innocent*, "Duke's faculty not only failed to stand up for procedural regularity, but a substantial faction of it joined the rush to judgment."[12]

Leading the rush was a professor of English and African American studies named Houston Baker Jr. In a public letter to the Duke administration, Baker denounced the entire team as the embodiment of "drunken white male privilege"[13] and demanded the immediate dismissal from the university of its members. Baker was among the eighty-eight faculty and staff who took out a full-page ad in the student paper condemning the accused "regardless of the results of the police investigation."[14] When the signers learned a few days later that DNA testing had failed to connect any member of the lacrosse team to Crystal Mangum, none of the eighty-eight backed down.

Not content to attack the players, faculty activists intimidated their colleagues into silence. For months, not a single one of the five hundred or so Duke arts and science faculty publicly supported the players. Not the bravest souls on the planet, professors feared if they were to defend the accused, they would be "smeared with charges of racism, sexism, classism, homophobia, or right wingism." And they were right. When one chemistry prof did finally speak out, and this only after the players' innocence had been established, the head of women's studies program promptly accused him of racism in a letter to the school newspaper.[15] On the contemporary campus, there is no more fearsome charge.

Despite the one player's racial taunt, the media chose to run with the class angle in their giddy coverage of the incident. This was not unusual. Although generally respectful of earned wealth, the media have long used rich kids as foils in the larger American morality play. In her gothic account of an apocryphal rape on the University of Virginia campus, for instance, *Rolling Stone* reporter Sabrina Rubin Erdely saw villainy in the hearts of the school's "toned, tanned and overwhelmingly blond students." Here, she suggested, a rapist of means could ply his trade with impunity. "The more privileged he is," Erdely quoted attorney Wendy Davis as saying, "the more likely the woman has to die before he's held accountable."[16]

Reporters of Erdely's generation had been nurtured on films in which rich jocks hound their class inferiors. In the collective media mind, the Duke lacrosse players slipped right into the paradigm established by *The Karate Kid*, *The Outsiders*, *Breaking Away*, *Revenge of the Nerds*, and other anti-classist pop hits. These films had created their own mythology. Aware of its power, archetypal rich jock Cameron Winklevoss explains to a partner in the movie *Social Network* that if he and his twin publicly attack Facebook founder Mark Zuckerberg, it would look "like my brother and I are in skeleton costumes chasing the Karate Kid around a high school gym."[17]

Although loudly averse to stereotyping in general, the news media carved out a wide exception to this rule for the Duke case. *New York Times* columnist Selena Roberts spoke for many when she described the whole team, including its one black player, as "a group of privileged players of fine pedigree entangled in a night that threatens to belie their social standing as human beings." The fact that Roberts was herself white and lived in one of America's pricier burgs did not deter her from accusing her own. *Newsweek* also fueled the stereotype, describing the "strutting" players as "a familiar breed on elite campuses." CNN's Nancy Grace was equally tough on these "rich kids." So too were Grace's invited guests, among them psychologist Dr. Patricia Saunders, who blindly accused the players of "underlying prejudice, and elitism, and classism, as well as probable racism."[18]

In fact, more than half the players did come from upper-middle-class families or better. Many did plan on heading to Wall Street after graduation. However, there was no evidence they flaunted their wealth, and plenty of evidence they behaved better than members of other major sports teams at Duke and other universities. Regardless, their perceived privilege stoked the media to near madness.

Initially, the *New York Times* resisted the rush to judgment. Taking the lead for the *Times* was sportswriter Joe Drape. Early on, he sniffed a hoax and told his editors as much. His reporting encouraged the defenders of the accused, and they fed him more inside information, hoping he would set the story straight. Drape never got the chance. As he informed the Duke people, he was "having problems with the editors." The "problems" were sufficient that they replaced him with reporters Rick Lyman and Duff Wilson, whose "politically correct politics," according to Taylor and Johnson, routinely trumped the facts. Sports columnist Roberts complemented the reporting with opinions righteously indifferent to the truth. "The message was clear," wrote Taylor and Johnson. "Lynch the privileged white boys and due process be damned."[19]

In time, the case against the three accused players began to erode. The DNA tests cleared them early on. Mangum's story slowly collapsed in on itself. And Nifong's behavior grew more erratic. Campus neo-puritans, however, stubbornly refused to acknowledge the contrary evidence and continued to slander the players in the face of it. The media, the *Times* in particular, stuck to their narrative. On August 25, 2006, nearly six months after the incident, the *Times* tried to shore up the case against the accused in a lengthy front-page story about this "tangled American opera of race, sex, and privilege."[20] Almost no one took the article seriously. Within hours of its appearance online, bloggers had waded through its errors and omissions and deconstructed the article to its preposterous pro-Nifong core.

As history records, there was no case. District Attorney Nifong built his prosecution of the three accused players on a foundation of suppressed evidence and outright lies. A year after the incident, North Carolina attorney general Roy Hooper dropped all charges against the players, declared them "innocent," and described them as victims of a "tragic rush to accuse."[21] The immediate consequences, however, were brutal. "This woman has destroyed everything I worked for in my life," Dave Evans, one of the accused, would tell Ed Bradley on CBS's *60 Minutes*. "She's put it on hold. She's destroyed two other families, and she's brought shame on a great university. And, worst of all, she's split apart a community and a nation on facts that just didn't happen and a lie that should have never been told."[22]

Mike Nifong fared even worse. His handling of the affair would cost him his job, his law license, his fortune, and even his freedom—at least for the day he served in the Durham County jail on a contempt charge. As to the unfortunate Crystal Mangum, she is now serving fourteen years in a North Carolina prison for the murder of her boyfriend.

The campus neo-puritans, of course, suffered not at all. Houston Baker, the players' most wild-eyed accuser, took a job soon afterwards as Distinguished University Professor in the English department at Vanderbilt. There, Tricia Dowd, the mom of one of the players, e-mailed him, asking him to reconsider his earlier claim that the boys had been given "license to rape, maraud, deploy hate speech and feel proud of themselves in the bargain." Baker responded by calling Dowd a "provacateur" [sic] who was "trying to get credit for a scummy bunch of white males!" He accused the players of living like "farm animals" and concluded that Dowd should forgive him if she really is "quite sadly, mother of a 'farm animal.'"[23] To be a neo-puritan, Dowd discovered, means never having to say you're sorry.

## CONTRACT KILLERS

In September 2014 Robert F. Kennedy Jr. joined the chaotic throngs marching through Manhattan in their Sisyphean protest against climate change. Although there were any number of targets Kennedy might have chosen, he focused his wrath on two aging brothers from Kansas. "They are enjoying making themselves billionaires by impoverishing the rest of us," ranted Kennedy. "Do I think the Koch brothers should be tried for reckless endangerment? Absolutely."[24]

One can forgive this aging dilettante for failing to understand free enterprise. His buccaneer grandfather swindled a good chunk of his fortune. But Kennedy should understand the family history well enough to know that granddad bought the presidency for Uncle Jack. Kennedy's wish to *imprison* a couple of honest billionaires for their above-board involvement in politics suggests that neo-puritanism, like heroin, rots the brain.

Fred Koch, the founding father of the Koch empire, would have been appalled if his son had turned out like young Kennedy. Fred did not raise his sons to be "country club bums."[25] So observed the left-leaning Daniel Schulman in his surprisingly fair Koch biography, *Sons of Wichita*. A lawyer by training, Kennedy knows something about criminal behavior. He fell into the environmental movement as part of his community service for, yes, a heroin bust. By contrast, the two Koch brothers who have run the business, Charles and David, both went to MIT, earned their master's degrees in chemical engineering, and worked their way up through the corporate ranks.

When Charles Koch entered the family business, it was doing about $70 million a year. When Kennedy attacked the brothers in 2014, Koch industries was doing about $115 billion and employing sixty thousand people. Because Koch Industries is a privately owned company, the second largest in America, the Kochs have not had to worry about meeting short-term shareholder expectations. This has allowed them to plow their profits back into the business, which they have run as a meritocracy, de-emphasizing job titles and emphasizing the creation of value. Unlike most companies demonized by the left—Goldman Sachs comes to mind—Koch Industries made its mark doing real, gritty, sweaty, mid-American kind of work. Koch has processed and transported and traded in oil, coal, fertilizer, pulp, fibers, polymers, building products, paper, electronic components, pollution control equipment, and beef.

Until the 1990s, when they were targeted by the Clinton administration, the Kochs did not even have a lobbyist in Washington. When the Kochs finally got in the game, their lobbyists did not, wrote Schulman, "shift their positions based on the political headwinds."[26] Unlike most DC influence peddlers, Koch's people stuck to their principles, lobbying for the free market ideals the Kochs have espoused from the beginning. These are the principles that the brothers take seriously. Charles, for instance, helped found and fund the libertarian Cato Institute, and David even ran for vice president in 1980 on the Libertarian Party ticket.

Although compatible with Republican positions on the economy, the

Kochs have historically hewed to the libertarian left of the party on other fronts. In 1968, for instance, the brothers ran a full-page ad in the *Wichita Eagle* urging America to "get out of Vietnam now." They have been soft on immigration, okay with gay marriage, and indifferent or hostile to most conservative social issues. David, who has spent most of his adult life in New York, gave $20 million to the Darwin-friendly Museum of Natural History in New York for the David H. Koch Hall of Human Origins, not exactly a conservative's idea of money well spent. David also gave $65 million to the Metropolitan Museum of Art, $100 million to Lincoln Center, and $100 million to the New York Public Library.[27]

Neither David's social liberalism nor his philanthropy cut him any slack with the city's neo-puritans. In 2011, when he took to the stage to introduce a production of *The Nutcracker* at the Brooklyn Academy of Music, a production he chipped in $2.5 million to sponsor, someone muttered loud enough to be heard, "He's an evil man."[28] And nothing provoked Koch critics quite like David's $100 million donation to build an ambulatory care center at New York-Presbyterian Hospital. "David Koch helps fund a facility in a neighborhood already lined with clinics and hospitals," said the befuddled head of the local union as her colleagues took to the street in protest. "Nurses see this as an assault on our patients."[29]

The Kochs did not become evil until David was very nearly seventy years old and Charles seventy-five. Seemingly overnight, and much to their surprise, they morphed from maverick entrepreneurs to what Schulman described as "crude caricature[s] of corporate fat cats subverting democracy and science as they secretly advanced their plutocratic agenda."[30] As to how the Kochs became evil, the answer is pretty simple. To counter the power of the tea party movement, propagandists on the left searched for someone to blame other than the millions of ordinary Americans angry with their government. The *New York Times* tried to oblige them by identifying likely puppeteers, but their early efforts failed to even mention the Koch brothers. In fact, there was no puppeteer. In Kansas City, for instance, a nineteen-year-old coed organized the initial tea party on April 15, 2009. She expected about 250 people to show up. More than 4,000 did. This was close to the norm across America.

Like many political organizations, the innocuous Koch-funded group, Americans for Prosperity (AFP), tried to latch onto the movement, but the AFP was a marginal player. "I've never been to a tea-party event," David Koch told *New York* magazine. "No one representing the tea party has ever even approached me."[31] No matter. As the 2010 midterms rolled around, a desperate White House looked for a sinner to pin the scarlet *C* on and found a pair of them in the Kochs. At a Texas fund-raiser, President Obama keyed in on the funding source behind the AFP. "You don't know if it's a foreign controlled corporation," he said. "You don't know if it's a big oil company or a big bank."[32]

Obama knew, and his henchmen were not shy about fingering the presumed kulaks in this rebellion against the state. Chief strategist David Axelrod called the Kochs out by name, describing them as "billionaire oilmen secretly underwriting what the public has been told is a grassroots movement."[33] Obama's allies in the media reinforced the theme. In October 2011 Brian Ross of ABC-TV chipped in with a breathless exposé, based on a report by Bloomberg Markets, called the "Secret Sins" of Koch Industries.[34]

"In a recent documentary, David Koch can be seen addressing tea party leaders and espousing American values," said Ross solemnly. ABC then cut to David at the podium saying, "The American dream of free enterprise, capitalism is alive and well." Ross sniffed out the hypocrisy. "But now questions are being raised about the American values of the source of the Koch brothers' wealth," he said. Apparently, employees of a French subsidiary had offered to bribe government officials several years earlier and were subsequently fired by Koch Industries, but that was sin enough for ABC to pillory the "secretive billionaire brothers" on national TV.

With the 2012 election looming, wrote Schulman, "It was as if President Obama were running against the Koch brothers." As the days melted down, Axelrod heated up the rhetoric against these "contract killers in super-PAC land."[35] Never mind that Democrats were being bankrolled by Wall Street, Hollywood, and rogue operatives like the "the man who broke the Bank of England," ruthless Hungarian-born financier George Soros. If the original Puritans rebelled against the buying and selling of indulgences, the neo-puritans optioned them on their own perverse futures market. Soros was hardly unique. Warren Buffett, Bill Gates, Mark Zuckerberg, and other billionaires had learned that a few well-publicized donations could buy lifetime exemptions from reprisal.

"I'm not sure it would ever cross Charles's mind," a Koch friend observed, "that a sitting president would single him out." The president's allies would do more than criticize. Hackers affiliated with the outfit called "Anonymous" tried to infiltrate the company's computer systems. Vandals defaced a Koch-funded math and science building at David's prep school alma mater, writing on its walls, "Money does not equal power." Other vandals defaced the David H. Koch Theater at Lincoln Center with the slogan, "I bought this theater so I could hide my evil deeds." The less cautious critics sent death threats—"The Koch brothers will Die!!!!!"—to Koch Industries. Both brothers had to hire security details for themselves and their families. It got so bad, in fact, that David felt obliged to send his children to school in a bulletproof car.[36]

Unlike so many of those tagged with a scarlet letter, the Kochs refused to yield. "With the left trying to intimidate the Koch brothers to back off their support for freedom," said Koch political strategist Richard Fink, "and signaling to others that is what happens if you oppose the administration and its allies, we have no choice but to continue to fight. We will not step back at all."[37]

## FINANCIAL GOMORRAH

Despite the few spiritual do-gooders hanging around the fringe, Occupy Wall Street was about as secular as a movement could possibly be. Still, its organizers turned to the Bible to capture the horror show that was American "corporatocracy." At one point, they fashioned a golden calf to mimic the iconic bull of Wall Street, a location the movement's initial blog post described as "the financial Gomorrah of America."[38] Gomorrah, of course, was one of the infamous twin cities described in Genesis, a deviant St. Paul to Sodom's degenerate Minneapolis. *Adbusters*, the Canadian organization that launched the Occupy movement, surely chose Gomorrah over Sodom, a city explicitly identified with homosexuality, to avoid offending their gay allies. Less was known of Gomorrah, other than that its sins, like Sodom's, were widely known to be "grievous" (Gen. 18:20). And for the Occupy people, the one truly grievous sin was greed—corporate greed, to be precise.

In June 2011, a month before the Occupy movement was born, former Massachusetts governor and hugely successful entrepreneur Mitt Romney announced his candidacy for president of the United States. In September of that year, President Obama made a pitch for his new JOBS Act. "Should we keep tax breaks for millionaires and billionaires? Or should we put teachers back to work so our kids can graduate ready for college and good jobs?" asked Obama, immediately before reminding his audience, "This isn't class warfare."[39]

A week after that speech, the Occupy crowd descended on lower Manhattan as a way of "bringing the perpetrators of the financial crash of 2008 to justice."[40] A month later, in a column titled "Occupy Wall Street Takes on Corporate Greed, aka Romney," Democratic strategist Brad Bannon casually shared with the readers of *US News & World Report* the way the pieces fit together. First, he noted that Obama's job speech rejecting "class warfare" was pretty much all about class warfare. The speech "hit the GOP for its affection for big business and its disdain for working Americans," Bannon explained.[41]

As in many wars, a nation would single out a given individual—the Hitler, the Tojo, the Saddam, the bin Laden, the Romney—to personify the evil of the enemy cause. "With his slicked-backed hair, the former Bay State governor even looks like the movie villain portrayed by Michael Douglas in Oliver Stone's *Wall Street* films," added Bannon. "Mitt Romney is Wall Street's avatar for campaign 2012." True, in

2008 Obama received more money from Wall Street—Goldman Sachs, Bank of America, Citigroup, UBS AG, JPMorgan Chase, and Morgan Stanley—than did any presidential candidate in a generation, but the media spared the public this unsettling bit of information.[42]

Confident the media had his back, Obama made the otherwise risky gamble to embrace the Occupy movement. "I understand the frustrations being expressed in those protests," Obama told ABC News in October 2011. "In some ways, they're not that different from some of the protests that we saw coming from the tea party. Both on the left and the right, I think people feel separated from their government. They feel that their institutions aren't looking out for them."[43]

Although Occupy Wall Street made the occasional jab at Obama, its spokespeople effectively introduced the themes the Democrats and the media would use to attack Romney. Among their favorite pejoratives was the word "obscene." MoveOn.org, for instance, claimed that Romney "made an obscene amount of money" from the auto company investments in his wife's blind trust.[44] On closer inspection, that "obscene" amount proved to be $15 million, about a day's pay for Bill Gates or Warren Buffet. *Gawker* lamented Romney's "obscene tax situation."[45] Apparently, he had made $45 million over the previous two years "doing absolutely nothing," other, of course, than risking capital in various entrepreneurial ventures. John Kerry and Ted Kennedy had done much the same except they leached their investment capital from wives and/or fathers. The *Washington Monthly*, for its part, complained in general about Romney's "obscene income."[46]

One tale of woe the media helped spread was so utterly Dickensian the word "obscene" scarcely did it justice. The story involved a Kansas City steel mill that employed more than forty-five hundred people at its peak in 1970, when owned by Armco Steel. The UK *Daily Mail* headlined its take on the saga, "The steel company deal that earned Mitt Romney millions while costing the government $44m and 750 people their jobs."[47]

In the way of background, Romney's Bain Capital became majority shareholder in the century-old company, renamed GS Technologies, in 1993. At the time, the mill's equipment was largely obsolete. Its competition worldwide was increasing in size and in sophistication. The employee base had dropped by more than 80 percent from its peak. And, critically, unlike many of its competitors, the mill had a union to deal with, a surly one at that. That Bain Capital would even attempt to rescue GS spoke to its faith in American enterprise.[48]

As readers of a certain age will recall, Ronald Reagan inherited an America deep in "malaise" when elected president in 1980. At the time, the future belonged to Japan—or so the nation was told. The wise men of American economics were encouraging businesses to mimic Japanese top-down "industrial policy" to compete. One of the wisest was future Clinton labor secretary Robert Reich. "Business enterprises," he argued in his 1983 best seller *The Next American Frontier*, "will largely replace geographic jurisdictions as conduits of government support for economic and human development."[49] Not all enterprises though. In Reich's America, federal largesse would descend like manna (with strings) only on those businesses that had willingly restructured themselves along approved lines. The idea of "picking winners" excited the Beltway brotherhood much as it would under Barack "Solyndra" Obama.

At the time at least, the Reichian model had little appeal beyond the I-495 loop. Walter Mondale, a Reichian enthusiast, carried just one state in the 1984 presidential election, his own Minnesota. In the rest of America, an entrepreneurial revolution was energizing the nation's would-be capitalists. Bain Capital and other private equity investors seized the momentum from the bureaucrats and saved the nation, at least temporarily, from Reichian mischief. The individual makeovers, however, have not all been pretty, and the GS Technologies deal was a case study of the same. The company went bankrupt in 2001. The question remained: who was responsible?

As the *Daily Mail* headline suggested, the media wanted to blame Romney, never mind that he had almost nothing to do with the deal on the front end, took a leave of absence immediately afterwards to run against Ted Kennedy for US Senate in Massachusetts, and left Bain altogether to rescue the Salt Lake City Olympics two years before GS Technologies went bankrupt. A high-level GS executive told me, "To be clear, Mitt himself was never involved in this investment at all, in any role except perhaps participating in the approval of the original investment." He added, "The spin of it makes me furious."[50]

Bain's goal at GS, as elsewhere, was to create wealth, with jobs being a by-product thereof. Said Howard Anderson, a professor at MIT's Sloan School of Management, Bain was "never interested in driving companies out of business." Added Steven Neil Kaplan, a professor at the University of Chicago Booth School of Business, "Their overall performance was terrific."[51] As even the media conceded, GS was no hit-and-run job. The company was paying dividends by 1994. That same year, management announced plans for a $98 million plant modernization. In 1995, Bain merged GS Technologies with a South Carolina firm to form one of America's largest mini-mill steel producers. Bain reinvested $16.5 million of its earlier dividend to pull the deal off. When a global corporate giant, the Rotterdam-based Mittal Steel, reportedly offered to buy the company out at a profit to Bain, the Bain-backed management turned the deal down. Bain wanted GS to succeed on its own terms as an American-owned company. In a stab at fairness, a Reuters hit piece quoted analyst Charles Bradford on GS Technologies' failure to survive. "If you look at the steel companies that went under at the time," said Bradford, "all of them were unionized."[52]

My contact, who preferred to remain anonymous for understandable reasons, was more blunt. "The true villain in this tale was the steelworkers' union," he told me. "They had crippled Armco-KC, as they had so many other once-great companies, and were hell-bent on frustrating Bain or anyone else in restoring sanity to the unreal world they had created." This former GS exec called the union "corrupt." As he told the story, union leaders were "ideologically committed to making sure that private equity could not replace the old management/ownerships that they had beaten into submission over decades." He added unsparingly, "They were prepared to commit suicide rather than let Bain succeed, and they achieved their goal."

In a 1997 strike at the plant, union peccadilloes included the shooting of bottle rockets at security guards, pounding on the windows of vehicles as they left the plant, and flattening the tires of nonunion trucks. According to my contact, Bain made its shares of mistakes. Its execs thought they could reason with the unions and out-negotiate Mittal Steel. They were wrong on both counts, and they paid the price.

Despite his renunciation of class warfare, Obama and his minions worked overtime to plant the scarlet *C* on Romney's chest. In May 2012, the Obama campaign ran an ad in several battleground states featuring a number of longtime union workers from GS claiming that a heartless Mitt Romney was personally responsible for ruining their lives. One of the men featured was a thirty-year veteran of the plant, named Joe Soptic. "Those guys are all rich," said Soptic. "They all have more money than they'll ever spend. Yet they didn't have the money to take care of the very people that made the money for them." The ad closed with a final heartrending plea from Soptic and a smiling Obama approving the message.[53]

In August 2012 the class war turned dirty. A pro-Obama super PAC, Priorities USA Action, created an ad blaming Romney and Bain Capital for the death of Joe Soptic's wife. "I lost my healthcare, and my family lost their healthcare. And, a short time after that, my wife became ill. I don't know how long she was sick and I think maybe she didn't say anything because she knew that we couldn't afford the insurance," said Soptic in the ad. "I do not think Mitt Romney realizes what he's done to anyone, and furthermore I do not think Mitt Romney is concerned."[54] One sympathetic blogger cast his judgment on Romney and his ilk with a quote from secular saint Charles Darwin: "If the misery of the poor be caused not by the laws of nature, but by our institutions, great is our sin."[55]

In neo-puritan circles, truth is simply not a virtue. Had it been, no one would have created this ad or approved it. For one, Soptic's wife was never covered under her husband's insurance plan. For another, Soptic lost his job in 2001, and his wife died in 2006. For a third, as explained, Romney had almost nothing to do with the steel plant deal. Worse than the crime, as they say, is the cover-up. When the ad collapsed under the weight of its own lies, Obama's people claimed no connection to it. Said White House spokesman Robert Gibbs on *Air Force One*, "We don't have any knowledge of the story of the family." This alibi quickly fell apart when it was revealed that the Obama campaign had used Soptic's story in a slide show earlier in 2012 and featured it in the earlier ad. In fact, Soptic himself had starred in a conference call hosted by Obama's deputy campaign manager, Stephanie Cutter. "Thank you, Joe," Cutter said at call's end. "We really appreciate you . . . sharing your experiences."[56]

As the 2012 campaign wound down, Team Obama hit the battleground states with an ad that even the Obama-friendly *Atlantic* described as "brutal." It began with an image of a confident Obama walking outside the White House. "I am Barack Obama, and I approve this message," said Obama in a voice-over. The ad then picked up the audio of Romney pilfered from a fund-raiser in which he talked about the "47 percent of the people who will vote for Obama no matter what." Under Romney's audio, the viewer saw black-and-white images of working people as grim and determined as those in Dorothea Lange's Depression-era catalog. From the looks of things, one could never guess that Romney was talking about people who did not work or that Obama had rejected "class warfare."

Filmmaker Michael Moore never pretended to abandon his holy war on the wealthy. He persisted in attacking "rich right-wing men," Romney most prominently, right down to the 2012 campaign wire. In late October of that year, Moore released an ad titled "the greatest generation" that was vulgar even by his own creepy standards.[57] In the ad, a half dozen cranky senior citizens vent their contrived spleen at Republican moneymen. One woman threatened to "cock punch" Romney, and another offered to "burn this mother f**ker down" if

Romney and pals managed to "steal" the election, there apparently being no legitimate way for Romney to win.

Two years after Obama's reelection, karma caught up with Moore and bit him in his ample butt. When his messy divorce spilled out into the public domain, the 1 percent got a hugely satisfying look at Moore's own "kulak tendencies." The chubby everyman, it seems, had a net worth north of $50 million. Much of this wealth was tied up in Moore's extravagant properties, most notably a New York City condo merged from three separate units and a ten-thousand-square-foot, lake-front home in Michigan. "What could be more ironic than the liberal, anti-capitalism firebrand Moore battling with his wife about an osten-tatious display of his wealth?" asked Abby Phillip of the *Washington Post*.[58] Al Gore's massive electric bills come to mind, but that is a story for another day.

# 7

# THE SCARLET *H*: HOMOPHOBE

"The twentieth-century martyrology, such as it is, is a canon of the politically correct," wrote influential *First Things* editor Father Richard John Neuhaus in 1993.[1] Not much has changed since. The martyrs the media celebrate today are those who suffered—or were at least inconvenienced—to advance the progressive cause. Each of the progressive subsets has its own martyrs. Each of these martyrs has his or her own cult, and many of the cults have their own hymn.

"I dreamed I saw Joe Hill last night," sang Pete Seeger, himself a Communist, of the early twentieth-century labor leader convicted of murdering a grocer and his son. Bob Dylan sang about Ruben "Hurricane" Carter, a black boxer convicted of "somethin' that he never done," namely, a triple homicide that he did, in fact, commit. "I never thought that wearing no hoodie could cost you your life," sang the rapper Plies about Trayvon Martin, overlooking the fact that Martin's unprovoked attack on George Zimmerman may have played a role in his death.

In the fall of 1998, hoping to advance the cause of gay rights and to help the Democrats in the upcoming midterm elections, gay activists were scanning the horizon for their own martyr and found one in a most unlikely place. As was true for progressive martyrs from Sacco and Vanzetti to Michael Brown, the story line did not come close to matching the reality, but in the able hands of neo-puritan propagandists, truth was what one could get away with.

## POSTER CHILD

In October 1998, on the windswept plains outside Laramie, Wyoming, Aaron McKinney pistol-whipped university student Matthew Shepard and left him to die. Within days, the media, Democrat strategists, gay activists, and the White House managed to turn Shepard into a martyr, collectively tracing his death to long-simmering societal hate. Jacob Marsden of the *Casper Star-Tribune* would later tell ABC's *20/20*, "I remember one of my fellow reporters saying to me, 'This kid's gonna be the new poster child for gay rights. Matt Shepard, gay bashed, symbol of the oppression of the gay community.'"[2] How right he was.

Much as they did years later with Trayvon Martin, the media depicted the twenty-one-year-old Shepard as a boy. In the words of *Newsweek*, he was a "slight, unassuming young homosexual . . . sweet tempered and boyishly idealistic." The *Denver Post* described Shepard as "a small, slight man who threatened nobody." He was not just a young gay man, but "everyone's son," including President Clinton's.[3]

Shepard was killed four weeks before the crucial 1998 midterm elections. Clinton's future was in the balance. The House of Representatives had authorized an impeachment inquiry into Clinton's sexual escapades and subsequent cover-up just a day before the Shepard story broke nationally. Even as Shepard lay in a coma, the always-opportunistic Clinton seized the moment to chastise those who questioned the progressive shift in sexual mores. "There is nothing more important to the future of this country than our standing together against intolerance, prejudice, and violent bigotry," said Clinton piously.[4] He would later compare Shepard's death to genocide in Bosnia.

Much to McKinney's undoubted surprise, Clinton subtly linked this soulless, fatherless, bisexual, meth-addled killer to the religious right and the Republican Party. Actress Anne Heche, then comedienne Ellen DeGeneres's gal pal, did so openly at a Washington, DC, vigil. "Mr. Trent Lott, Mr. Newt Gingrich, Mr. Jerry Falwell, how many Christs must bear the crosses until we learn that we are all children of God?" said Heche. "You preach in support of groups that encourage me to change who I am, to become more like you. I do not want to be like you."[5]

Like many other activists, Heche focused her rage on those Christians offering homosexuals the opportunity to change their lifestyles. Gay advocates argued that their orientation was as immutable as the color of an African American's skin. Maybe, maybe not. To the LGBT community's dismay, Heche married a man within three years of her proud declaration of immutability and would go on to have two children. That community was equally dismayed to learn that Chirlane McCray, proud author of the 1979 essay "I Am a Lesbian," married a fellow named Warren Wilhelm and would also have two children. With the possible exception of Michael Jackson, no African American has pulled an identity-switch quite as dramatic as these two women.[6] Speaking of identity switches, Wilhelm would rename himself Bill de Blasio and wreck neo-puritan terror on the NYPD as mayor of New York City.

Although songs would be written about Shepard, his cultists did not need them. They had Hollywood in their pocket. Shepard's death inspired three TV movies about his life. In each of them, his iconographers propped his body up against the fence to which he was tied and pictured his death as a crucifixion. The crucifixion meme was thoroughly implanted in progressive skulls well before the November 1998 election. At the DC vigil just two days after Shepard died, Heche claimed that the killers and their presumed allies "joined their ignorance with brutality, to crucify a young brilliant boy who they perceived to be such a threat." Not coincidentally, two of the Shepard movies premiered in the week before Easter. Of more lasting propaganda value was the Laramie Project, an ambitious educational program that exploited Shepard's death "to teach about prejudice and tolerance."[7]

For fifteen years, this martyr narrative went unchallenged. According to the legend, Shepard had never met McKinney before their chance meeting that fateful night in a Laramie bar. Claimed the *Denver Post*, Shepard "did nothing to provoke the attack except let his eventual assailants know he was gay."[8] The message coming from the media, which McKinney's friends echoed in a bizarre attempt to mitigate his guilt, was that this redneck homophobe beat Shepard to teach him not to solicit straight people.

This was pure progressive cant. In 2013, a brave gay journalist named Stephen Jimenez untold the accepted story of Shepard's death in a stunningly honest book titled *The Book of Matt*. As Jimenez revealed, Shepard and the bisexual McKinney, both meth dealers, had sex together on numerous occasions.

"Matthew was part of an interstate meth-trafficking circle," wrote Jimenez. McKinney was "first his friend and occasional sex partner, then his competitor and adversary, and finally his killer."[9] On the night in question, McKinney went on a meth-fueled rampage. He pistol-whipped the vulnerable Shepard for drug money; pistol-whipped his own partner, Russell Henderson; drove into town to rob Shepard's apartment, and then pistol-whipped a stranger who got in his way, fracturing his skull in the process.

From day one, the media told the story they wanted America to hear. Those few journalists who cared about the truth were hindered, wrote Jimenez, "by sealed court records and witnesses who had been ordered into silence." As a result, the public did not learn that Shepard was HIV-positive or that he had once been arrested for molesting two eight-year-old boys. Authorities "quietly concealed" his arrest record.[10]

Unprofessional as it was for the media to sanctify the victim, it was evil of them to demonize the accused. The prosecutors yielded to the pressure the media generated and sentenced McKinney and his partner, Russell Henderson, to prison for life without parole. McKinney no doubt deserved his fate. Henderson did not. He tried to stop the beating and got beaten by McKinney for his trouble. Having pled guilty to avoid the death penalty, he too will never get out of prison. Asked Jimenez, "Did the enormous political, media, and financial pressures that overtook the Shepard case usurp Russell's right to a fair trial?"[11] The answer, Jimenez strongly suggested, was yes.

A gay activist of long standing, Jimenez spent fifteen years researching the story, fifteen thankless years. "This is absolutely disgusting," wrote one reviewer on Amazon eager to plant a scarlet *H* on Jimenez. "The right's sick attempt to declare the Matthew Shepard murder was not a hate crime is not just pushing a bigoted political agenda, it is a slap in the face to his memory and his family."[12] Jimenez plowed on despite the threats, the rejection, and the criticism. He argued correctly that it did a "disservice to Matthew's memory to freeze him in time as a symbol, having stripped away his complexities and frailties as a human being."[13] The media rewarded Jimenez by ignoring his book. The Laramie Project website has yet to recognize his existence.

At the end of the John Ford classic *The Man Who Shot Liberty Valance*, the local newspaper editor (in an unnamed state very much like Wyoming) hears that Sen. Ranse Stoddard did not shoot the criminal Valance, as he was long reputed to have done. Upon learning this, the editor throws the evidence of the same in the fire. When Stoddard asks him why, the editor replies, "This is the West, sir. When the legend becomes fact, print the legend."[14] For Matthew Shepard, the legend lives on.

## PANSY-ASSED

In 1958 writer Alvin Schwartz introduced a character named "Bizarro" to jazz up the *Superman* comic franchise. "I was striving, you might say," Schwartz noted, "for that mirror-image, that opposite. And out of a machine which would reveal the negative Superman, came the mirror image." By his very nature, Bizarro did everything the exact opposite way a rational person would. On at least one occasion he explained why: "Me unhappy! Me don't belong in world of living people! Me don't know difference between right and wrong—good and evil!"

If there is a difference between Bizarro and nationally prominent anti-bullying guru Dan Savage, it is largely in self-awareness, advantage Bizarro. At the 2012 National High School Journalism Convention in Seattle, Savage viciously bullied an audience of well-mannered teens with a rant so crazily hateful it would make a Jeremiah Wright homily sound like the Sermon on the Mount.[16] In the process, he showed the world just how comfortable supporters of the gay agenda had become in professing their Christophobia. Indeed, of all the progressive sects, none is as relentlessly anti-Christian as the gay rights movement. A Muslim nation that stones gay men to death provokes less outrage among gay-friendly activists than does a Christian who declines to bake a cake for a gay wedding, and that is not an exaggeration.

"We can learn to ignore the bullshit in the Bible about gay people," Savage instructed the captive teens. After all, he insisted in a Bizarro-worthy twist on history, the Bible was "a radically pro-slavery document." That revelation would have come as news to Christian abolitionists like William Wilberforce or civil rights activists like the Reverend Martin Luther King Jr., but then again, Savage did not really care about slavery. What he cared about was sex. "What are the odds that the Bible got something as complicated as human sexuality wrong?" he asked the teens, then answered his own question, "100 percent."

Savage mockingly compared the Bible's sanctions on homosexuality to those on masturbation, menstruation, and eating shellfish. When several of the students bravely walked out in protest, Savage showed them the backside of the neo-puritanical hand. "It's funny, as someone who's on the receiving end of beatings that are justified by the Bible," he said clumsily, "how pansy-assed some people react when you push back."

Savage grasped Christianity about as well as he did the concept of bullying. It was not some Old Testament crustacean-phobe who defined marriage for Christians, but Jesus Christ himself, and he did so in a loving fashion. In the Gospel of Mark (10:6–9), Jesus, citing Genesis, introduced an essential understanding of God's plan for man. "But from the beginning of the creation God made them male and female," he told the Pharisees, who were testing him on the subject of divorce. "For this cause shall a man leave his father and mother, and cleave to his wife; and they twain shall be one flesh: so then they are no more twain, but one flesh. What therefore God hath joined together, let not man put asunder."

Many Americans, Christians included, fail to understand the critical notion of complementarity in Jesus' expressed idea of "one flesh." Then too, many Americans, those in Hollywood especially, have overlooked the "put asunder" part of the contract, both in their own lives and in the life of the culture. What they fail to understand, they fail to defend, including the inarguable reality that over the past two millennia, the stable, male-female, two-parent family has helped the Judeo-Christian West create a culture and economy unparalleled in world history.

The sophisticated left knows this. "The great foe of Socialism, of the communistic idea of society, is the family," the *New York Times* opined a century ago. "Marriage is the flower of individualism. As the family grows and its cost increases, its need of an independent income becomes vital. The ideal family man is the capitalist, the 'good provider.'" The *Times* cited as authority famed social philosopher William Graham Sumner, who argued in his 1907 book, *Folkways*, "Every socialist who can think is forced to go on to a war on marriage and the family."[17]

In their ceaseless war against the family, progressive activists overlooked for many years the subversive potential of gay rights, especially gay marriage. They generally wrote off the movement as frivolous and bourgeois. Indeed, in 1969, the *New York Daily News* headlined its coverage of the watershed Stonewall rebellion, "Homo Nest Raided, Queen Bees Are Stinging Mad."[18] Even the insurrection-friendly *Village Voice* dismissed Stonewall as the "Great Faggot Rebellion."[19] These responses represented something of a progressive norm. As testament to the same, postrevolutionary Cuban leaders flagrantly attempted to purge their country of homosexuality, which they believed to be as much a by-product of capitalism as homelessness or hedge funds. Leftist poster boy Che Guevara was particularly keen on "reeducating" gay and effeminate men and dispatched thousands, without charge or trial, to prison camp for reeducation.

In his book, *Before Night Falls*, gay author Reinaldo Arenas documented his conviction by Cuban authorities on the charge of "ideological deviation." He escaped prison, tried to flee that worker's paradise on an inner tube, and was subsequently caught and assigned to the island's most brutal prison, there to endure several years of torture and abuse before being dispatched to America on the infamous Mariel boat-lift. "The difference between the Communist system and the capitalist system," Arenas wrote, "is that when they give you a kick in the ass, in the Communist system you have to applaud, in the capitalist system, you can scream."[20] Arenas died of AIDS in 1990. He did not live to see the day that neo-puritans would demand applause for the very acts that got him arrested.

After the collapse of the Soviet Union, progressive activists took up the cause of gay rights as part of the larger switch from revolution to "anti-racism." (The how and when of this would make a book in itself.) Given their continuing embrace of Castro's Cuba and their current alliance with radical Islam, these activists would seem to have little long-term interest in the welfare of their new gay friends. No, what excites them is the opportunity to use gay issues to divide America against itself. Gay marriage is a particularly potent wedge issue. As Dan Savage made clear to his young audience, or certainly tried to, those who accept biblical truth had better get used to wearing the scarlet *H*.

## DUMB BITCH

"Next, let's have California, Carrie Prejean," said Billy Bush, host of the Miss USA 2009 pageant. The tall, twenty-one-year-old blonde strode nervously to the center stage. One of five finalists, she hoped to avoid the kind of embarrassment that befell many a would-be beauty queen on the Q & A portion of such contests. In the 2007 Miss Teen USA pageant, for instance, Miss South Carolina cruised to YouTube immortality when asked to explain why one-fifth of all Americans could not find their own country on a map.

"I personally believe that U.S. Americans are unable to do so because, uhmmm, some people out there in our nation don't have maps," said the unfortunate Lauren Upton, "and uh, I believe that our, I, education like such as uh, South Africa, and uh, the Iraq, everywhere like such as, and I believe that they should, uhhh, our education over here in the US should help the US, uh, should help South Africa, it should help the

Iraq and the Asian countries so we will be able to build up our future, for us."[21] Historically, this was the kind of question contestants got, and Upton's was the kind of answer that contestants, at least occasionally, gave. Prejean reached into the bowl hoping to acquit herself well, better than Upton, at least.

A few years earlier, no celebrity judge would have dared to ask the question that Prejean drew: "Vermont recently became the 4th state to legalize same-sex marriage. Do you think every state should follow suit. Why or why not?"[22] A few years before that, no celebrity judge would have accused Prejean of "homophobia" for her answer. The word was all but unknown. Its first recorded use was in a 1969 article titled "He-Man Horse Shit" in a precociously sleazy tabloid called *Screw*. The two gay activists who wrote the article employed the "phobia" suffix to suggest that heterosexuals avoided certain behaviors and pastimes—poetry, art, touching, and so on—out of the fear that others might think them homosexual.[23]

They had borrowed the term from gay-friendly psychologist George Weinberg. At that time, mental health professionals were beginning to rethink their take on homosexuality, often under duress. In May 1970, for instance, local gay provocateurs stormed the American Psychiatric Association (APA) meeting in San Francisco, shouting insults, disrupting meetings, snatching microphones from trembling hands, all the while insisting that they be heard. "Psychiatry has waged a relentless war of extermination against us," shouted one activist. In confusing these timid docs with the SS, he was hardly unique. From the beginning of the insurrection, neo-puritans, gay and straight, would undermine their foes' defenses with Nazi allusions until they skulked away or surrendered.

The shrinks were not remotely man enough to fight back. They were keening for their own private Vichy before the San Francisco meeting was halfway through. By December 1973, they had fully capitulated. The APA's Board of Trustees voted overwhelmingly that month to remove homosexuality from the *Diagnostic Manual of Mental Disorders*. With the upward thrust of a few wrinkled hands, they opted for collaboration, declaring gayness to be something other than an illness.[24] At about that same time, Weinberg was subtly redefining "phobia" to mean something other than "fear." When he had first used the term "homophobia" in print in 1971 in the weekly newsletter *Gay*, he defined it as the "the dread of being in close quarters with homosexuals—and in the case of homosexuals themselves, self-loathing." So defined, the "phobia" part made some sense. That would not last. In his 1972 book, *Society and the Healthy Homosexual*, Weinberg laid the groundwork for an expanded definition of the word, one that had little to do with fear and everything to do with politics.

By 2009 politics infested events as historically innocuous as a Miss USA pageant. Ironically, the celebrity judge who drafted Prejean's question was born to parents who had fled the same island hellhole Arenas had. If Arenas had gotten his butt kicked in Cuba, Perez Hilton made his name by kicking butt in America. Born Mario Armando Lavandeira in Miami, Hilton had rechristened himself in homage to airhead celebrity Paris Hilton and gossiped his way to fame, if not fortune, through his supremely catty blog. Well before he turned thirty, Hilton emerged as the mainstream media's "bad-boy darling go-to gay."[25]

A natural neo-puritan, Hilton prided himself on "outing" those celebrities who chose not to share their sexual inclinations with the world. In 2006, he had scored a media hit when he forced former *Doogie Howser* star Neil Patrick Harris to admit his homosexuality. "We are so proud (despite the naysayers) in having a hand in bringing about change," Hilton boasted at the time. "We've said it before and we will say it again: the closet no longer exists if you are a celebrity or a politician!"[26]

The bully boy tactics of this self-styled "gossip gangsta" did not thrill everyone in the gay community. Many had problems with the ethics of forcing private individuals to reveal their sexuality. "What purpose does it serve?" asked gay comedy writer Bruce Vilanch. Hilton and other "gay people for a living" seemed to forget, said Vilanch, that most homosexuals had day jobs and did not appreciate having their privacy rights shredded. Writing in *Salon*, Japhy Grant believed the straight media cottoned to Hilton because he fulfilled the stereotype of "the bitchy gay man who has all the dish," a homosexual equivalent of "Stepin Fetchit."[27] Grant missed Hilton's real value: he was doing the neo-puritan's dirty work in advancing the gay agenda.

It took thirty feet-dragging years for Hollywood to realize Sidney Poitier might make for better box office than the shiftless black characters played by Fetchit and others, but one would not know this by watching the Oscars. In March 2006, George Clooney showed just how perversely self-congratulatory Hollywood could be. "We're the ones who talked about AIDS when it was just being whispered, and we talked about civil rights when it wasn't really popular," said Clooney, inventing history as he talked. "This Academy, this group of people gave Hattie McDaniel an Oscar in 1939 when blacks were still sitting in the backs of theaters."[28] In the aptly titled *South Park* episode "Smug Alert," the creators ran Clooney's speech unaltered. Black director Spike Lee got in his licks too. As Lee pointed out, Hattie McDaniel played the archetypal "Mammy" in a movie that championed the *Southern* cause in the Civil War. Said Lee, for once making sense, "To use that as an example of how progressive Hollywood is is ridiculous."[29]

If a little sluggish on the civil rights front, the always-insecure denizens of Hollywood were eager to reaffirm their place among the elect on the subject of gay rights. They had some atoning to do. The same evening as the Clooney smug alert, gay caballero movie *Brokeback Mountain* failed to win the Oscar for Best Picture. "We should have known conservative heffalump academy voters would have rather different ideas of what was stirring contemporary culture," said bitter *Brokeback* author and neo-puritan scold Annie Proulx. "Next year we can look to the awards for controversial themes on the punishment of adulterers with a branding iron in the shape of the letter A, runaway slaves, and the debate over free silver."[30] Proulx was not far off in her predictions. The historical drama *12 Years a Slave* would win the Best Picture Oscar a few years later.

A California ballot measure in 2008 gave Hollywood the chance to redeem itself. Proposition 8 defined marriage as a contract between one man and one woman and drove red carpetfuls of celebrities, Hilton Perez among them, out to the streets in protest. Complicating their mission was Hollywood heartthrob Barack Obama. A few months before the 2008 election, the opportunistic candidate told California pastor Rick Warren, "I believe that marriage is the union between a man and a woman. Now, for me as a Christian, it's also a sacred union. God's in the mix." With Obama at the top of the ticket, black and Latino voters turned out in record numbers and helped pass Proposition 8.

With its passage, the Hollywood Hills shook with a fury not felt since the Northridge earthquake. "At some point in our lifetime," prophesied the ever-smug Clooney, "gay marriage won't be an issue, and everyone who stood against this civil right will look as outdated as George Wallace standing on the school steps keeping James Hood from entering the University of Alabama because he was black."[31] By the time Prejean pulled her lethal question from the seemingly benign bowl three months after the election, wrathful neo-puritans had seized control of the Hollywood square. If God was still "in the mix" elsewhere, in Tinseltown he was surely not.

"Well, I think it's great that Americans are able to choose one way or the other," said Prejean awkwardly to a TV audience of some seven million people. "We live in a land where you can choose same-sex marriage or opposite marriage. You know what, in my country, in my family, I think I believe that marriage should be between a man and a woman, no offense to anybody out there. But that's how I was raised and I believe that it should be between a man and a woman."[32] As soon as she gave her answer, Prejean could tell from the reaction of the judges, especially Perez, that this was not what they wanted to hear. "He looked absolutely devastated," Prejean remembered.[33] Although her answer mirrored the president's on that same question, the judges were not hearing Barack Obama. They were hearing George Wallace. The fitting had already begun for Prejean's scarlet *H*.

Firebrand Hilton took the lead. He reportedly gave Prejean a "zero" vote on her answer, which likely cost her the Miss USA crown. She would be judged first runner-up. "If that girl would have won Miss USA I would have gone up on stage, I shit you not," Hilton boasted on his blog, "and snatched that tiara off her head." Hilton's rants grew progressively more obscene because no one of consequence in his world objected. Hollywood's anger was directed instead at Prejean. "A lot of people are mad at you," her gay manager texted her, to discourage her from attending the coronation ball. "I'm afraid of what might happen to you. You really shouldn't come." He apologized not to Prejean for the invectives his allies hurled at her—Nazi, bigot, bitch, c***—but to Perez for Prejean's answer. Her female coach meanwhile apologized to the sponsors.[34] Over the next several months Prejean would suffer any number of insults and indignities culminating in the loss of her Miss California crown. The pretext for this anti-Christian tiara snatch was Prejean's alleged failure to cooperate with the Miss California executives then scheming to take her crown away.

After Prejean was bushwhacked at the Miss USA contest, the media dug into her virtual Dumpster almost as eagerly as they had dug into Sarah Palin's literal one. They delighted in shocking themselves with the prurient tidbits they unearthed—photos of her modeling lingerie, reports of a breast enhancement, a graphic home video. These were the kind of discoveries that usually advance an actress's career, but not Prejean's. Reporters saw in Prejean what the lions saw huddled before them in the Colosseum—fresh Christian meat.

In 2010, when Prejean married Oakland Raiders quarterback Kyle Boller, virtually every article alluded to her scarlet *H*. "The 23-year-old's nuptials come more than a year after she made scandalous comments about gay marriage at the 2009 Miss USA pageant," reported the *New York Daily News*.[35] In 2011, when announcing the birth of the Bollers' baby girl, *Hollywood Life* reminded its readers that Prejean had "shocked the nation" with her answer to Perez's question.[36]

In truth, neither "shocked" nor "scandalous" would seem to be the mot juste for a statement with which most Americans then agreed, including the liberal president. Lost in the retelling of this story was the fact that the live audience applauded Prejean's answer. In their ascendancy, however, the neo-puritans had lost all fear and much common decency. They would not let up. In 2012, when the couple decided to sell their home at a loss, not unusual in that particular California boom-bust cycle, *TMZ* headlined its article on the sale, "Opposite Sex Husband Sells SD Mansion for Loss."[37] Of one thing Prejean could be certain, the scarlet *H* would follow her to the grave.

## VILE SCUM

In 2014 Janna Darnelle (not her real name), a thirty-five-year-old mother of two, proved that a woman did not have to be a celebrity to be handed a scarlet *H*. By this time, any abandoned wife and mother could qualify. All it took was for a husband to run off with a man—and for the wife to protest.

The downward spiral began in 2007, when Janna's husband of ten years heeded the call of nature and dumped her for his newfound boyfriend. Completely blindsided by the announcement, Janna begged him to stick it out for the sake of their two young children and the life they had built together. Alas, the fellow's newly embraced identity did not allow for the continuation of the family unit. "We had become disposable," wrote Janna. "Being gay trumped commitment, vows, responsibility, faith, fatherhood, marriage, friendships, and community."[38] Swept up in the gay rights movement, the husband demanded equal custody of the children and took the dispute to court to get his way. Janna believes the judge, who openly sympathized with her husband, hoped to establish the case as a precedent to influence future ones. At one point, he told her husband, "If you had asked for more, I would have given it to you."

The husband and his lover went on to "marry" before their West Coast state redefined marriage. After the act became legal, the couple staged a second ceremony with the children in attendance. *USA Today* covered the ceremony in a celebratory photo essay without Darnelle's knowledge or permission. Her husband then moved into his lover's gay-friendly condo complex, where they launched their "non-exclusive" relationship. How, Janna wondered, would her adolescent son learn to deal with girls when he was surrounded by men who sought sexual gratification from each other? "How will he learn to treat girls with care and respect when his father has rejected them and devalues them?" she asked. "How will he embrace his developing masculinity without seeing his father live out authentic manhood by treating his wife and family with love, honoring his marriage vows even when it's hard?"

Janna asked these and other questions in a September 2014 column she wrote for Salt Lake City's *Deseret News*, later republished in the journal *Public Discourse*. She ended the column with a plea that America "defend marriage as being between one man and one woman." Given her experience, this request should not have seemed extreme. At the time, the citizens in only a handful of states had voted to authorize gay marriage, but they and their allies elsewhere were hell-bent on having their way.

The most driven of the neo-puritan incendiaries was a gay provocateur who blogged obsessively under the name "Scott Rose." Commented Rose on a gay blog mocking Janna, "Hopefully, Janna will let go of her prejudices so that she doesn't humiliate herself and the children any further."[39] On that same blog, Janna's husband weighed in and shared his ex-wife's real name. He also included a photo of himself, his partner, and his two children that purported to show "how happy ALL 4 of us are."

A question as to why the husband posted Janna's name generated a slew of wrathful responses. So consistent were they in tone that they sounded as if they had come from a mean gay version of *The Little Rascals* storied "He-Man Woman-Haters Club." Said one respondent to the questioner, "The vile scum Janna Darnelle was not simply writing about her 'horrible experience,' you insufferable tool. She was engaging with vicious anti-gay forces who seek to maintain, bring, and further harm into the lives of MILLIONS of gay people and their children!" In that no gay comment section would be complete without at least one Nazi reference, the fellow added, "I can only imagine your deep concern had Adolf Hitler written vicious screeds about Jews under a pen name." Others who commented called Janna "disgruntled," "a bitter, vindictive ex-spouse," a "horrible person," a "lunatic," and "a woman even a straight man couldn't get away from fast enough." Several of the respondents referred to her lament as a "screed," Rose among them. As to Janna's husband, Rose had this to say: "Best wishes and lots of love to your family!"

In the midst of the comments, Rose would jump back in repeating Janna's real name lest anyone overlook it. Not content to defame her on the Internet, Rose reportedly harassed Janna with threatening messages and left the following subversive dig on her employer's Facebook page.

> This is a COMPLAINT against [. . .], an executive assistant in [. . .]. Under the nom de plume of "Janna Darnelle," [. . .] has published a horrifying, defamatory anti-gay screed on the website "Public Discourse." The first problem would be that she is creating a climate of hostility for eventual gay elders and/or their visiting friends and relatives. The second problem would be that in the screed, she comes off as being unhinged. Her public expressions of gay-bashing bigotry are reflecting very poorly on LLC.[40]

Many respondents launched into unprovoked jabs at Christians, the word *Christian* almost inevitably modified by the adjective "so-called." Said one, "[Christians] claim they love everyone, as long as that everyone follows lockstep in those so-called Christian beliefs." Said another to Janna's husband, "It sounds to me like your ex-wife HAS embraced her 'god' and her faith. And like every other believer in god, that's . . . herself (as demonstrated by science)." Curiously, in her article Janna did not once imply she was a Christian. Her critics assumed that anyone who protested desertion by a would-be gay husband had to be some backwater Bible-thumper. In 2014 who else dared to complain?

## THE REFUSENIKS

Andrea Peyser of the *New York Post* referred to these people as "refuseniks." Although originally applied to Soviet Jews who were refused permission to emigrate to Israel, the word has evolved to mean anyone who protests an injustice by refusing official orders. The American-born Peyser used the term knowingly. Her parents met while serving in the Israeli army. She also used it appropriately. Her "refuseniks" faced a punitive state apparatus keen on suppressing religious dissent. Even in America, as Cardinal George feared, authorities had begun to tell ordinary people "what they must personally think"—or else.

In a November 2014 article, Peyser profiled one couple deep in the "or else" stage, Cynthia and Robert Gifford of New York State.[41] For the previous twenty-five years, the Giffords had lived and worked on a farm near Albany. They and their two children hosted the occasional wedding ceremony, but the farm was better known for an annual fall festival that featured kid-friendly attractions, like a corn maze and pig racing.

In 2012 Cynthia took a call from a young woman she had never met. As the two spoke, the woman's female partner recorded the conversation without, of course, informing Cynthia. Although the Giffords have had gay employees, and even a transgendered one, Cynthia politely told the caller that, given the Giffords' devout Christian beliefs, they could not in good conscience host a same-sex wedding ceremony on their property.

The would-be newlyweds did not overly worry about the Giffords' faith or their conscience. They promptly took the tape to the New York State Division of Human Rights and filed a formal complaint. An administrative law judge from the Bronx, Migdalia Pares, did not much concern herself with the Giffords' faith either. Pares declared their farm a "public accommodation" and ruled the Giffords had violated state law by discriminating against the offended lesbians. She fined them $10,000 and ordered them to pay the pair $1,500 each for their "mental anguish." The two women had no trouble finding another venue, but the Giffords may never find peace of mind. "This is scary," said Cynthia. "It's scary for all Americans." To keep the powers that be off their backs, the Giffords gave up hosting weddings altogether.

For all their travails, the Giffords fared better than Melissa and Aaron Klein. The couple operated a storefront bakeshop, Sweet Cakes by Melissa, in the considerably more combative environment of metropolitan Portland, Oregon. In February 2013, these Christian parents of five refused to bake a wedding cake for another lesbian couple. The lesbians promptly filed a civil rights complaint against the Kleins, and their supporters set out to cripple their business. Their tactics included death threats, vandalizing the bakery's vehicle on several occasions, and intimidating the clients and vendors listed on the shop's website. "They have an odd way of showing tolerance," quipped Aaron of his local neo-puritans.[42] Overwhelmed, the Kleins moved their business home in August of that year but were unable to list their phone number because of the constant harassment. With the clientele whittled down to family and friends, thirty-five-year-old Aaron took a job driving a garbage truck to support the family.

The *Huffington Post* reported the business closure with admirable restraint, a virtue not all its readers shared.[42] As is true in the comments section of most progressive sites reporting on gay issues, the anti-Christian animus overwhelms. The consistency of tone and message makes the skeptic wonder whether all such posts everywhere weren't written by the same snarky, self-righteous, twentysomething. Following is a sample right off the top:

> If the practice of your faith hinges on the degradation and humiliation of God's creations, might I suggest you've missed the mark entirely?

> Allowing discrimination is not freedom of religion, it's bigotry.

> The constant self-victimization of religious zealots has become quite tedious.

> Their religion is really a metaphor for "I'm a bigot and I hate gays and lesbians."

> So basically what they said is "We find homosexuals disgusting and we

refuse to serve them, but it's not discrimination because our religion says it's okay."

We don't serve your kind here, because in our holy book, GAWD said "thou shalt not bake cakes for people like that."

Wouldn't a religious exemption from anti discrimination laws have been nice for every bigot?

Of course, the Kleins never expressed any hatred of gays and never refused any gay person service. They simply refused to bake a cake honoring a practice contrary to their faith. Ironically, at the time Melissa turned the couple's request down, Oregon defined marriage as the union between one man and one woman, a constitutional amendment approved overwhelmingly by the many "bigots" of Oregon just nine years earlier. The fact that civilizations from the beginning of time have defined marriage thus mattered not at all to the preening neo-puritans of Portland. They were altogether ready to slap a scarlet *H* and worse on this young couple. "Wanna discriminate against somebody based on your religion?" wrote one aspiring Torquemada. "Be prepared to be investigated, fined, and potentially shut down."

Although the apparatchiks of the local gay rights movement sank the business, they only succeeded in strengthening the Kleins' faith. "What they are doing is proving the Bible to be true," Klein told me. He cited the "destructive heresies" anticipated in 2 Peter 2:9: "The Lord knows how to deliver the godly out of temptations and to reserve the unjust under punishment for the day of judgment" (NKJV). At the time of this writing, however, the Kleins were facing a more immediate judgment, specifically, a $135,000 fine, not easily paid on a garbage man's salary.

The neo-puritans of Colorado proved no more tolerant of the faith of their cake makers than did their Oregonian brethren. Jack Phillips had been making wedding cakes at his suburban Denver store, Masterpiece Cakeshop, for nearly twenty years when his life took a turn for the absurd. A devout Christian, Phillips welcomed all comers to his shop, but as a rule he declined to make his custom-designed "masterpieces" for events that conflicted with his faith, Halloween included.

In July 2012 two men came to his shop wanting a cake to celebrate their same-sex wedding. Phillips politely explained he would make any other kind of baked goods they might want, but not a wedding cake. Besides, he noted, Colorado did not recognize same-sex marriages. The easily offended couple promptly rushed to the Colorado Division of Civil Rights. There they complained of being rejected from a public accommodation because of their sexual orientation. "Being discriminated against is a form of personal invalidation," one of the husbands-to-be told the media. "It's being degraded and put on a lower level than other people in society."[44] Why gay couples continually allowed themselves to be "degraded" by the rare Christian refusenik seemed odd only to those who presumed their intentions to be innocent. They rarely were.

When the case went public, Nicolle Martin, Phillips's pro bono attorney, thought reason would prevail. A "recovering liberal feminist," Martin believed that on hearing her client's argument for creative and religious freedom, anyone who honored the Constitution would see his side of the story. "I was a little naïve," she confessed. The hate and vitriol Phillips faced, "this new McCarthyism," took her by surprise. "I have come full circle to realize," she noted, "that if you conflict with prevailing liberal orthodoxy, they will root you out. They will find you."[45]

Phillips refused to back down. As he explained in his own defense, the free speech clause of the First Amendment protected him from being compelled to use his artistic talents in an objectionable way, and he rightly saw himself as an artist. The motto of his shop, after all, reads, "Jack Phillips creates a masterpiece! Custom designs are his specialty." The free expression of religion clause in that same amendment immunized him even further—or so he thought. The Commission thought otherwise and ordered Phillips to "cease and desist" from discriminating against same-sex couples.

Phillips appealed the decision to the Colorado Civil Rights Commission, and the commissioners upheld the original decision and then some. They ordered Phillips not only to sell wedding cakes to whomever, but also to provide his employees with "comprehensive staff training" on Colorado's antidiscrimination laws, to provide the state with quarterly reports on "remedial measures taken," and to document the number of patrons denied service and the reasons why.[46]

The chair of the Colorado Civil Rights Commission, a black attorney named Katina Banks, signed the damning decree. Unmentioned in the reporting was that a year earlier, Banks and her female sweetheart had posted the story of their relationship on a "freedom to marry" site. "We want to be married to express our love and commitment," Banks lamented, "and we could do that if we went somewhere else where it's allowed—but it would have no meaning here where we live."[47] They lived in the same place at the same time as the gay couple demanding a cake from Phillips. How, Phillips wondered, was he to educate his staff in an act that had "no meaning"? He and Martin were not about to capitulate in any case. "We plan to fight this," said Martin, "and we plan to go down swinging."

The Commission's Orwellian edict caused just enough unease among liberals that more than a few felt obliged to rationalize it. "This is what [Phillips] should have done originally," argued one respondent on the *Huffington Post*. "Not make wedding cakes a part of his business."[48] In other words, when Phillips started his cake-making business in 1994, two years *before* President Clinton signed the Defense of Marriage Act into law, he should have anticipated this 180-degree turn in the party line and launched a cake business that did not include wedding cakes. This is the kind of progressive logic Woody Allen parodied in his 1971 film *Bananas*. "All citizens will be required to change their underwear every half-hour," said Allen's accidental commissar, Fielding Mellish. "Underwear will be worn on the outside so we can check." Yes, absurd law always requires checking.

Phillips refused to be intimidated. Unlike the Kleins, he had a mature enough business to withstand state persecution, at least for the immediate future. "There's civil disobedience," he said, reflecting on his options. "We'll see what happens. I'm not giving up my faith. Too many people have died for this faith to give it up that easily."[49] A lot of Coloradans apparently agreed. Inspired by his stand, they began buying so many cookies and brownies that Phillips, temporarily at least, did not have to make any wedding cakes.

To paraphrase anti-Nazi pastor Martin Niemoller, "First they came for the bakers." No one thought they would come for the pastors, at least not so soon. The neo-puritan elders continually assured their media pals they had no such intention. In Idaho, that guarantee lasted as long as it took to find a gay couple willing to be "degraded" by some unsuspecting Christian minister. "Many have denied the idea that pastors would ever be forced to perform ceremonies that are completely at odds with their faith," said Jeremy Tedesco, an attorney with Alliance Defending Freedom (ADF), "but that's what is happening here—and it's happened this quickly."[50]

Sure enough, just two days after federal judges struck down the state's ban on same-sex marriages, city officials in Coeur d'Alene were demanding that a pair of Christian ministers join a gay couple in matrimony or something like it. Given the pattern nationwide, one sensed an unseen hand behind the demand. The local bureaucrats did not have to see the hand to feel the push. They capitulated before the gay couple could say, "ACLU."

Donald and Evelyn Knapp, the couple who own and operate the Hitching Post Wedding Chapel, held their ground. They were not about to scrap a two-thousand-year-old tradition at the whim of a federal judge and some antsy local bureaucrats. Given that they performed specifically Christian services with frequent references to the Bible, they saw their enterprise as something more timeless than a "public accommodation." Faced with a $1,000-a-day fine and a threatened trip to the hoosegow, the Knapps contacted the ADF and sued the city. In the small miracles department, the city backed off its demands, calling the whole thing a "misperception."[51] Christians around the world did not misperceive anything. They saw exactly what was going on and showed city officials that, in Idaho at least, they could still bring more heat than the local media and the Rainbow Coalition. The national media knew enough to back off.

In Houston, a neo-puritan vanguard also got a little too far ahead of its media supply train. There, the lesbian mayor of Houston, Annise Parker, and her staff cracked down on local pastors who were protesting a transgender-friendly equal rights ordinance. At someone's request, city attorneys subpoenaed "all speeches, presentations, or sermons related to [the equal rights ordinance], the Petition, Mayor Annise Parker, homosexuality, or gender identity prepared by, delivered by, revised by, or approved by you or in your possession."[52] Not since Governor Winthrop drove Ann Hutchinson out of the Massachusetts Bay Colony for her sermons "traducing" the colony's ministers had a public official so flagrantly suppressed religious expression.

The huge public outcry that followed cowed Parker into claiming she had been unaware of the subpoenas until after they were sent. "This is an issue that has weighed heavily on my mind for the last two weeks," said Parker. "I decided that withdrawing the subpoenas is the right thing to do. It addresses the concerns of ministers across the country who viewed the move as overreaching."[53] Taking Parker at her word, two weeks passed before she realized state censorship of a preacher's sermon might be a bit of constitutional overreach. If one sentiment captured the state of the neo-puritan mind circa 2014, this was it.

If Parker learned a lesson, few of her fellow pro-gay travelers seemed to. With each passing month activists found new reasons to accuse the unenlightened of bigotry. Italian designers Domenico Dolce and Stefano Gabbana, both gay themselves, found themselves in the cross-hairs of movement snipers for daring to question same-sex marriage and gay adoption. The media exploded. Accusations flew. Boycotts followed. The State of Indiana passed its own Religious Freedom Restoration Act. The media exploded. Accusations flew. Boycotts followed. And throughout it all, the neo-puritans rubbed their hands in righteous glee.

## HORRIBLE VALUES
Since opening its first restaurant in 1967, Chick-fil-A's modus operandi

had the nation's investment bankers scratching their heads. They never quite understood why a fast-food operation would close on what might have been its most profitable day, Sunday. If the bankers did not understand, it is likely because they had not met a Christian businessman who took his faith as seriously as CEO Dan Cathy. "[We are] based on biblical principles," said Dan Cathy of the Cathy family business model, "asking God and pleading with God to give us wisdom on decisions we make about people and the programs and partnerships we have. And He has blessed us."[54]

In 2012 the company needed all the blessings God could shower. For more than a year, neo-puritan shock troops had been doing their damnedest to take Chick-fil-A down. The controversy began in January 2011 when a Chick-fil-A franchise in south central Pennsylvania donated food to a Christian marriage retreat. The Pennsylvania Family Institute (PFI), which sponsored the retreat, happened to endorse traditional marriage. Connecting the dots, an obscure, amateurish blog, *Towleroad*—"a site with homosexual tendencies"—ran an article headlined "If You're Eating Chick-fil-A, You're Eating Anti-Gay." The most offensive quote the blog could dig up from PFI head Michael Geer was this: "The only way that we can get the people to decide this issue is through the ballot box. Marriage as defined as between a man and a woman has proven to be the best for the health, education and welfare of children."[55] That was provocation enough for *Towleroad* and just the kind of news the *New York Times* found fit to print.

In a lengthy article, the *Times* led its readers to believe that news of this Chick-fil-A marketing gesture in the middle of nowhere "lit up gay blogs around the country." Although seemingly neutral, the *Times* put "Jesus Chicken" on notice that the gay community was watching. "It literally leaves a bad taste," one entrepreneur/drama queen told the *Times*, "because I know the people who are putting this food in my mouth actively loathe me."[56]

Democratic operatives could say only so much about Chick-fil-A through 2011 and into 2012. The reason was simple enough: President

Obama was still on record endorsing traditional marriage. True to form, Vice President Biden seemed to have forgotten what his "marriage equality" marching orders were. When questioned on *Meet the Press* in early May 2012, Biden said he was "absolutely comfortable" with homosexual couples having the same marital rights as heterosexual couples.[57] "I think you may have just gotten in front of the president on gay marriage," Biden's communications director suggested on the trip back from the studio.[58] Biden had indeed. Obama staffers were in a panic. While their man was still "evolving" on the subject, Biden was standing as upright as the *Homo sapiens sapiens* on the far right side of the evolution chart.

To catch up, the White House promptly arranged a soft-lit, soft-ball interview with then crypto-lesbian Robin Roberts on ABC's *Good Morning America*.[59] Roberts, who would "come out" soon after, did not disappoint. Just three days after Biden's impromptu curveball, she asked—as if she did not know the answer in advance—"So, Mr. President, are you still opposed to same-sex marriage?" After much hemming and hawing, Obama finally conceded, "At a certain point, I've just concluded that—for me personally, it is important for me to go ahead and affirm that—I think same-sex couples should be able to get married." With an election looming, this born-again federalist somehow convinced himself it was "healthy" for states to work on the issue locally.

"It's not being worked out on the state level," protested Roberts impulsively. "We saw that Tuesday in North Carolina, the 30th state to announce its ban on gay marriage." By a whopping 61 to 39 percent margin, in fact, North Carolina voters rejected same-sex marriage and civil unions, and this in a state Obama carried in 2008. In passing a constitutional amendment, North Carolina would seem to have "worked out" the issue to its own liking. For neo-puritans like Roberts, however, "worked out" meant something completely different. It meant having a state swallow their dogma whether the citizens wanted to or not.

Nothing if not political, Obama allowed that some traditional marriage supporters were not mean-spirited. This had to come as a shock to gay advocates who could imagine no motive other than hate, but soul sister Roberts caught the cue. "Especially in the black community," she clarified. Said Obama, "Absolutely." Dissenters in the white community got no such pass. Indeed, with Obama now fully evolved, progressives felt free to call them "knuckle-dragging homophobes"[60] and worse.

Dan Cathy had more to do with his time than monitor trends on Twitter. Two months after Obama's conversion, he thought it still respectable to endorse traditional marriage. In July 2012, when asked about the subject by an obscure Baptist journal, Cathy answered, "We are very much supportive of the family—the biblical definition of the family unit."[61] Once this interview surfaced, inquisitors dug into the record and found a more provocative radio interview with Cathy from a month earlier. On this equally obscure show, Cathy had elaborated, "As it relates to society in general, I think we are inviting God's judgment on our nation when we shake our fist at Him and say, 'We know better than You as to what constitutes a marriage.'"[62]

Just days after Cathy's remarks surfaced, Thomas Menino, mayor of the city that gave Hester her scarlet *A*, validated Cardinal George's thesis that government had begun "using civil law to impose its own form of morality on everyone." Menino sent Cathy—and likely every media outlet in America—a letter urging him to rethink his plan to locate a Chick-fil-A in Boston. "There is no place for discrimination on Boston's Freedom Trail, and no place for your company alongside it," said Menino, whose idea of "freedom" meant court-imposed same-sex marriage at a time when even its proponents conceded the issue had no chance of winning a public vote.[63]

Chicago politicians trumped Menino's gassy rhetoric with time-honored political thuggery. If alderman Joe Moreno could not use civil rights law to block the opening of Chick-fil-A's first freestanding facility in Chicago, he threatened to use the city's notorious zoning ordinances. There surely had to be some traffic and congestion issues Moreno could throw in Chick-fil-A's way. Mayor Rahm Emanuel, Obama's former chief of staff, had Moreno's back. "If you're gonna be part of the Chicago community, you should reflect Chicago values," said Emanuel,[64] oblivious to the reality of how the phrase "Chicago values" played to an America that had grown up watching *The Untouchables*.

If Dan Cathy waffled a bit in the spotlight, his supporters did not, former Arkansas governor Mike Huckabee most notably. It saddened Huckabee that a Christian company had to face so much "vicious hate speech and intolerant bigotry."[65] To bolster Chick-fil-A's defenses in the escalating culture war, Huckabee called for a Chick-fil-A Appreciation Day. The day proved to be prodigiously successful. Customers lined up out the door and around the block in one location after another and proudly posted pictures of these lines on Facebook and Twitter. "While we don't release exact sales numbers, we can confirm reports that it was a record-setting day," said a company spokesman.[66]

During Chick-fil-A Appreciation Day, the neo-puritans stewed. One of them, the CFO of a small start-up called Vante, braved the long lines to express the street-level zeitgeist of the movement. So confident was Adam Smith he was on the right side of history, in fact, that he recorded and proudly posted on YouTube a video of his quest to get a free cup of water.[67] As he waited in the drive-through line, Smith mused, "An antigay breakfast sandwich always tastes better when it's full of hate." He then shared his convictions with an admirably restrained Chick-fil-A clerk named Rachel.

"You know why I'm getting my free water, right?" he asked her. "I do not," said Rachel. "Because Chick-fil-A is a hateful corporation," Smith answered. Over her painfully polite defense, he pontificated, "I don't know how you live with yourself and work here. I don't understand it. This is a horrible corporation with horrible values. You deserve better." Staying true to her training, Rachel answered, "I hope you have a really nice day." Said Smith in parting, "I will. I just did something really good. I feel purposeful. Thank you so much." So desperate was Smith for purpose in his life that he found it, or thought he did, bullying a clueless teen. His company, Vante, thought otherwise. It fired him.

A few weeks later, LGBT volunteer Floyd Corkins II took the quest for purpose a brutal step further. With a gun in one hand and a bag of Chick-fil-A in another, Corkins stormed the offices of the Family Research Council (FRC) in Washington and opened fire on the FRC's black security guard, Leo Johnson, who tried to block his way. Although shot in the arm, Johnson managed to tackle and subdue Corkins and prevent what could have been a massacre. After his arrest, Corkins told authorities he wanted to "kill as many as possible and smear the Chick-fil-A sandwiches in victims' faces." He had chosen FRC for its support of Chick-fil-A. In his pants' pocket he had a list of the other pro-Chick-fil-A targets. According to FRC president Tony Perkins, the listing of the FRC as a "hate group" by the Southern Poverty Law Center put a bull's-eye on its back.[68]

Not surprisingly, the media paid little attention to the shooting incident and even less to Corkins's motive. They stuck to the preferred narrative that the gay rights movement was benign and that Cathy had damaged his brand by opposing it. A *Huffington Post* headline from January 2013 showed just how myopic their worldview was: "Chick-fil-A Sales Soar in 2012 Despite Bad PR."[69] Thanks in no small part to that same "bad PR," a year later Chick-fil-A passed KFC to become the nation's leading provider of chicken to go.

Unlike Dan Cathy, Brendan Eich did not have a customer base that shared his values. A week after taking the CEO job at the Mozilla Corporation, the fifty-three-year-old Eich sat for an interview with *CNET*. He did so to save his job. Although a legendary figure in Silicon Valley—Eich created the computer language JavaScript—the young and/or wired were clamoring for his head. They had discovered that in 2008 Eich had held the same position on marriage that Obama had. Eich, however, had made the mistake of backing up his conviction with cash—specifically, a thousand-dollar donation to help pass California Prop 8, the proposition that reaffirmed traditional marriage.

Once Obama "evolved" on this issue, neo-puritans insisted anyone could—and everyone should—do the same. The seventy thousand who signed a petition demanding Eich "make an unequivocal statement of support for marriage equality" certainly seemed to think so. It was not enough that he accept a position contrary to his faith. To gain their grudging approval, Eich had to endorse "marriage equality" wholeheartedly. "If he cannot, he should resign," read the petition. "And if he will not, the board should fire him immediately."[70]

As chief architect and cofounder of Mozilla, a nonprofit organization dedicated to keeping the Web open and free, Eich had no interest in pulling the organization down around him. And so he scrambled to save both Mozilla and his job. He came to his interview well coached in neo-puritan patois. "When people learned of the donation, they felt pain. I saw that in friends' eyes, who are LGBT. I saw that in 2012. I am sorry for causing that pain." Then Eich swiveled to show how his own principles fit within Mozilla's imagined culture. "If Mozilla cannot continue to operate according to its principles of inclusiveness," he continued, "where you can work on the mission no matter what your background or other beliefs, I think we'll probably fail."[71]

"War is peace," wrote George Orwell in *1984*. "Freedom is slavery. Ignorance is strength." An updated 2014 version might have added, "Exclusion is inclusion." Two days after the interview, Eich was gone. "We didn't move fast enough to engage with people once the controversy started," said executive chairwoman Mitchell Baker in her mea culpa to the Mozilla community. "We're sorry. We must do better."[72] Not fast enough? She and her fellow board members set a land speed record for booting a CEO. They slapped a scarlet *H* on Eich and pressured him to resign within ten days of his taking over. It is hard to imagine they could have destroyed the career of a trusted colleague much quicker than that. "Our organizational culture reflects diversity and inclusiveness," Baker prattled on. "We welcome contributions from everyone regardless of age, culture, ethnicity, gender, gender-identity, language, race, sexual orientation, geographical location and religious views. Mozilla supports equality for all."

Many of those who weighed in on the brouhaha on tech sites made comments like, "I don't feel sorry for a hateful bigot who got what was coming to him."[73] But if Mitchell and her colleagues counted on a monolithic response from the tech community, they misjudged that community. For every commenter who endorsed the coerced resignation of Eich, several protested the "rush to fascism." Said one, "You're entitled to your own opinion as long as it agrees with the liberals." Said another, "Eich's rights to free speech and association have been violated." Still another addressed the obvious irony of Eich's departure: "So does that mean that Obama has to resign too?" Others saw right through the empty sanctimony of Mitchell's position. "Compelling Eich to resign for his views on same-sex marriage is an absolute outrage! His resignation sends a clear message to me that the notion of inclusiveness and openness laid out in the Mozilla Manifesto is hogwash." Liberal *Forbes* tech contributor Tony Bradley may well have captured the reigning spirit in the headline of his piece, "Backlash against Brendan Eich Crossed a Line."[74] That it did. Whether anything was learned remained to be seen.

## NEW CREATION

In October 2013 Phil Robertson, the patriarch of the *Duck Dynasty* clan and a costar of the most successful reality-TV show in the history of cable television, agreed to sit for an interview with Drew Magary of *GQ* magazine.[75] "Hey, what does GQ stand for?" asked Robertson at the beginning of the interview, a question that quickly established the cultural divide between them.

The story Robertson told Magary was compelling. A good old boy from backwoods Louisiana, Robertson gave up his quarterback slot at Louisiana Tech—a guy named Terry Bradshaw took over—because quarterbacking interfered with duck hunting. This being the sixties, and Robertson being just another "immoral man," he yielded to the siren song of the "sinful revolution" before turning his life over to Jesus. That turn saved his marriage and started him on a wildly improbable road to entrepreneurial success making duck calls.

As part of their deal with A&E, the Arts and Entertainment channel, Robertson insisted that the network acknowledge and respect the family's faith. According to Robertson, A&E said they wanted a show about family values, and, as he knew, "the best family values come about when God is involved." A&E obliged, and the show succeeded beyond anyone's best projections. "The Robertsons are immensely likable. They're funny. They look cool," said Magary of Phil and his many kin. Their style and their faith, he noted, made them "ideal Christian icons: beloved for staking out a bit of holy ground within the mostly secular, often downright sinful, pop culture of America."

For all his professed fondness for the Robertsons, Magary, much like Jeff Pearlman with John Rocker, tried his best to undermine them. A young and proudly vulgar Australian American, Magary did not share Pearlman's obvious anti-Christian animus. Nor had he staked out a position on the rainbow coalition's front lines. Rather, he had found his own profane niche in what he called "the godless part of America," and he knew how enthusiastically its denizens would cheer the sacking of the *Duck Dynasty* QB. His first question to Phil—"Do you think homosexual behavior is a sin?"—was calculated to do just that.

"Start with homosexual behavior and just morph out from there," said Phil. "Bestiality, sleeping around with this woman and that woman and that woman and those men." Magary then quoted Robertson's paraphrase of 1 Corinthians 6: "Don't be deceived. Neither the adulterers, the idolaters, the male prostitutes, the homosexual offenders, the greedy, the drunkards, the slanderers, the swindlers—they won't inherit the kingdom of God. Don't deceive yourself. It's not right" (vv. 9–10).

Robertson was not far off. The International Standard Version of this passage reads, "You know that wicked people will not inherit the kingdom of God, don't you? Stop deceiving yourselves! Sexually immoral people, idolaters, adulterers, male prostitutes, homosexuals" (v. 9). As Robertson would later explain, homosexuality was just one of several sins in the Corinthians list. It was not "elevated" above any of the other sins. When Magary asked whether homosexuality was a "sin," Robertson wondered where else he could have turned for an answer but the Bible.

Although Magary noted the Corinthians reference, few others would acknowledge Robertson's source. As to his personal take on homosexual acts, Robertson did his best to avoid common vulgarisms, but that somehow made his explanation all the more memorable. "It seems like, to me, a vagina—as a man—would be more desirable than a man's anus," said Phil artlessly. "That's just me. I'm just thinking: There's more there! She's got more to offer. I mean, come on, dudes! You know what I'm saying? But hey, sin: It's not logical, my man. It's just not logical." He did not have to say any more. Although Magary highlighted Robertson's answers to questions about Mitt Romney and health insurance, no one much cared. The kindling had been lit.

When the interview leaked out in December 2013, the response was painfully predictable. First came the deranged headlines. "Phil from 'Duck Dynasty' Rips Homosexuals . . . Man Ass Can't Compare to Vagina," said TMZ.[76] Then came the denunciations and implicit threats from the various gay rights groups. "Phil's decision to push vile and extreme stereotypes," GLAAD's Wilson Cruz told *Variety*, "is a stain on A&E and his sponsors who now need to reexamine their ties to someone with such public disdain for LGBT people and families."[77] A mere four hours after posting Robertson's remarks and GLAAD's threat, *Variety* was reporting the capitulation of A&E Networks, the parent company of A&E. To much acclaim, the network put the show on indefinite hiatus. "His personal views in no way reflect those of A&E Networks, who have always been strong supporters and champions of the LGBT community," said a spokesman.[78] Two days later, Cracker Barrel, the country store and restaurant chain whose executives obviously had no clue about its customer base, announced it was pulling *Duck Dynasty* products from its shelves.

Cracker Barrel rolled first. Fewer than forty-eight hours after removing selected *Duck Dynasty* items that "might offend some of our guests," the company made a groveling apology to its customers. "Our intent was to avoid offending, but that's just what we've done," the company wrote. "You flat out told us we were wrong. We listened."[79]

A&E was not far behind. More than 250,000 fans signed a petition demanding Robertson's reinstatement. High-profile political figures, such as Louisiana governor Bobby Jindal, decried the network's obvious anti-Christian bias. And, most critically, the Robertsons stood their ground. They told the suits at A&E they could suspend Phil if they liked, but without their patriarch, there would be no show—period.

On December 27, nine days after suspending Robertson, a doubly humiliated A&E lifted the suspension. "It resonates with a large audience because it is a show about family," said an A&E spokesman, "a family that America has come to love. As you might have seen in many episodes, they come together to reflect and pray for unity, tolerance and forgiveness. These are three values that we at A&E Networks also feel strongly about."[80] The folks at GLAAD were not appeased. "Phil Robertson should look African American and gay people in the eyes and hear about the hurtful impact of praising Jim Crow laws and comparing gay people to terrorists," said the organization. Of course, Robertson had not praised Jim Crow, but activists from the various progressive subsets had long made a habit of aligning their cause with the civil rights movement. "If dialogue with Phil is not part of next steps," GLAAD continued, "then A&E has chosen profits over African American and gay people—especially its employees and viewers."[81] A&E wasn't listening. GLAAD did not have the highest-rated show on its network, and too few GLAAD supporters watched *Duck Dynasty* to matter.

The Robertsons, Phil included, refrained from criticizing the network or the antagonists during this whole fandango. They took their faith seriously enough to hold their tongues. As Phil explained, quoting Corinthians 6, the fruit of the Holy Spirit is "love, joy, peace, patience, kindness, goodness, fruitfulness, gentleness, and self-control."[82] They were not about to sacrifice these fruits for profit or revenge.

# 8

# AVENGING ANGELS

I n the early morning hours of December 20, 2014, after shooting his girlfriend in the stomach, Ismaaiyl Brinsley, an ex-con and aspiring jihadist, boarded a bus in Baltimore bound for New York City. He was a man on a mission. After arriving in New York, Brinsley posted online precisely what that mission was. "I'm putting wings on pigs today," he wrote. "They take 1 of ours . . . let's take 2 of theirs." His post cited two men whom the media had improbably elevated to martyrdom in the last few months, Michael Brown and Eric Garner, and closed with a much-too-accurate prediction, "I'm putting pigs in a blanket."[1]

Two hours later, Brinsley secured his own place in the hard-left pantheon when he shot and killed NYPD officers Wenjian Liu and Rafael Ramos before taking his own life. Brinsley's jihad followed a month of marches and less savory madness, the most visible in those cities with a hard-left base—San Francisco, Oakland, Berkeley, New York. Five days earlier, on New York's Fifth Avenue, marchers abandoned the passive "Hands up, don't shoot" mantra for the proactive "What do we want? Dead cops! When do we want it? Now!"[2] They did not have to wait long before they got their way.

In an insightful *City Journal* article, Heather Mac Donald dissected the "big lie" at the heart of this most recent madness, namely, that police pose an ongoing existential threat to black America. "The highest reaches of American society promulgated these untruths and participated in the mass hysteria," wrote Mac Donald.[3] Those reinforcing the lie included New York City mayor Bill de Blasio, Attorney

General Holder, President Obama, and just about every media talking head not employed by Fox News. As Mac Donald observed, young black men were at least thirty times more likely to be killed by another young black man than by a police officer and ten times more likely to be murdered than young men of any other race. Said Mac Donald, "None of those killings triggered mass protests; they are deemed normal and beneath notice."

The mass protests, like those around the death of Sacco and Vanzetti, had little to do with racism, less to do with black lives mattering, and nothing to do with solving problems. Protest organizers hoped to cause problems, to provoke reaction, to hasten their long march through the West's institutions. The Comintern may have passed into history, but its evil spawn have lived on. "We will not let recent tragic moments derail this movement," said an unblushing member of the hard-left Answer Coalition after the death of the two NYPD cops. "This is the revolution and we will not be repressed."[4]

The NYPD assassination and other recent events suggest that progressivism may be moving beyond its neo-puritan phase. No longer content to brand enemies with a letter, neo-puritan shock troops now threaten to brand those enemies with bullets. Although the psychos are the ones pulling the trigger—Brinsley in New York, Corkins at the FRC in Washington, Nidal Malik Hasan at Fort Hood—thousands endorse this insanity behind their balaclavas and Twitter tags.

In Europe, the situation is more ominous still. In many countries, the state has already assumed the power to punish unorthodox speech, and Islamic terrorists are ready to make that punishment capital. The murderous January 2015 assault on the Parisian satire magazine *Charlie Hebdo* merely continued a tradition that began with the assassinations of Pim Fortuyn and Theo Van Gogh. If the Islamic assassins in Paris, like Brinsley in New York, troubled the more respectable among progressives, it was by getting too far ahead of the moral curve. Their cause may have been just—"The future must not belong to those who slander the prophet of Islam," Obama reminded the United Nations in September

2012—but their lack of subtlety was embarrassing.[5]

For all the millions marching in Paris or tweeting "Je suis Charlie" from their Tribeca lofts, what seems undeniable is that "liberalism" of the Atticus Finch school is dead. Today, progressives are not the ones standing outside the jailhouse, shotgun reluctantly in hand, protecting the "mockingbird" within. No, they are the mob in front, clamoring for the mockingbird's head. That mockingbird could be George Zimmerman or Darren Wilson or Brendan Eich or Clarence Thomas or the Duke lacrosse players or Molly Norris or some pariah yet unknown. The neo-puritan hunt for new offenders has not ceased or even slowed.

Almost uniquely among those who have been assigned a scarlet letter in recent years, Phil Robertson seems to understand the religious nature of the conflict at hand. He sees it as one between the "politically correct" and the "biblically correct," between the "new man" of the progressive imagination and the "new creation in Christ"[6] that he and others strive to become. This is the same struggle Solzhenitsyn and Whittaker Chambers identified, but Robertson, unhardened by history, expects to win. He does not fear the enemy. In fact, he does not fear evil. "We're all sinners," he readily concedes. "We never, ever judge someone on who's going to heaven, hell," he told *GQ*'s Magary. "That's the Almighty's job. We just love 'em, give 'em the good news about Jesus—whether they're homosexuals, drunks, terrorists. We let God sort 'em out later."[7]

As Robertson sees things, the "hate" neo-puritans impute to those who resist their call is in reality a hatred of God. He knows whereof he speaks. Robertson was once a hater himself. Now repentant, his goal is not to make enemies. His goal is to make converts. He knows that to make them, he has to be heard. And to be heard, he has to speak out. "I judge no person and condemn no one," says Robertson. "I only want America's culture to change for the better."[8] That change, Robertson knows, will come only when many others do what he does—tell the truth, tell it loudly, and refuse to back down.

Although he sets an excellent example, Robertson does not have voice enough to change the culture. No individual does. To reverse the progressive tide will take a thousand acts of courage or more. It is not a task we can leave to others. We must be more than Charlie Hebdo for a day or two. Every day, we must be the wedding cake maker in Colorado, the cartoonist in Seattle, the cop in New York, the college president in Massachusetts. We must let these good souls know that their scarlet letters are ours. We must stand beside them on their scaffolds and give them courage to hold firm.

If we act soon enough and stand strong enough, we can shame the neo-puritan mob into submission. If we hesitate, it will take a whole lot more than shame.

# NOTES

## CHAPTER 1: MAN'S SECOND-OLDEST FAITH

1. Margaret Sanger, *Pivot of Civilization* (Chapel Hill, NC: Project Gutenberg, 2008), chap. 7.
2. Whittaker Chambers, *Witness* (Washington, DC: Regnery, 2001), 9, 11.
3. Ibid., 15.
4. Barry Gewen, "The Dominant Writer of the Twentieth Century?" *New York Times*, August 13, 2008, http://artsbeat.blogs.nytimes.com/2008/08/13/the-dominant-writer-of-the-20th-century/?_r=0.
5. Douglas Birch, "Solzhenitsyn, chronicler of Soviet gulag, dies," *USA Today*, August 3, 2008, http://usatoday30.usatoday.com/news/world/2008-08-03-3387415391_x.htm.
6. Alexander Solzhenitsyn, "A World Split Apart," trans. I. A. Ilovayskaya, June 8, 1978, http://www.lib.ru/PROZA/SOLZHENICYN/s_world_engl.txt_with-big-pictures.html.
7. Shelby Steele, *White Guilt: How Blacks and Whites Together Destroyed the Promise of the Civil Rights Era* (New York: HarperCollins, 2006), 150.
8. Ibid., 115.
9. Peter Hitchens, *The Rage Against God: How Atheism Led Me to Faith* (Grand Rapids: Zondervan, 2010), 39, 120, 25.
10. Ayaan Hirsi Ali, *Infidel* (New York: Simon & Schuster, 2007), 292.
11. Walter Russell Mead, "Living Large in a Shrinking Cocoon," *American Interest*, December 21, 2014, http://www.the-american-interest.com/2014/12/21/living-large-in-a-shrinking-cocoon/.
12. Ibid.
13. Cheryl Chumley, "Barbara Walters admits 'we' thought Obama was 'the next messiah,'" *Washington Times*, December 18, 2013, http://www.washingtontimes.com/news/2013/dec/18/barbara-walters-admits-we-thought-obama-was-next-m/.
14. Francis Cardinal George, "A tale of two churches," *Catholic New World*, September 7–20, 2014, http://www.catholicnewworld.com/cnwonline/2014/0907/cardinal.aspx.
15. Nathaniel Hawthorne, *The Scarlet Letter* (New York: Plain Label Books, 2005), 96.
16. Mead, "Living Large."
17. Joseph Bottum, "The Spiritual Shape of Political Ideas," *Weekly Standard*, December 1, 2014, http://www.weeklystandard.com/articles/spiritual-shape-political-ideas_819707.html?page=3.
18. Alexandra Pelosi, *Fall to Grace*, HBO Documentary Films, 2014.
19. Hawthorne, *The Scarlet Letter*, 176.

20. Flannery O'Connor, *Wise Blood* (New York: Farrar, Straus and Giroux, 1990), 101.

21. "Duncan criticises 'Tory Taleban,'" BBC News, July 18, 2005, http://news.bbc.co.uk/2/hi/uk_news/politics/4692145.stm.

22. Ann Heche, speech at Matthew Shepard vigil, Washington, DC, October 14, 1998, http://www.oocities.org/hollywood/1777/theview.html.

23. Steele, *White Guilt*, 9.

24. Hitchens, *Rage against God*, 169.

25. Mark Steyn, *Lights Out: Islam, Free Speech and the Twilight of the West*, Nook ed. (Woodsville, NH: Stockade, 2009), 201.

26. Phil Robertson, *UnPHILtered: The Way I See It* (New York: Howard, 2014), 14.

27. Steele, *White Guilt*, 63.

28. Robertson, *UnPHILtered*, 20.

29. Steyn, *Lights Out*, 310.

30. Hawthorne, *The Scarlet Letter*, 149.

31. Andrei Volkov, "Dostoevsky Did Say It: A Response to David E. Cortesi (2011), Secular Web, http://infidels.org/library/modern/andrei_volkov/dostoevsky.html.

32. Bill Ayers, *Fugitive Days: Memoirs of an Antiwar Activist* (Boston: Beacon Press, 2001), 105.

33. Hawthorne, *Scarlet Letter*, 473.

34. Michael Kaufman, "Solzhenitsyn, Literary Giant Who Defied Soviets, Dies at 89," *New York Times*, August 4, 2008.

35. Ibid.

## CHAPTER 2: THE SCARLET R: RACIST

1. Katherine Ann Porter, *The Never-Ending Wrong* (London: Secker & Warburg, 1977), 19.

2. Ion Mihai Pacepa and Ronald Rychlak, *Disinformation: Former Spy Chief Reveals Secret Strategies for Undermining Freedom, Attacking Religion, and Promoting Terrorism* (Washington, DC: WND Books, 2013), 44.

3. Paul Cassell, "Why Michael Brown's best friend's story isn't credible, *Washington Post*, December 2, 2014, http://www.washingtonpost.com/news/volokh-conspiracy/wp/2014/12/02/why-michael-browns-best-friends-story-is-incredible/.

4. "Department of Justice Report Regarding the Criminal Investigation into the Shooting Death of Michael Brown by Ferguson, Missouri Police Officer Darren Wilson," Department of Justice Memorandum, March 4, 2015, http://www.justice.gov/usao/moe/news/2015/march/DOJ%20Report%20on%20Shooting%20of%20Michael%20Brown.pdf.

5. Stephen Koch, *Double Lives* (New York: Enigma, 2004), 40.

6. Ibid., 45–48.

7. "US embassy marchers condemn Ferguson shooting," BBC News, November 26, 2014, http://www.bbc.com/news/uk-england-london-30220409.

8. "Ferguson police officer who killed black teen resigns," *Daily Sabah*, November 30, 2014, http://www.dailysabah.com/americas/2014/11/30/ferguson-police-officer-who-killed-black-teen-resigns.

9. "As protests continue, some in Ferguson try to move on," CBS News, November 28, 2014, http://www.cbsnews.com/news/ferguson-protesters-disrupt-shoppers-for-second-day/.

10. Alex Kekauoha, "Oakland reacts to grand jury decision in Ferguson with protests, freeway shutdown," *Oakland North*, November 24, 2014, https://oaklandnorth.net/2014/11/24/oakland-reacts-to-grand-jury-decision-in-ferguson-shooting-with-protests-freeway-shutdown/.

11.  Jean Pasco, "Sinclair Letter Turns Out to Be Another Expose," *Los Angeles Times*, December 24, 2005, http://articles.latimes.com/2005/dec/24/local/me-sinclair24.

12.  Aurelius, "CUNY Professor: Darren Wilson Symbolizes "Racist, Repressive Capitalism,'" *Pundit Press*, November 26, 2014, http://thepunditpress.com/2014/11/26/cuny-professor-darren-wilson-represents-racist-repressive-capitalism/.

13.  Chauncey DeVega, "Darren Wilson's Testimony Reads Like Ramblings of a Paranoid White Supremacist," *AlterNet*, November 25, 2014, http://www.alternet.org/civil-liberties/darren-wilsons-testimony-reads-ramblings-paranoid-white-supremacist.

14.  Barack Obama, "A More Perfect Union," video transcript, March 18, 2008, http://constitutioncenter. org/amoreperfectunion/.

15.  Shelby Steele, *White Guilt: How Blacks and Whites Together Destroyed the Promise of the Civil Rights Era* (New York: HarperCollins, 2006), 6.

16.  Joseph Bottum, "The Spiritual Shape of Political Ideas," *Weekly Standard*, December 1, 2014, http://www.weeklystandard.com/articles/spiritual-shape-political-ideas_819707.html?page=2.

17.  Nathaniel Hawthorne, *The Scarlet Letter* (New York: Plain Label Books, 2005), 149.

18.  Richard Goldstein, "Earl L. Butz, Secretary Felled by Racial Remark, Is Dead at 98," *New York Times*, February 4, 2008, http://www.nytimes.com/2008/02/04/washington/04butz.html.

19.  Ibid.

20.  Eric Pace, "Jimmy (the Greek) Snyder, 76, is Dead; a Sports Oddsmaker," *New York Times*, April 22, 1996, http://www.nytimes.com/1996/04/22/sports/jimmy-the-greek-snyder-76-is-dead-a-sports-oddsmaker.html.

21.  George Vecsey, "Motivation Key Factor with Athletes," *New York Times*, April 27, 1989.

22.  Pace, "Jimmy (the Greek) Snyder, 76, is Dead."

23.  Richard Goldstein, "Al Campanis Is Dead at 81; Ignited Baseball over Race," *New York Times*, June 22, 1998, http://www.nytimes.com/1998/06/22/us/al-campanis-is-dead-at-81-ignited-baseball-over-race.html.

24.  Ibid.

25.  Roxane Gay, "Paula Deen's racism isn't shocking at all," *Salon*, June 20, 2013, http://www.salon.com/2013/06/20/paula_deens_racism_isnt_shocking_at_all/.

26.  "Controversy has often dogged Don Imus," Associated Press, April 13, 2007, http://www.today.com/id/18081950#.VKxYX5hKHgx.

27.  Jake Tapper, "The skeletons and suits in Sharpton's closet," *Salon*, June 20, 2003, http://www.salon.com/2003/06/21/sharpton_7/.

28.  Deeptl Hajela, "Imus takes his lumps on Sharpton's show," *USA Today*, April 9, 2007, http://usatoday30.usatoday.com/life/theater/2007-04-09-739667894_x.htm.

29.  Bill Carter, "Radio Host Is Suspended over Racial Remarks," *New York Times*, April 10, 2007, http://www.nytimes.com/2007/04/10/business/media/10imus.html.

30.  "CBS Fires Don Imus over Racial Slur," CBS News, April 12, 2007, cached at Free Republic, http://www.freerepublic.com/focus/news/1816406/posts.

31.  Kareem Abdul-Jabbar, "Welcome to the Finger-Wagging Olympics," *Time*, April 28, 2014, http://time.com/79590/donald-sterling-kareem-abdul-jabbar-racism/.

32.  Bill Plaschke, "NBA makes the right move regarding Donald Sterling," *Los Angeles Times*, April 29, 2014, http://touch.latimes.com/#section/-1/article/p2p-80050738/.

33.  Dan Berman, "President Obama: Alleged Donald Sterling remarks 'incredibly offensive,'" *Politico*, April 27, 2014, http://www.politico.com/story/2014/04/president-obama-donald-sterling-remarks-106062.html.

34. Jonathan Last, "Virtues, Past & Present," *Weekly Standard*, November 10, 2014, http://www.weeklystandard.com/articles/virtues-past-present_817763.html.

35. Dakota Smith, "Los Angeles NAACP president defends Clippers owner Donald Sterling's record on minorities but calls remarks 'devastating,'" *Los Angeles Daily News*, April 28, 2014, http://www.dailynews.com/sports/20140428/los-angeles-naacp-president-defends-clippers-owner-donald-sterlings-record-on-minorities-but-calls-remarks-devastating.

36. Abdul-Jabbar, "Finger-Wagging."

37. Pacepa and Rychlak, *Disinformation*, 35.

38. Michael Fletcher, "U.S. Investigates Suspicious Fires at Southern Black Churches," *Washington Post*, February 8, 1996, http://www.washingtonpost.com/wp-srv/national/longterm/churches/reaction.htm.

39. Michael Fumento, "It's Smoke and Mirrors," *Wall Street Journal*, July 8, 1996, http://fumento.com/arson/wsjfire.html.

40. Linda Yglesias, "Flames of Hate Racism Blamed in Shock Wave of Church Burnings," *New York Daily News*, May 19, 1996, http://www.nydailynews.com/archives/news/flames-hate-racism-blamed-shock-wave-church-burnings-article-1.724066.

41. Pacepa and Rychlak, *Disinformation*, 3, 1.

42. Fumento, "It's Smoke and Mirrors."

43. Kevin Sack, "Links Sought in an 'Epidemic of Terror,'" *New York Times*, May 21, 1996, http://www.nytimes.com/1996/05/21/us/links-sought-in-an-epidemic-of-terror.html.

44. Bill Clinton, "Radio Address to Americans," June 8, 1996, http://usembassy-israel.org.il/publish/press/whouse/archive/june/wh1_6-11.htm.

45. "Vivid Childhood Memories a Clinton Fabrication," *Daily Republican*, June 10, 1996, B2, http://www.dailyrepublican.com/clintonfabrication.html.

46. Fred Bayles, "Records Show Little Evidence to Link Church Fires, Racism Arsons up for Both Black and White Churches, Data Indicates," Associated Press, July 5, 1996, http://newsok.com/records-show-little-evidence-to-link-church-fires-racism-arsons-up-for-both-black-and-white-churches-data-indicates/article/2546234.

47. Michael Fumento, "Politics and Church Burnings," *Commentary*, October 1, 1996, https://www.commentarymagazine.com/article/politics-and-church-burnings/.

48. Jenny Beth Martin and Mark Meckler, "On being labeled as 'racist,'" Politico, July 14, 2010, http://www.politico.com/news/stories/0710/39745.html.

49. "Join the Debate," Politico, July 20, 2010, http://www.politico.com/arena/archive/an-iced-tea-party.html#91E3D9D5-C40D-440C-9D48-1C50CBC60C87.

50. "Health reform leaves political rifts unhealed," NBC News, March 22, 2010, http://www.nbcnews.com/video/nightly-news/35992924#35992924.

51. William Douglas, "Tea party protesters scream 'nigger' at black congressman," McClatchy DC, March 20, 2010, http://www.mcclatchydc.com/2010/03/20/90772_rep-john-lewis-charges-protesters.html?rh=1.

52. "Carson and Lewis Down the Steps at Cannon from Many Angles," YouTube video, 4:56, posted by Larry O'Connor, April 27, 2010, https://www.youtube.com/watch?v=5y17LKXBrkk.

53. Courtland Milloy, "Congressmen show grace, restraint in the face of disrespect," *Washington Post*, March 24, 2010, http://www.washingtonpost.com/wp-dyn/content/article/2010/03/23/AR2010032304018.html.

54. See "Capitol Hill Conspiracy," YouTube video, 4:55, posted by Jack Cashill, March 30, 2010, https://www.youtube.com/watch?v=c0UIUdDMbeU.

55. Douglas, "Tea party protestors."
56. Brian Beutler, "Tea Partiers Call Lewis 'N****r', Frank 'F****t', At Capitol Hill Protest," *TPM*, March 20, 2010, http://talkingpointsmemo.com/dc/tea-partiers-call-lewis-n-r-frank-f-t-at-capitol-hill-protest.
57. William Douglas, "Tea party protesters call Georgia's John Lewis 'nigger,'" McClatchy DC, March 20, 2010, http://www.mcclatchydc.com/2010/03/20/90774/tea-party-protesters-call-georgias.html.
58. Douglas, "Tea party protestors."
59. "Tea Party Protesters Dispute Reports of Slurs, Spitting against Dem Lawmakers," Fox News, March 22, 2010, http://www.foxnews.com/story/2010/03/22/tea-party-protesters-dispute-reports-slurs-spitting-against-dem-lawmakers/.
60. Jack Cashill, "Anatomy of a Racial Smear," *American Thinker*, March 24, 2010, http://www.americanthinker.com/articles/2010/03/anatomy_of_a_racial_smear_1.html.
61. Milloy, "Congressmen show grace."
62. Maureen Dowd, "Hail the Conquering Professor," *New York Times*, March 23, 2010, http://www.nytimes.com/2010/03/24/opinion/24dowd.html.
63. Bob Herbert, "An Absence of Class," *New York Times*, March 22, 2010, http://www.nytimes.com/2010/03/23/opinion/23herbert.html.
64. Frank Rich, "The Rage Is Not about Health Care," *New York Times*, March 27, 2010, http://www.nytimes.com/2010/03/28/opinion/28rich.html.
65. "Olbermann: GOP self-destruction imminent," NBC News, March 22, 2010, http://www.nbcnews.com/id/35990654/ns/msnbc-countdown_with_keith_olbermann/t/olbermann-gop-self-destruction-imminent/#.VKxxkZhKHgw.
66. Phillip Roth, *The Human Stain* (New York: Houghton Mifflin, 2000), 6.
67. Robby Soave, "Prof corrects minority students' capitalization, is accused of racism," *Daily Caller*, November 26, 2013, http://dailycaller.com/2013/11/26/prof-corrects-minority-students-capitalization-is-accused-of-racism/.
68. Elie Mystal, "Racist T-Shirts on Campus? Only If You Bother to Think about It," *Above The Law*, November 22, 2013, http://abovethelaw.com/2013/11/racists-t-shirts-on-campus-only-if-you-bother-to-think-about-it/.
69. Joel Brinkley, "Despite Increasing prosperity, Vietnam's appetites remain unique," *Chicago Tribune*, February 1, 2013, http://articles.chicagotribune.com/2013-02-01/opinion/sns-201301291330--tms--amvoicesctnav-c20130129-20130129_1_dog-meat-da-nang-meat-eaters.
70. "Stanford University: Remove Joel Brinkley, No Place for Racism, *Fascinasians*, http://fascinasiansblog.com/post/42533899856/stanford-university-remove-joel-brinkley-no.
71. Paul Cheung, "AJA condemns Joel Brinkley's column about Vietnam, *AAJA*, February 7, 2013, http://www.aaja.org/joel-brinkley-column/.
72. Steele, *White Guilt*, 21.
73. F. Erik Brooks, *Pursuing a Promise: A History of African Americans at Georgia Southern University* (Macon, GA: Mercer University Press, 2006), 106.
74. Howard Segal, "Ohio State's Gordon Gee and UMaine's Dale Lick: loose lips sink presidencies," *Education: Future Imperfect* (blog), June 8, 2013, http://educationfutureimperfect.bangordailynews.com/2013/06/08/ohio-states-gordon-gee-and-umaines-dale-lick-loose-lips-sink-presidencies/.
75. Lyn Riddle, "Maine Official Is Criticized for Comment on Blacks in Sports," *New York Times*, April 1, 1989, http://www.nytimes.com/1989/04/01/us/maine-official-is-criticized-for-comment-on-blacks-in-sports.html.

76. Jon Entine, "The DNA Olympics—Jamaicans Win Sprinting 'Genetic Lottery'—and Why We Should All Care," *Forbes.com*, August 12, 2012, http://www.forbes.com/sites/jonentine/2012/08/12/the-dna-olympics-jamaicans-win-sprinting-genetic-lottery-and-why-we-should-all-care/.

77. Rate My Professors, "Howard Segal," http://www.ratemyprofessors.com/ShowRatings.jsp?tid=7301.

78. Segal, "Ohio State's Gordon Gee and UMaine's Dale Lick."

79. Jerry Kirshenbaum, "Ill Chosen Words," *Sports Illustrated*, August 9, 1993, http://www.si.com/vault/1993/08/09/129093/ill-chosen-words.

80. "Racial Remark Stalls Job Seeker," *New York Times*, July 22, 1993, http://www.nytimes.com/1993/07/22/us/racial-remark-stalls-job-seeker.html.

81. Jeff Pearlman, "I want Tim Tebow to fail," http://www.jeffpearlman.com/i-want-tim-tebow-to-fail/.

82. Bob Tebow Evangelistic Association, http://www.btea.org/.

83. "Super Bowl 2010 Commercial—Tim Tebow & Mom," YouTube video, 0:32, posted by "coolguy9822," February 7, 2010, https://www.youtube.com/watch?v=7O18zLQ3TQA.

84. Pearlman, "I want Tim Tebow to fail."

85. Jeff Pearlman, "A Reporter's Tale: The John Rocker Story 15 Years Later," *The Bleacher Report*, April 14, 2014, http://www.chatsports.com/mlb/a/A-Reporters-Tale-The-John-Rocker-Story-15-Years-Later-2-9610172.

86. Jeff Pearlman, "At Full Blast Shooting outrageously from the lip, Braves closer John Rocker bangs away at his favorite targets: the Mets, their fans, their city and just about everyone in it," *Sports Illustrated*, December 27, 1999, http://www.si.com/vault/1999/12/27/271860/at-full-blast-shooting-outrageously-from-the-lip-braves-closer-john-rocker-bangs-away-at-his-favorite-targets-the-mets-their-fans-their-city-and-just-about-everyone-in-it.

87. Thomas Barrabi, "'Survivor' 2014 Cast: Ex-MLB Pitcher John Rocker to Appear on Show after Racist Comments," *International Business Times*, August 28, 2014, http://www.ibtimes.com/survivor-2014-cast-ex-mlb-pitcher-john-rocker-appear-show-after-racist-comments-1672498.

88. John Rocker, in a phone interview with the author, August 30, 2014.

89. Pearlman, "A Reporter's Tale."

90. Jack Cashill, *Sucker Punch: The Hard Left Hook That Dazed Ali and Killed King's Dream* (Nashville: Nelson Current, 2006), 10.

91. Ibid., 35–36.

92. Mark Kram, *Ghosts of Manila: The Fateful Blood Feud Between Muhammad Ali and Joe Frazier* (New York: HarperCollins, 2001), 16.

93. Mike Marqusee, Redemption Song: Muhammad Ali and the Spirit of the Sixties (London: Verso, 1999), 175.

94. Ferdie Pacheco, *Blood in My Coffee: The Life of a Fight Doctor* (New York: Sports Publishing, 2005), 125.

95. Cashill, *Sucker Punch*, 130.

96. Ibid., 137.

97. Ibid., 130.

98. William Nack, "'The Fight's Over, Joe' More Than Two Decades after They Last Met in the Ring, Joe Frazier Is Still Taking Shots at Muhammad Ali, but This Time It's a War of Words," *Sports Illustrated*, September 30, 1996, http://www.si.com/vault/1996/09/30/208924/the-fights-over-joe-more-than-two-decades-after-they-last-met-in-the-ring-joe-frazier-is-still-taking-shots-at-muhammad-ali-but-this-time-its-a-war-of-words.

99. Cashill, *Sucker Punch*, 131.

100. Ibid., 132–35.

101. Marqusee, *Redemption Song*, 216.

102. Thomas Hauser, *Muhammad Ali: His Life and Times* (New York: Open Road Media, 2012), 225.

103. Cashill, *Sucker Punch*, 171.

104. Ibid., 172.

105. Ibid.

106. Richard J. Herrnstein and Charles Murray, *The Bell Curve: Intelligence and Class Structure in American Life* (New York: Simon & Schuster, 1994), 272.

107. Ibid., 315.

108. Daniel Goleman, "Richard Herrnstein, 64, Dies; Backed Nature over Nurture," *New York Times*, September 16, 1994, http://www.nytimes.com/1994/09/16/obituaries/richard-herrnstein-64-dies-backed-nature-over-nurture.html.

109. Ibid.

110. "Charles Murray: The Bell Curve," *C-SPAN Booknotes*, December 4, 1994, http://www.booknotes.org/FullPage.aspx?SID=61965-1.

111. Herrnstein and Murray, *The Bell Curve*, 311.

112. Bob Herbert, "In America; Throwing a Curve," *New York Times*, October 26, 1994, http://www.nytimes.com/1994/10/26/opinion/in-america-throwing-a-curve.html.

113. Russell Jacoby and Naomi Glauberman, *The Bell Curve Debate: History, Documents, Opinions* (New York: Times Books, 1995), 240.

114. "Charles Murray," *C-SPAN Booknotes*, December 4, 1994.

115. Herrnstein and Murray, *Bell Curve*, 297.

116. Jacoby and Glauberman, *The Bell Curve Debate*, 241.

117. Ibid., 247–48.

118. Charles Lane, "The Tainted Sources of 'The Bell Curve,'" *New York Review of Books*, December 1, 1994, http://www.nybooks.com/articles/archives/1994/dec/01/the-tainted-sources-of-the-bell-curve/.

119. Buzz Bissinger, "Shattered Glass," *Vanity Fair*, September 1998, http://www.vanityfair.com/magazine/archive/1998/09/bissinger199809.

120. Herrnstein and Murray, *The Bell Curve*, 297.

121. "Margaret Sanger—20th Century Hero," *Planned Parenthood Report*, http://www.plannedparenthood.org/files/7513/9611/6635/Margaret_Sanger_Hero_1009.pdf.

122. Margaret Sanger, *Pivot of Civilization* (Chapel Hill, NC: Project Gutenberg, 2008), chaps. 1, 12.

123. *Buck v. Bell*, May 2, 1927, FindLaw, http://caselaw.lp.findlaw.com/scripts/getcase.pl?court=US&vol=274&invol=200.

124. "Margaret Sanger Is Dead at 82; Led Campaign for Birth Control," *New York Times*, September 7, 1966, http://www.nytimes.com/learning/general/onthisday/bday/0914.html.

125. Southern Poverty Law Center website, http://www.splcenter.org/what-we-do.

126. Ken Silverstein, "The Church of Morris Dees," *Harper's*, November 2000, http://www.americanpatrol.com/SPLC/ChurchofMorrisDees001100.html.

127. "Charles Murray," Extremist Files, Southern Poverty Law Center, accessed February 18, 2015, http://www.splcenter.org/get-informed/intelligence-files/profiles/Charles-Murray.

128. "Parallels with McCann case—OJ Detective Mark Fuhrman on Oprah 2010," YouTube video, 46:35, posted by "HiDeHo4," October 11, 2010, https://www.youtube.com/watch?v=519jra2RLEc.

129. Mark Fuhrman, *Murder in Brentwood* (Washington: Regnery, 1997), 11.

130. Ibid., 18, 23.

131. Ibid., 22.

132. Ibid., 24.

133. Ibid., 102.

134. Johnnie Cochran, *A Lawyer's Life* (New York: St. Martin's Press, 2002), 103.

135. Fuhrman, *Murder in Brentwood*, xv.

136. "Testimony of Mark Fuhrman, Witness for the Prosecution, March 9–16, 1995," http://law2.umkc. edu/faculty/projects/ftrials/Simpson/fuhrman1.htm; "Excerpts from the Fuhrman Tapes," http:// web.mit.edu/dryfoo/www/Info/fuhrman.html.

137. Vincent Bugliosi, "Foreword," in Fuhrman, *Murder in Brentwood*, xii.

138. Cochran, *A Lawyer's Life*, 104.

139. Fuhrman, Murder in Brentwood, 231.

140. Cochran, *A Lawyer's Life*, 107.

141. "Excerpts of Marcia Clark's Closing Arguments," *New York Times*, September 27, 1995, http:// www.nytimes.com/books/97/06/15/reviews/clark-excerpts.html.

142. Bugliosi, "Foreword," ix.

143. Ibid., xvi.

144. Greg Krikorian, "Co-Workers Paint Different Portrait of Mark Fuhrman: LAPD: In contrast to racist boasts on tapes, black, Latino colleagues describe a hard-working, unbiased cop," *Los Angeles Times*, November 8, 1995, http://articles.latimes.com/1995-11-08/news/mn-771_1_mark-fuhrman.

145. Chris Smith, "Dominick Dunne vs. Robert Kennedy," *New York*, February 21, 2011, http://nymag. com/nymetro/news/crimelaw/features/n_8816/.

146. Jack Cashill, *If I Had a Son: Race, Guns, and the Railroading of George Zimmerman* (Washington, DC: WND Books, 2013), 68–77; Stephanie Condon, "Obama: 'If I had a son, he'd look like Trayvon,'" CBS News, March 23, 2012, http://www.cbsnews.com/news/obama-if-i-had-a-son-hed-look-like-trayvon/.

147. President Barack Obama speaking to Angelo Cataldi on 610 WIP in Philadelphia about a speech he made at the National Constitution Center and as reported by Dan Gross, "Obama on WIP: My grandmother's a 'typical white person,'" Philly.com, March 20, 2008, http://www.philly.com/ philly/blogs/phillygossip/Obama_on_WIP_My_grandmothers_a_typical_white_person.html.

148. Elizabeth Flock, Who is George Zimmerman? More information emerges about the shooter of Trayvon Martin, *Washington Post*, March 21, 2012.

149. Richard Perez-Pena, "Survivor Recounts Horror of Attack in Newark Schoolyard," *New York Times*, April 29, 2010, http://www.nytimes.com/2010/04/30/nyregion/30newark.html?_r=0.

150. Scott McDonnell, "George Zimmerman rips Sanford police in audio from 2011 meeting," BayNews 9, May 23, 2012, http://baynews9.com/content/news/articles/cfn/2012/5/23/zimmerman_new_ audio.html.

151. Cashill, *If I Had a Son*, 91–98.

152. Jack Cashill, "George Zimmerman, Media Malpractice, and NBC," *American Thinker*, July 2, 2014, http://www.americanthinker.com/articles/2014/07/george_zimmerman_media_malpractice_and_ nbc.html.

153. "Martin Family Lawyer Likens Trayvon to Medgar Evers and Emmett Till," Real Clear Politics, Video, July 14, 2013, http://www.realclearpolitics.com/video/2013/07/14/martin_family_lawyer_ likens_trayvon_to_medgar_evers_and_emmett_till_.html.

## CHAPTER 3: THE SCARLET D: DENIER

1. All Bottum quotes in this section are from Joseph Bottum, "The Spiritual Shape of Political Ideas," *Weekly Standard*, December 1, 2014, 3, http://www.weeklystandard.com/articles/spiritual-shape-political-ideas_819707.html?page=3.

2. Joe Romm, "Michael Crichton, world's most famous global warming denier, dies," *ThinkProgress*, November 5, 2008, http://thinkprogress.org/climate/2008/11/05/203302/michael-crichton-worlds-most-famous-global-warming-denier-dies/.

3. All Crichton quotes in this section are taken from Michael Crichton, "Remarks to the Commonwealth Club," September 15, 2003, http://perc.org/articles/remarks-commonwealth-club.

4. Matt Novak, "The Population Bomb: Scenario 3 (1970)," *Paleo-Future*, July 18, 2007, http://paleo-future.blogspot.com/2007/07/population-bomb-scenario-3-1970.html.

5. Rachel Carson, *Silent Spring*, anniv. ed. (New York: Houghton Mifflin, 2002), 174; see also, for example, pages 16, 24, 30, 40, among others.

6. Jack Cashill, *Hoodwinked: How Intellectual Hucksters Have Hijacked American Culture* (Nashville: Nelson Current, 2009), 199–206.

7. "John McConnell," http://www.earthsite.org/john.htm.

8. "Earth Day," *Apologetics Index*, http://www.apologeticsindex.org/e12.html.

9. John McConnell, "Earth Day Proclamation," the WorldPeace Peace Page, June 21, 1970, http://www.johnworldpeace.com/edproc.html.

10. Ira Einhorn, *Prelude to Intimacy* (lulu.com, 2005), 180.

11. Ibid.

12. Steve Lopez, "TIME Archive: The Ira Einhorn Case," *Time*, September 29, 1997, http://content.time.com/time/nation/article/0,8599,168382-1,00.html.

13. Dave Lindorff, "For Ira Einhorn, a fate worse than death," *Salon*, October 18, 2002, http://www.salon.com/2002/10/18/einhorn_2.

14. "Nation: A Memento Mori to the Earth," *Time*, May 4, 1970, http://content.time.com/time/magazine/article/0,9171,943782,00.html.

15. Paul Kengor, "Happy Earth Day . . . and Lenin Day," *American Spectator*, April 22, 2013, http://spectator.org/articles/55727/happy-earth-day...-and-lenin-day.

16. See the Earth Day SF page, http://www.earthdaysf.org/earth-day.html.

17. "Earth Day San Francisco," Vimeo video, 1:28:15, posted by evox Television Networks, April 19, 2014, http://vimeo.com/92622635.

18. Juliet Elperin and Scott Clement, "New Post-ABC News poll: Keystone XL project overwhelmingly favored by Americans," *Washington Post*, March 7, 2014, http://www.washingtonpost.com/politics/new-post-abc-news-poll-keystone-xl-project-overwhelmingly-favored-by-americans/2014/03/06/d74c58c6-a4a1-11e3-a5fa-55f0c77bf39c_story.html.

19. William Pendley, *Sagebrush Rebel: Reagan's Battle with Environmental Extremists and Why It Matters Today* (Washington: Regnery, 2013), chap. 5.

20. James Watt, "The Religious Left's Lies," *Washington Post*, May 21, 2005, http://www.washingtonpost.com/wp-dyn/content/article/2005/05/20/AR2005052001333.html.

21. Jack Anderson, "Watt affair smells of Watergate," *Florence Times Daily*, May 6, 1982, http://news.google.com/newspapers?nid=1842&dat=19820506&id=gsYhAAAAIBAJ&sjid=x50FAAAAIBAJ&pg=2724,2512263.

22. "Good Vibrations: In Defense of the Beach Boys," *History, Art & Archives* (blog), June 27, 2013, http://history.house.gov/Blog/Detail/15032396974.

23. Phil McCombs, "Watt Outlaws Rock Music on Mall for July 4," *Washington Post*, April 6, 1983, A1.

24. Phil McCombs and Richard Harrington, "Watt Sets Off Uproar with Music Ban," *Washington Post*, April 7, 1983, A1, A17.

25. "Good Vibrations."

26. Francis X. Clines, "Watt Reverses Ban on Rock Music at Concert," *New York Times*, April 8, 1983, http://www.nytimes.com/1983/04/08/us/watt-reverses-ban-on-rock-music-at-concert.html.

27. Jim Jerome, "The Close of an Endless Summer," *People*, January 16, 1984, http://www.cinetropic.com/blacktop/people/.

28. Francis X. Clines, "Watt Asks That Reagan Forgive 'Offensive' Remark about Panel," *New York Times*, September 23, 1983, http://www.nytimes.com/1983/09/23/us/watt-asks-that-reagan-forgive-offensive-remark-about-panel.html.

29. "Bill Moyers to receive 2004 Global Environmental Citizen Award," EurekAlert! November 30, 2004, http://www.eurekalert.org/pub_releases/2004-11/potn-bmt113004.php.

30. "The Lessons of the Alar Scare," *Chicago Tribune*, June 14, 1989, http://articles.chicagotribune.com/1989-06-14/news/8902090470_1_alar-apple-juice-natural-carcinogens.

31. Bill Moyers, "Blind Faith," speech reprinted in *These Times*, February 2005, http://www.thirdworldtraveler.com/Religion/Blind_Faith.html.

32. Watt, "The Religious Left's Lies."

33. Ibid.

34. Christopher Buckley, *Thank You for Smoking: A Novel* (New York: Random House, 2010), 232.

35. All headlines reported by Anthony Watts, "A brief history of climate panic and crisis . . . both warming and cooling," *WUWT* (blog), July 29, 2014, http://wattsupwiththat.com/2014/07/29/a-brief-history-of-climate-panic-and-crisis-both-warming-and-cooling/.

36. Walter Sullivan, "Scientists Ask Why World Climate Is Changing; Major Cooling May Be Ahead," *New York Times*, May 21, 1975, http://query.nytimes.com/mem/archive-free/pdf?res=9A01EEDC1239E63BBC4951DFB366838E669EDE.

37. All Michael Crichton quotes in this section are from "Aliens Cause Global Warming," his lecture at the California Institute of Technology, January 17, 2003, http://stephenschneider.stanford.edu/Publications/PDF_Papers/Crichton2003.pdf.

38. R. P. Turco et al., "Nuclear Winter: Global Consequences of Multiple Nuclear Explosions," *Science*, December 1983, http://www.sciencemag.org/content/222/4630/1283.

39. Austin Bay, "The 1983 Euro-Missile Crisis: Last Great Battle of the Cold War?" *Strategy Page*, November 5, 2013, https://www.strategypage.com/on_point/20131105222327.aspx.

40. Barack Obama, "Breaking the War Mentality," *Sundial*, March 10, 1983, http://www.columbia.edu/cu/computinghistory/obama-sundial.pdf.

41. Crichton, "Aliens Cause Global Warming."

42. Frank Roylance, "Burning oil wells could be disaster, Sagan says," *Baltimore Sun*, January 23, 1991, http://articles.baltimoresun.com/1991-01-23/news/1991023131_1_kuwait-saddam-hussein-sagan/2.

43. Joe Witte, "Kuwait Oil Fires Didn't Alter the Climate," *New York Times*, September 15, 1992, http://www.nytimes.com/1992/09/29/opinion/l-kuwait-oil-fires-didn-t-alter-the-climate-593092.html.

44. "Statement of Dr. James Hansen, Director, NASA Goddard Institute for Space Studies," *Guardian*, June 23, 2008, http://image.guardian.co.uk/sys-files/Environment/documents/2008/06/23/ClimateChangeHearing1988.pdf.

45. Stephen Schneider, Interview, *Discover*, October 1989, 45–48.

46. Russell Cook, "The First, the Last, and the Only Accusation against Skeptics. Repeat It Often, Inexplicable Errors Are Optional," GelbspanFiles.com, http://gelbspanfiles.com/?p=326.

47. Roger Ebert, "Al Gore Plays Leading Man," *Roger Ebert Interviews*, May 28, 2006, http://www.rogerebert.com/interviews/al-gore-plays-leading-man.

48. Cook, "The First, the Last, and the Only Accusation against Skeptics."

49. Eoin O'Carroll, "Why are they calling it 'climate change' now?" *Christian Science Monitor*, September 8, 2009, http://www.csmonitor.com/Environment/Bright-Green/2009/0908/why-are-they-calling-it-climate-change-now.

50. "A Sensitive Matter," *Economist*, March 30, 2013, http://www.economist.com/news/science-and-technology/21574461-climate-may-be-heating-up-less-response-greenhouse-gas-emissions.

51. Ellen Goodman, "No Change in Political Climate," Boston.com, February 9, 2007, http://www.boston.com/news/globe/editorial_opinion/oped/articles/2007/02/09/no_change_in_political_climate/.

52. Dennis Prager, "On Comparing Global Warming Denial to Holocaust Denial," *Townhall.com*, February 13, 2007, http://townhall.com/columnists/dennisprager/2007/02/13/on_comparing_global_warming_denial_to_holocaust_denial.

53. Bjorn Lomborg, *The Skeptical Environmentalist: Measuring the Real State of the World* (Cambridge: Cambridge University Press, 2001), 266.

54. Ibid., 259.

55. Ibid., 323. Italics in original.

56. Crichton, "Aliens Cause Global Warming."

57. "Bjørn Lomborg's comments to the 11-page critique in January 2002 *Scientific American*," *Scientific American*, February 16, 2002, http://www.scientificamerican.com/media/pdf/lomborgrebuttal.pdf.

58. Buckley, *Thank You for Smoking*, 9.

59. Iain Gately, *Tobacco: A Cultural History of How an Exotic Plant Seduced Civilization* (New York: Grove, 2007), 38.

60. "The Reports of the Surgeon General: The 1964 Report on Smoking and Health," Profiles in Science, http://profiles.nlm.nih.gov/ps/retrieve/Narrative/NN/p-nid/60.

61. Stephanie Levitt, "Office Hours: Professor John F. Banzhaf III," *Nota Bene*, October 19, 2011, http://www.thenotabene.org/2011/10/office-hours-professor-john-f-banzhaf-iii-by-stephanie-levitt/.

62. Buckley, *Thank You for Smoking*, 38.

63. U.S. EPA, Respiratory Health Effects of Passive Smoking (Also Known as Exposure to Secondhand Smoke or Environmental Tobacco Smoke ETS)," 1992, EPA website, http://cfpub.epa.gov/ncea/cfm/recordisplay.cfm?deid=2835.

64. James E Enstrom and Geoffrey C Kabat, "Environmental tobacco smoke and tobacco related mortality in a prospective study of Californians, 1960–98," *BMJ*, May 28, 2008, http://heartland.org/sites/all/modules/custom/heartland_migration/files/pdfs/23332.pdf.

65. Emily Badger, "It Really Only Took about 20 Years for the U.S. to Turn Smokers into Pariahs," *Atlantic*, July 10, 2013, http://www.citylab.com/politics/2013/07/it-really-only-took-about-20-years-us-turn-smokers-pariahs/6155/.

66. Marlene Cimons, "Support-Seeking Smokers Take a Drag on the Internet," *Los Angeles Times*, August 4, 1998, http://articles.latimes.com/1998/aug/04/news/mn-10033.

67. Jonathan Last, "Virtues, Past & Present," *Weekly Standard*, November 10, 2014, http://www.weeklystandard.com/articles/virtues-past-present_817763.html.

68. Leo McKinstry, "Moral panic over smoking that led to fostering ban," *Express*, September 9, 2011, http://www.express.co.uk/comment/columnists/leo-mckinstry/270033/Moral-panic-over-smoking-that-led-to-fostering-ban.

69. Scott Dunn, "Smoking police charge Wiarton councillor again," *Owens Sound Sun Times*, August 1, 2014, http://www.owensoundsuntimes.com/2014/08/01/smoking-police-charge-wiarton-councillor-again.

70. Ben Hubbard, "Life in a Jihadist Capital: Order with a Darker Side," *New York Times*, July 23, 2014, http://www.nytimes.com/2014/07/24/world/middleeast/islamic-state-controls-raqqa-syria.html?emc=edit_tnt_20140723&nlid=60534081&tntemail0=y&_r=2.

## CHAPTER 4: THE SCARLET S: SEXIST

1. Jender, "The Life of a woman in philosophy," *What Is It Like to Be a Woman in Philosophy* (blog), October 23, 2012, https://beingawomaninphilosophy.wordpress.com/2012/10/23/the-life-of-a-woman-in-philosophy/.

2. David Mamet, *Oleanna* (New York: Vintage eBooks, 1993), 38, 32.

3. Mick LaSalle, "The Long Lost David Mamet Interview, from 1994," *SFGate*, January 31, 2014, http://blog.sfgate.com/mlasalle/2014/01/31/the-long-lost-david-mamet-interview-from-1994/.

4. Emil Tonkovich, phone interviews with author, August–September, 2014.

5. Robert Jerry, memo to file, May 21, 1991.

6. Jerry, letter to student, June 28, 1991.

7. Jean Younger, sworn affidavit, September 11, 1991.

8. Shelly White, sworn affidavit, April 28, 1992.

9. Mike Davis, memo to Chancellor Budig et al., October 29, 1991.

10. Ric Anderson, "Former student details allegation," *Lawrence Journal-World*, September 3, 1992, 3A, http://news.google.com/newspapers?nid=2199&dat=19920903&id=P20zAAAAIBAJ&sjid=5uYFAAAAIBAJ&pg=6511,616289.

11. Arthur Miller, *The Crucible*, posted online by the Chandler Unified School District (Chandler, AZ), http://www.cusd80.com/cms/lib6/AZ01001175/Centricity/Domain/4860/The%20Crucible_full%20text_adobe_format.pdf.

12. Letter, signed October 31, 1991.

13. "KU Hearing Committee Report: Findings of Fact," July 30, 1993.

14. "KU Hearing Committee Report: Dissenting Opinion," July 30, 1993.

15. The professors in question were Fred Lovitch, William Westerbeke, and George Coggins. Lovitch resigned his position as chancellor's chair in protest of the unfair process.

16. Camille Paglia, "The Strange Case of Clarence Thomas and Anita Hill," in *Sex, Art, and American Culture* (New York, Vintage, 1992), 46–48.

17. "Clarence Thomas: The Justice Nobody Knows," *60 Minutes*, September 27, 2007, http://www.cbsnews.com/news/clarence-thomas-the-justice-nobody-knows/8/.

18. Bernadette Waterman Ward, "Abortion as a Sacrament: Mimetic Desire and Sacrifice in Sexual Politics," *Contagion: Journal of Violence, Mimesis, and Culture* 7 (Spring 2000): 18–35.

19. "A Radical Bows Out," *Forerunner*, August 29, 1999, http://www.forerunner.com/fyi/ft082999.htm.

20. Sofia Vasquez-Mellado, "'Abortion is sacred!': Bare-breasted Femen activists attack Madrid Cardinal," *LifeSiteNews*, February 4, 2014, https://www.lifesitenews.com/news/abortion-is-sacred-bare-breasted-femen-activists-attack-madrid-cardinal.

21. Clarence Thomas, *My Grandfather's Son: A Memoir* (New York: HarperCollins, 2007), 60.

22. Ethan Bronner, "A Conservative Whose Supreme Court Bid Set the Senate Afire," *New York Times*, December 20, 2012, http://www.nytimes.com/2012/12/20/us/robert-h-bork-conservative-jurist-dies-at-85.html?pagewanted=all&_r=1&.

23. Stephen Shapiro, "Background and Ability Qualify Thomas for Court," *Christian Science Monitor*, September 12, 1991, http://www.csmonitor.com/1991/0912/12181.html.

24. David Brock, "The Real Anita Hill," *American Spectator*, March 1992.

25. Anita Miller, ed., *The Complete Transcripts of the Clarence Thomas–Anita Hill Hearings* (Chicago: Chicago Review Press, 2005), 87.

26. Ibid., 111.

27. Brock, "The Real Anita Hill."

28. Miller, *The Complete Transcripts of the Clarence Thomas–Anita Hill Hearings*, 14.

29. Brock, "The Real Anita Hill."

30. Miller, *The Complete Transcripts of the Clarence Thomas–Anita Hill Hearings*, 64.

31. Ibid., 23–25.

32. Ibid., 105.

33. Nathaniel Hawthorne, *The Scarlet Letter* (New York: Plain Label Books, 2005), 102.

34. Miller, The Complete Transcripts of the Clarence Thomas–Anita Hill Hearings, 117.

35. Ibid., 118.

36. Paglia, "The Strange Case of Clarence Thomas and Anita Hill."

37. Brock, "The Real Anita Hill."

38. David Brock, "Book on Anita Hill Greeted by Hysteria," *New York Times*, June 14, 1993, http://www.nytimes.com/1993/06/14/opinion/l-book-on-anita-hill-greeted-by-hysteria-593093.html.

39. "The Justice Nobody Knows," *60 Minutes.*

40. Jocelyn Noveck, "Anita Hill in Spotlight Again as New Film, 'Anita,' Opens," *Huffington Post*, March 22, 2014, http://www.huffingtonpost.com/2014/03/22/anita-hill-spotlight-anew-film-anita-opens_n_5012568.html.

41. Scott Whitlock, "Journalist Barbara Walters Is 'Honored to Meet' Anita Hill, Her 'Heroine,'" *NewsBusters*, March 19, 2014, http://newsbusters.org/blogs/scott-whitlock/2014/03/19/journalist-barbara-walters-honored-meet-anita-hill-her-heroine.

42. "The Conversation: Anita Hill and Clarence Thomas, Nearly 20 Years Later," ABC News, October 20, 2010, http://abcnews.go.com/WN/clarence-thomas-anita-hill-decades/story?id=11928941.

43. Paglia, "The Strange Case of Clarence Thomas and Anita Hill."

44. "Women know less about politics than men worldwide," *Guardian*, July 11, 2013, http://www.theguardian.com/news/datablog/2013/jul/11/women-know-less-politics-than-men-worldwide.

45. "October 16, 2012, Debate Transcript," *Commission on Presidential Debates*, http://www.debates.org/index.php?page=october-1-2012-the-second-obama-romney-presidential-debate.

46. Suzi Parker, "Mitt Romney's 'binders full of women,'" *Washington Post*, October 17, 2012, http://www.washingtonpost.com/blogs/she-the-people/wp/2012/10/17/mitt-romneys-binders-full-of-women/.

47. Tom Shine, "Rep. Darrell Issa Bars Minority Witness, a Woman, on Contraception," *ABC News*, February 16, 2012, http://abcnews.go.com/blogs/politics/2012/02/rep-darrell-issa-bars-minority-witness-a-woman-on-contraception-2/.

48. "Transcript: Sandra Fluke testifies on why women should be allowed access to contraception and reproductive health care," *WTF?! (What the Folly?!)* (blog), February 23, 2012, http://www.whatthefolly.com/2012/02/23/transcript-sandra-fluke-testifies-on-why-women-should-be-allowed-access-to-contraception-and-reproductive-health-care/.

49. Julie Rovner, "Law Student Makes Case for Contraceptive Coverage," *Shots* (blog), February 23, 2012, http://www.npr.org/blogs/health/2012/02/23/147299323/law-student-makes-case-for-contraceptive-coverage.

50. Linda Lowen, "Rush Limbaugh's Comments and Sandra Fluke's Testimony—Fact vs. Fiction," *Women's Issues*, http://womensissues.about.com/od/reproductiverights/a/Rush-Limbaughs-Comments-And-Sandra-Flukes-Testimony-Fact-Vs-Fiction.htm.

51. Allison McGevna, "David Letterman Slammed for Sex Jokes about Palin's Teen Daughter," *Fox News*, June 11, 2009, http://www.foxnews.com/entertainment/2009/06/11/david-letterman-slammed-sex-jokes-palins-teen-daughter/.

52. Geoffrey Dickens, "Networks That Skipped Bashir's Gross Attack on Palin Were Outraged by Limbaugh Fluke Joke," *NewsBusters*, December 4, 2013, http://newsbusters.org/blogs/geoffrey-dickens/2013/12/04/networks-skipped-bashirs-gross-attack-palin-were-outraged-limbaugh.

53. Grace Wyler, "And Here's Mitt Romney's Mealy-Mouthed Response to Rush Limbaugh's 'Slut' Attacks," *Business Insider*, March 2, 2012, http://www.businessinsider.com/rick-santorum-says-rush-limbaugh-slut-comments-are-absurd-2012-3.

54. "Jaco Report: Full Interview with Todd Akin," Fox2now, August 19, 2012, http://fox2now.com/2012/08/19/the-jaco-report-august-19-2012/.

55. "Charles Jaco Talks with Senator Claire McCaskill," Fox2now, September 7, 2012, http://fox2now.com/2012/09/07/charles-jaco-talks-with-senator-claire-mccaskill/.

56. Todd Akin, *Firing Back: Taking on the Party Bosses and the Media Elite to Protect Our Faith and Freedom* (Washington, DC: WND Books, 2014), 128–29.

57. Eugene J. Kanin, "False Rape Allegations," *Archives of Sexual Behavior* 23, no. 1 (February 1994): 81, http://falserapearchives.blogspot.com/2009/06/archives-of-sexual-behavior-feb-1994.html.

58. "Clinton "in fact" raped Juanita—the *Wall Street Journal*: Full Transcript of *NBC Dateline* report on Juanita Broaddrick," http://shadowgov.com/Clinton/DNBCJuanitaTranscript.html.

59. Michael Isikoff, *Uncovering Clinton: A Reporter's Story* (Pittsburgh, PA: Three Rivers Press, 1999), 256.

60. Carl Limbacher, "Paula Jones Suspected Clinton Had Role In Mysterious Deaths," Newsmax.com, April 17, 1999, http://rense.com/politics2/paula.htm.

61. "Jones v. Clinton: Cast of Characters," CNN.com, http://www.cnn.com/ALLPOLITICS/resources/1998/clinton.jones/characters.html.

62. Akin, *Firing Back*, 130.

63. Blaine Harden, "Joseph Kennedy Ends Gubernatorial Bid," *Washington Post*, August 29, 1997, http://www.washingtonpost.com/wp-srv/politics/campaigns/keyraces98/stories/ma082997.htm.

64. Nina Burleigh, *New York Observer*, July 20, 1998.

65. Akin, *Firing Back*, 130.

66. "Obama, Sandra Fluke Now Fundraising on 'Legitimate Rape,'" *PJ Media*, August 22, 2012, http://pjmedia.com/tatler/2012/08/22/obama-sandra-fluke-now-fundraising-on-legitimate-rape/.

67. Akin, *Firing Back*, 169.

68. Stanley Rothman et al., "Politics and Professional Advancement among College Faculty," *The Forum* 3, no. 1 (2005), http://www.cwu.edu/~manwellerm/academic%20bias.pdf.

69. Jennifer Schuessler, "A Star Philosopher Falls, and a Debate over Sexism Is Set Off," *New York Times*, August 2, 2013, http://www.nytimes.com/2013/08/03/arts/colin-mcginn-philosopher-to-leave-his-post.html?pagewanted=all&_r=0.

70. Sarah Kuta, "CU-Boulder reports pervasive sexual harassment within philosophy department," *Daily Camera*, January 31, 2014, http://www.dailycamera.com/cu-news/ci_25035043/cu-sexual-harassment-philosophy-department.

71. Jender, "Who's ready for the gang bang?" (October 25, 2011), https://beingawomaninphilosophy.wordpress.com/2011/10/25/whos-ready-for-the-gang-bang/; "Not as women-friendly as it looks" (October 28, 2011), https://beingawomaninphilosophy.wordpress.com/?s=Not+as+women-friendly+as+it+looks; and "Does your husband know you won't cook dinner every night?" (August 18, 2012) on *What Is It Like to Be a Woman in Philosophy?* (blog).

72. Anonymous, "I Had an Affair with My Hero, a Philosopher Who's Famous for Being 'Moral,'" *Thought Catalog*, April 26, 2014, http://thoughtcatalog.com/anonymous/2014/04/i-had-an-affair-with-my-hero-a-philosopher-whos-famous-for-being-moral/.

73. ProtectingLisbeth, "The Moral Philosopher and His Illicit International Affairs," *ProtectingLisbeth*, May 5, 2014, https://protectinglisbeth.wordpress.com/2014/05/05/the-moral-philosopher-and-his-illicit-international-affairs/.

74. All details up to the next note are from Anonymous, "I Had an Affair with My Hero."

75. ProtectingLisbeth, "The Moral Philosopher and His Illicit International Affairs."

76. Anonymous, "I Had an Affair with My Hero."

77. Edmund Burke, *The Quotations Page*, http://www.quotationspage.com/quote/40838.html.

78. Tom Wolfe, *I Am Charlotte Simmons* (New York: Farrar, Strauss & Giroux, 2004), 179.

79. Nathan Harden, *Sex and God at Yale* (New York: Thomas Dunne Books, 2012), 11, 29.

80. Anonymous, "I Had an Affair with My Hero."

81. ProtectingLisbeth, "The Moral Philosopher and His Illicit International Affairs."

82. Brenda Hughes Neghaiwi, "Harassment victims speak," *Yale Daily News*, September 30, 2011, http://yaledailynews.com/blog/2011/09/30/harassment-victims-speak/.

83. ProtectingLisbeth, "The Moral Philosopher and His Illicit International Affairs."

84. Ibid.

85. Thomaspogge.com.

86. Justin, "Yale Seeks Information about Sexual Misconduct," *Daily Nous*, May 12, 2014, http://dailynous.com/2014/05/12/yale-seeks-information-about-sexual-misconduct/.

87. Charlotte Allen, "The Professor's Tale," *Weekly Standard*, July 30, 2014, http://m.weeklystandard.com/articles/professor-s-tale_795390.html.

88. Eric Schliesser, "Why I Donated to Fund a Lawsuit against a Fellow Professional Philosopher," *Digressions&Impressions* (blog), May 11, 2014, http://digressionsnimpressions.typepad.com/digressionsimpressions/2014/05/why-i-donated-to-fund-a-lawsuit-against-a-fellow-professional-philosopher.html.

89. Lawrence H. Summers, "Remarks at NBER Conference on Diversifying the Science & Engineering Workforce," http://www.harvard.edu/president/speeches/summers_2005/nber.php.

90. Marcella Bombardieri, "Summers' remarks on women draw fire," Boston.com, January 17, 2005, http://www.boston.com/news/education/higher/articles/2005/01/17/summers_remarks_on_women_draw_fire/?page=full.

91. Daniel Hemel, "Summers' Comments on Women and Science Draw Ire," *Harvard Crimson*, http://www.thecrimson.com/article/2005/1/14/summers-comments-on-women-and-science/?page=2.

92. Sam Dillon, "Harvard Chief Defends His Talk on Women," *New York Times*, January 18, 2005, http://www.nytimes.com/2005/01/18/national/18harvard.html.

93. Lawrence H. Summers, "Letter from President Summers on women and science," Office of the President, Harvard, January 19, 2005, http://www.harvard.edu/president/speeches/summers_2005/womensci.php.

94. Bombardieri, "Summers' remarks on women draw fire."

95. Stephen E. Sachs, "FOCUS: We Are Not Spineless," *Harvard Crimson*, February 18, 2005, http://www.thecrimson.com/article/2005/2/18/focus-we-are-not-spineless-harvard/.

96. Larry Summers, "Letter to the Faculty Regarding NBER Remarks," February 17, 2005, http://www.harvard.edu/president/speeches/summers_2005/facletter.php.

97. Tina Wang, "The Worlds That Started the War," *Harvard Crimson*, June 9, 2005, http://www.thecrimson.com/article/2005/6/9/the-worlds-that-started-the-war/?page=2.

98. Charles Murray, "Sex Ed at Harvard," *New York Times*, January 23, 2005, http://www.nytimes.com/2005/01/23/opinion/23murray.html.

99. Steven Pinker, "Sex Ed," *New Republic*, February 14, 2005, http://www.newrepublic.com/article/sex-ed.

100. Alan Finder et al., "President of Harvard Resigns, Ending Stormy 5-Year Tenure," *New York Times*, February 22, 2006, http://www.nytimes.com/2006/02/22/education/22harvard.html?pagewanted=all.

101. Marcella Bombardieri and Maria Sacchetti, "Summers to step down, ending tumult at Harvard," Boston.com, February 22, 2006, http://www.boston.com/news/education/higher/articles/2006/02/22/summers_to_step_down_ending_tumult_at_harvard/?page=full.

102. Matt Berman, "What Potential Fed Front-Runner Larry Summers Said about Women," *National Journal*, July 24, 2013, http://www.nationaljournal.com/politics/what-potential-fed-front-runner-lawrence-summers-said-about-women-20130724.

103. David Dayen, "Larry Summers will destroy the economy (again)," *Salon*, July 24, 2013, http://www.salon.com/2013/07/24/sexist_larry_summers_will_destroy_the_economy/.

104. Annalyn Kurtz and Hibah Yousuf, "Larry Summers withdraws name for Fed chair job," CNN, September 16, 2013, http://money.cnn.com/2013/09/15/news/economy/fed-chair-larry-summers-withdraws/.

105. Josh Eidelson, "Ally assails White House 'sexism' on treatment of Yellen," *Salon*, September 24, 2013, http://www.salon.com/2013/09/24/ally_assails_white_house_sexism_on_treatment_of_yellen/.

106. Martha Duffy, "The Bete Noire of Feminism: Camille Paglia," *Time*, January 13, 1992, http://content.time.com/time/magazine/article/0,9171,974660,00.html.

107. Camille Paglia, "Academic, Heal Thyself," *New York Times*, March 6, 2006, http://www.nytimes.com/2006/03/06/opinion/06paglia.html?_r=0.

108. Camille Paglia, *Sexual Personae: Art and Decadence from Nefertiti to Emily Dickinson*, vol. 1 (New Haven: Yale University Press, 1990), 37.

109. Ibid., 38.

110. Camille Paglia, "It's a Man's World, and It Always Will Be," *Time*, December 16, 2013, http://ideas.time.com/2013/12/16/its-a-mans-world-and-it-always-will-be/.

111. Noel Sheppard, "Despicable: MSNBC's Bashir Wishes Sarah Palin Would Be Defecated, Urinated On," *NewsBusters*, November 15, 2013, http://bit.ly/18nCTS2.

112. "CNN Anchor Laughs at Bristol Palin Describing Assault: 'The Best Audio We've Ever Come Across,'" *Real Clear Politics Video*, October 22, 2014, http://www.realclearpolitics.com/video/2014/10/22/cnn_anchor_laughs_at_bristol_palin_describing_assault_the_best_audio_weve_ever_come_across.html.

113. Alan Shipnuck, *The Battle for Augusta National: Hootie, Martha, and the Masters of the Universe* (New York: Simon & Schuster, 2004), 7.

114. Ibid., 2, 42.

115. Christine Brennan, *Best Seat in the House: A Father, a Daughter, a Journey Through Sports* (New York: Simon & Schuster, 2006), 238.

116. Ibid., 239.

117. Ibid.

118. Ibid., 240–41.

119. Ibid., 244.

120. Shipnuck, *The Battle for Augusta National*, 45, 5–6.

121. Ibid., 9–10.

122. Frank Litsky, "GOLF; Women's Group Vows to Pressure Augusta," *New York Times*, July 13, 2002, http://www.nytimes.com/2002/07/13/sports/golf-women-s-group-vows-to-pressure-augusta.html.

123. Shipnuck, *The Battle for Augusta National*, 11.

124. Doug Ferguson, "Women's Group Targets CBS," *USA Today*, August 31, 2002, http://usatoday30.usatoday.com/sports/golf/masters/2002-08-31-masters-cbs_x.htm.

125. Clifton Brown and Thomas Bonk, "Augusta Steadfast," *SunSentinel*, November 12, 2002, http://articles.sun-sentinel.com/2002-11-12/sports/0211110586_1_martha-burk-william-hootie-johnson-woman.

126. Richard Sandomir, "GOLF; Citing Role of Women in War, Burk Raises Pressure on Augusta," *New York Times*, March 27, 2003, http://www.nytimes.com/2003/03/27/sports/golf-citing-role-of-women-in-war-burk-raises-pressure-on-augusta.html.

127. Ibid.

128. George Vecsey, "Sports of The Times; The Sporting World Could Certainly Use a Few More Martha Burks," *New York Times*, April 16, 2003, http://www.nytimes.com/2003/04/16/sports/sports-times-sporting-worlhttp:/www.nytimes.com/2003/04/16/sports/sports-times-sporting-world-could-certainly-use-few-more-martha-burks.htmld-could-certainly-use-few-more-martha-burks.html.

129. Damon Hack, "Augusta's Payne Has No Plans to Meet Burk," *New York Times*, May 9, 2006, http://www.nytimes.com/2006/05/09/sports/golf/09masters.html?_r=0.

130. Elisabeth Bumiller, "Avid Golfer Rice Jumps a Barrier Again," *New York Times*, August 20, 2012, http://www.nytimes.com/2012/08/21/sports/golf/condoleezza-rice-joins-augusta-national-golf-club.html?_r=0.

131. Emma Fitzsimmons, "Condoleezza Rice Backs Out of Rutgers Speech after Student Protests," *New York Times*, May 3, 2014, http://www.nytimes.com/2014/05/04/nyregion/rice-backs-out-of-rutgers-speech-after-student-protests.html.

## CHAPTER 5: THE SCARLET I: ISLAMOPHOBE

1. Glenn Davis, "Breitbart Takes On Beck, Trump, and Shirley Sherrod on *Real Time* w/ Bill Maher," *Mediaite*, April 29, 2011, http://www.mediaite.com/tv/andrew-breitbart-real-time-bill-maher/.

2. Sam Harris, "Can Liberalism Be Saved from Itself?" Samharris.org, http://www.samharris.org/blog/item/can-liberalism-be-saved-from-itself.

3. Ibid.

4. Sam Harris, The End of Faith: Religion, Terror, and the Future of Reason (New York: W. W. Norton, 2005), 178.

5. Jack Cashill, *2006: The Chautauqua Rising* (Dunkirk, NY: Olin Frederick, 2000), 126.

6. Mark Tooley, "The National Council of Churches does a dictator's bidding," *Weekly Standard*, February 14, 2000.

7. Paul Brandeis Raushebush, "Don't Mess with Joan Brown Campbell," *Huffington Post*, October 17, 2013, http://www.huffingtonpost.com/paul-raushenbush/dont-mess-with-joan-brown_b_3773609.html.

8. Jason Rodriquez, "Chautauqua Community Weighs In on Mosque Debate," *Jamestown Post-Journal*, August 8, 2010.

9. Geert Wilders, *Marked for Death: Islam's War against the West and Me* (Washington, DC: Regnery, 2012), 133.

10. Steven Emerson, "CAIR Exposed as IAP Offshoot, CAIR Followed Pro-Hamas Agenda from the Start," *IPT News*, March 24, 2008, http://www.usmessageboard.com/threads/council-for-islamic-american-relations-ciar-who-they-are-and-whats-their-goal.182984/.

11. Joan Brown Campbell, "Brown comments on Cashill statement," *Chautauquan Daily*, July 27–28, 2002, 4a.

12. Abdur-Rahman Muhammad, "Whether or not Ground Zero mosque is built, U.S. Muslims have access to the American Dream," *New York Daily News*, September 5, 2010, http://www.investigativeproject.org/2164/whether-or-not-ground-zero-mosque-is-built-us#.

13. "Moderate Muslims Speak Out on Capitol Hill," *IPT News*, October 1, 2010, http://www.investigativeproject.org/2217/moderate-muslim-speak-out-on-capitol-hill.

14. Muhammad, "Whether or not Ground Zero mosque is built, U.S. Muslims have access to the American Dream."

15. Mark Steyn, *Lights Out: Islam, Free Speech and the Twilight of the West*, Nook ed. (Woodsville, NH: Stockade, 2009), 33.

16. "Moderate Muslims Speak Out on Capitol Hill."

17. Dr. Dominique Clement et al., "The Evolution of Human Rights in Canada," Canadian Human Rights Commission, 2012, http://www.chrc-ccdp.ca/sites/default/files/ehrc_edpc-eng.pdf.

18. "Canadian Human Rights Act," Justice Laws website, accessed February 20, 2015, http://laws-lois.justice.gc.ca/eng/acts/H-6/section-13-20021231.html.

19. Steyn, *Lights Out*, 13, 221

20. Ibid., 21, 254.

21. Ibid., 55, 61.

22. Ibid., 326.

23. Mark Steyn, "Soggy Berries, Soggy Tories," *SteynOnline*, June 13, 2014, http://www.steynonline.com/6418/soggy-berries-soggy-tories.

24. Steyn, *Lights Out*, 286.

25. Christopher Hitchens, "Stand up for Denmark," *Slate*, February 21, 2006, http://www.slate.com/articles/news_and_politics/fighting_words/2006/02/stand_up_for_denmark.html.

26. David Itzkoff, "'South Park' Episode Altered after Muslim Group's Warning," *New York Times*, April 22, 2010, http://www.nytimes.com/2010/04/23/arts/television/23park.html?_r=0.

27. Caitlin Brody, "Are Trey Parker and Matt Stone Just Assholes?" *Flavorwire*, April 22, 2010, http://flavorwire.com/85603/are-trey-parker-and-matt-stone-just-assholes.

28. Molly Norris, MollyNorris.com, April 20, 2010. No longer accessible. See also Jimmy Orr, "Creators of 'Everybody Draw Muhammad Day' drop gag after everybody gets angry," *Los Angeles Times*, April 26, 2010, http://latimesblogs.latimes.com/washington/2010/04/creators-of-everybody-draw-muhammad-day-abandon-effort-after-it-becomes-controversial.html.

29. Michael Cavna, "Apologetic 'Draw Muhammad' cartoonist urges 'Draw Al Gore' instead," *Washington Post*, April 30, 2010, http://voices.washingtonpost.com/comic-riffs/2010/04/apologetic_draw_muhammad_carto.html.

30. Brian Stelter, "Cartoonist in Hiding after Death Threats," *New York Times*, September 16, 2010, http://www.nytimes.com/2010/09/17/us/17cartoon.html.

31. Daniel Person, "Innocence of Muslims Has Echoes of 'Everybody Draw Muhammed Day,'" *Seattle Weekly*, September 13, 2012, http://www.seattleweekly.com/dailyweekly/2012/09/innocence_of_muslims_has_echos.php.

32. Donovan Slack, "Hillary Clinton condemns Benghazi attack," Politico 44, September 12, 2012, http://www.politico.com/politico44/2012/09/hillary-clinton-condemns-benghazi-attack-135265.html.

33. Associated Press, "'Book of Mormon' creators now pushing the edge on Broadway," mLive website, June 11, 2011, http://www.mlive.com/tv/index.ssf/2011/06/book_of_mormon_creators_now_pu.html.

34. Nakoula Basseley Nakoula, phone interview with the author, May 4, 2014.

35. Ian Lovett, "Man Linked to Film in Protests Is Questioned," *New York Times*, September 15, 2012, http://www.nytimes.com/2012/09/16/world/middleeast/man-linked-to-film-in-protests-is-questioned.html.

36. Tom Bevan, "What the President Said about Benghazi," Real Clear Politics, November 30, 2012, http://www.realclearpolitics.com/articles/2012/11/30/what_the_president_said_about_benghazi_116299.html.

37. Christian Toto, "David Letterman Mocks Pope, Catholic Church," Breitbart, July 24, 2013, http://www.breitbart.com/big-hollywood/2013/07/24/letterman-mocks-pope-crowd-not-amused/.

38. Adam Nagourney and Serge Kovaleski, "Man of Many Names Is Tied to a Video," *New York Times*, September 13, 2012, http://www.nytimes.com/2012/09/14/us/origins-of-provocative-video-are-shrouded.html.

39. Josh Gerstein, "Activists troubled by White House call to YouTube," Politico, September 14, 2012, http://www.politico.com/blogs/under-the-radar/2012/09/activists-troubled-by-white-house-call-to-youtube-135618.html.

40. Nakoula, interview with author.

41. Ibid.

42. Thomas Friedman, "Bush Finds Threat to Murder Author 'Deeply Offensive,'" *New York Times*, February 22, 1989, http://www.nytimes.com/1989/02/22/world/bush-finds-threat-to-murder-author-deeply-offensive.html.

43. Christopher Hitchens, cited in Christopher Rollason, "Hitchens, Rushdie and Said: A Tangled Triad," *Dr. Christopher Rollason Bilingual Culture Blog*, January 31, 2011, https://rollason.wordpress.com/2011/01/31/hitchens-rushdie-and-said-a-tangled-triad/.

44. Wilders, *Marked for Death*, 9.

45. "The death of Fortuyn," *Arab News*, May 8, 2002, http://www.arabnews.com/node/220705.

46. Wilders, *Marked for Death*, 142.

47. Ayaan Hirsi Ali, *Infidel* (New York: Simon & Schuster, 2007), 31, 187.

48. Ibid., 224, 290.

49. Ibid., 269–70.

50. Ibid., 295, 303.

51. Ibid., 309–11.

52. "Theo van Gogh/Ayaan Hirsi Ali: 'Submission' pt 1," YouTube video, 10:51, posted by "aryanpower14," December 14, 2007, https://www.youtube.com/watch?v=aGtQvGGY4S4.

53. Wilders, *Marked for Death*, 208.

54. Ibid., 11–12.

55. Hitchens, "Stand up for Denmark."

56. Wilders, *Marked for Death*, 189.

57. Ibid., 187–92, 6.

58. "Statement of Geert Wilders during His Interrogation by the State Police," Gatestone Institute, December 9, 2014, http://www.gatestoneinstitute.org/4940/geert-wilders-police-interrogation.

59. Wilders, *Marked for Death*, 190.

60. Richard Perez-Pena, "Women's Rights Activist Criticizes Brandeis's Decision to Cancel Her Honorary Degree," *The Lede* (blog), April 9, 2014, http://thelede.blogs.nytimes.com/2014/04/09/womens-rights-activist-criticizes-brandeiss-decision-to-cancel-her-honorary-degree/.

61. Richard Perez-Pena and Tanzina Vega, "Brandeis Cancels Plan to Give Honorary Degree to Ayaan Hirsi Ali, a Critic of Islam," *New York Times*, April 8, 2014, http://www.nytimes.com/2014/04/09/us/brandeis-cancels-plan-to-give-honorary-degree-to-ayaan-hirsi-ali-a-critic-of-islam.html?_r=0.

62. Wilders, *Marked for Death*, 4.

## CHAPTER 6: THE SCARLET C: CLASSIST

1. "Rick Santelli: Tea Party," *Freedom Eden*, February 19, 2009, http://freedomeden.blogspot.com/2009/02/rick-santelli-tea-party.html.

2. "For the Love of Money," *The Brian Lehrer Show*, March 11, 2010, http://www.wnyc.org/story/32737-for-the-love-of-money/.

3. *Roger and Me*, script, http://www.script-o-rama.com/movie_scripts/r/roger-and-me-script-transcript.html.

4. Liz Robbins, "Tax Day Is Met with Tea Parties," *New York Times*, April 15, 2009, http://www.nytimes.com/2009/04/16/us/politics/16taxday.html?_r=0.

5. Stephane Courtois and Mark Kramer, eds., *The Black Book of Communism: Crimes, Terror, Repression* (Cambridge, MA: Harvard University Press, 1999), 164.

6. Stuart Taylor Jr. and KC Johnson, *Until Proven Innocent: Political Correctness and the Shameful Injustices of the Duke Lacrosse Case*, Nook ed. (New York: Thomas Dunne, 2007), 25.

7. Ibid., 34, 36–37

8. Ibid., 133.

9. Ibid., 32.

10. Ibid., 77.

11. Joseph Bottum, "The Spiritual Shape of Political Ideas," *Weekly Standard*, December 1, 2014, http://www.weeklystandard.com/articles/spiritual-shape-political-ideas_819707.html?page=3.

12. Taylor and Johnson, *Until Proven Innocent*, 14, 143.

13. Ibid., 106.

14. "Duke Case: The Listening Statement," *The Johnsville News*, November 10, 2006, http://johnsville.blogspot.com/2006/11/duke-case-listening-statement.html.

15. Taylor and Johnson, *Until Proven Innocent*, 128, 129.

16. Sabrina Rubin Erdely, "A Rape on Campus: A Brutal Assault and Struggle for Justice at UVA," *Rolling Stone*, November 19, 2014, http://www.rollingstone.com/culture/features/a-rape-on-campus-20141119.

17. Aaron Sorkin, *The Social Network* (screenplay), http://flash.sonypictures.com/video/movies/thesocialnetwork/awards/thesocialnetwork_screenplay.pdf.

18. Taylor and Johnson, *Until Proven Innocent*, 147, 15, 150, 152.

19. Ibid., 147.

20. Ibid., 308.

21. Ibid., 407.

22. "Duke Rape Suspect Speaks Out," *60 Minutes*, October 11, 2006, http://www.cbsnews.com/news/duke-rape-suspects-speak-out/.

23. Peter Applebome, "After Duke Prosecution Began to Collapse, Demonizing Continued," *New York Times*, April 15, 2007, http://select.nytimes.com/2007/04/15/nyregion/15towns.html?_r=0.

24. Cheryl Chumley, "RFK Jr. wants law to 'punish global warming skeptics," *Washington Times*, September 23, 2014, http://www.washingtontimes.com/news/2014/sep/23/robert-kennedy-jr-we-need-laws-punish-global-warmi/.

25. Daniel Schulman, *Sons of Wichita: How the Koch Brothers Became America's Most Forceful and Private Dynasty* (New York: Grand Central Publishing, 2014), 19.

26. Ibid., 235.

27. Ibid., 92, 330–31.

28. Ibid., 267.

29. Daniel Greenfield, "SEIU, Insane Leftists Protests $100 Mil Koch Donation," *Frontpage Mag*, March 11, 2014, http://www.frontpagemag.com/2014/dgreenfield/seiu-insane-lefitsts-protests-100-mil-koch-donation-to-hospital/.

30. Schulman, *Sons of Wichita*, 257.

31. Andrew Goldman, "The Billionaire's Party," *New York*, July 25, 2010, http://nymag.com/news/features/67285/.

32. Schulman, *Sons of Wichita*, 258.

33. Ibid., 259.

34. Brian Ross and Cindy Galli, "Report: 'Secret Sins' of Koch Industries," *ABC News*, October 7, 2011, http://abcnews.go.com/Blotter/koch-industries-report-reveals-secret-sins/story?id=14676652.

35. Schulman, *Sons of Wichita*, 293.

36. Ibid., 272–74.

37. Ibid., 275.

38. "#OccupyWall Street: A Shift in Revolutionary Tactics," *Adbusters*, July 13, 2011, https://www.adbusters.org/blogs/adbusters-blog/occupywallstreet.html#comments.

39. "Address by the President to a Joint Session of Congress," September 8, 2011, http://www.whitehouse.gov/the-press-office/2011/09/08/address-president-joint-session-congress.

40. "A New Global Economic Order, *Adbusters*, September 7, 2011, https://www.adbusters.org/blogs/adbusters-blog/occupywallstreet-less-two-weeks-away.html.

41. Brad Bannon, "Occupy Wall Street Takes on Corporate Greed, aka Romney," *U.S. News & World Report*, October 20, 2011, http://www.usnews.com/opinion/blogs/brad-bannon/2011/10/20/occupy-wall-street-takes-on-corporate-greed-aka-romney.

42. Ed Morrissey, "Guess which President has raked in the most Wall Street bucks in a generation?" *Hot Air* (blog), October 10, 2011, http://hotair.com/archives/2011/10/10/guess-which-president-has-raked-in-the-most-wall-street-bucks-in-a-generation/.

43. Devin Dwyer, "Obama: Occupy Wall Street 'Not That Different' from Tea Party Protests," *Political Punch* (blog), October 18, 2011, http://abcnews.go.com/blogs/politics/2011/10/obama-occupy-wall-street-not-that-different-from-tea-party-protests/.

44. Marika, "Remember That Auto Bailout Romney Hated? He Made an Obscene Amount of Money from It," MoveOn.org, October 19, 2012, http://front.moveon.org/remember-that-auto-bailout-romney-hated-he-made-an-obscene-amount-of-money-from-it/#.VLRFQ5hKHgx.

45. Jim Newell, "Your Guide to Romney's Obscene Tax Situation," *Gawker*, January 24, 2012, http://gawker.com/5878851/your-guide-to-mitt-romneys-obscene-tax-situation.

46. Steven Benen, "Mitt Romney's Tax Transparency Problem: Earns Obscene Income While Paying Way Less Than the Middle Class," *Washington Monthly*, December 27, 2011, http://bit.ly/1G3cgot.

47. "Revealed: The steel company deal that earned Mitt Romney millions while costing the government $44m and 750 people their jobs," *Daily Mail*, January 6, 2012, http://www.dailymail.co.uk/news/article-2083337/Mitt-Romney-earned-millions-steel-company-deal-cost-government-44m.html.

48. Jack Cashill, "Not Even Bain Capital Could Save KC's Armco Steel," *Ingram's Magazine*, February, 2012, http://www.cashill.com/regional/not_even_bain.htm.

49. Robert Reich, *The Next American Frontier* (New York: Penguin, 1984), 248.

50. Anonymous GS executive, in a phone interview with the author, January 9, 2012.

51. "Facts Strained in 'King of Bain,'" FactCheck.org, January 13, 2012, https://www.factcheck.org/2012/01/facts-strained-in-king-of-bain/.

52. Andy Sullivan and Greg Roumeliotis, "Special Report: Romney's steel skeleton in the Bain closet," Reuters, January 6, 2012, http://www.reuters.com/article/2012/01/06/us-campaign-romney-bailout-idUSTRE8050LL20120106.

53. Becky Bowers and Molly Moorhead, "Obama ad claims Romney, Bain left misery in wake of GST Steel takeover," PolitiFact.com, May 16, 2012, http://www.politifact.com/truth-o-meter/statements/2012/may/16/barack-obama/obama-ad-claims-romney-bain-left-misery-wake-gst-s/.

54. Olivier Knox, "Pro-Obama ad ties Romney to woman's death from cancer," ABC News, August 7, 2012, http://abcnews.go.com/Politics/OTUS/pro-obama-ad-ties-romney-womans-death-cancer/story?id=16947016.

55. "Ivorybill," commenting on Jed Lewison, "Romney Campaign," *Daily Kos*, August 8, 2012, http://www.dailykos.com/story/2012/08/08/1117978/-Romney-campaign-Bain-layoff-victim-should-have-moved-to-Massachusetts-to-get-health-insurance#.

56. "Obama campaign caught in lie over Joe Soptic, possible violation of law," *examiner.com*, August 10, 2012, http://www.examiner.com/article/obama-campaign-caught-lie-over-joe-soptic-possible-violation-of-law.

57. Mytheos Holt, "Michael Moore's Latest Ad Vows to 'C**k Punch' Mitt Romney," *The Blaze*, October 30, 2012, http://bit.ly/1zjK3Fc.

58. Abby Phillip, "Liberal filmmaker Michael Moore's conservative neighbors gawk, revel in his messy divorce," *Washington Post*, July 22, 2014, http://www.washingtonpost.com/blogs/style-blog/wp/2014/07/22/liberal-filmmaker-michael-moores-conservative-neighbors-gawk-revel-in-his-messy-divorce/.

## CHAPTER 7: THE SCARLET H: HOMOPHOBE

1. Richard John Neuhaus, "Public Square," *First Things*, November 1993, http://www.firstthings.com/article/1993/11/speaking-for-the-common-good.

2. "New Details Emerge in Matthew Shepard Murder," ABC News, November 26, 2004, http://abcnews.go.com/2020/story?id=277685.

3. Stephen Jimenez, *The Book of Matt: Hidden Truths about the Murder of Matthew Shepard*, Nook ed. (Hanover, NH: Steerforth, 2013), 13.

4. Bill Clinton, "Statement by the President," March 5, 1999, http://clinton6.nara.gov/1999/03/1999-03-05-statement-by-the-president-on-death-of-billy-jack-gaither.html.

5. Ann Heche, Washington, D.C., at the Matthew Shepard vigil, October 14, 1998.

6. Megan Barnes, "Chirlane McCray Wonders Why Her 1979 'I Am a Lesbian' Essay Didn't Get More Attention," *Village Voice*, June 24, 2014, http://blogs.villagevoice.com/runninscared/2014/06/she_was_a_lesbian_chirlane_mccray_tells_the_voice_how_her_past_affects_her_role_in_city_hall.php.

7. Elyse Sommer, "The Laramie Project," *CurtainUp*, http://www.curtainup.com/laramieproject.html.

8. Quoted in Jimenez, *The Book of Matt*, 251.

9.   Ibid., 327.

10.  Ibid., 344.

11.  Ibid., 304.

12.  *The Book of Matt*, Amazon customer reviews, http://www.amazon.com/The-Book-Matt-Matthew-Shepard/product-reviews/1586422146?pageNumber=13.

13.  Jimenez, *The Book of Matt*, 341.

14.  AFI's 100 Years . . . 100 Movie Quotes Nominees, quote 222, http://www.afi.com/Docs/100Years/quotes400.pdf.

15.  "Bizarro," *Supermanica, the Encyclopedia of Supermanic Biography*, http://supermanica.wiki/index.php/Bizarro.

16.  The Savage quotes that follow are from "Dan Savage discusses bible at High School Journalism convention," YouTube video, 3:20, posted by "bandroadie95," April 27, 2012, https://www.youtube.com/watch?v=ao0k9qDsOvs.

17.  "Socialism and Marriage, *New York Times*, December 1, 1911, http://timesmachine.nytimes.com/timesmachine/1911/12/01/issue.html.

18.  Jerry Lisker, "Homo Nest Raided, Queen Bees Are Stinging Mad," *New York Daily News*, July 6, 1969, http://www.pbs.org/wgbh/americanexperience/features/primary-resources/stonewall-queen-bees/.

19.  Walter Troy Spencer, "Too much my dear," *Village Voice*, July 10, 1969, http://news.google.com/newspapers?nid=1299&dat=19690710&id=u-wjAAAAIBAJ&sjid=K4wDAAAAIBAJ&pg=1707,293555.

20.  Reinaldo Arenas, *Before Night Falls* (New York: Profile, 2010), 139.

21.  "Miss Teen USA 2007—South Carolina answers a question," YouTube video, 0:48, posted by "IRamzayI," August 24, 2007, https://www.youtube.com/watch?v=lj3iNxZ8Dww.

22.  "Miss California Blows It with Her Anti-Gay Answer," YouTube video, 4:13, posted by "The Young Turks," April 20, 2009, https://www.youtube.com/watch?v=8GD75J_Ph8Y.

23.  Gregory M. Herek, "'Beyond Homophobia': Thinking about Sexual Prejudice and Stigma in the Twenty-First Century, *Sexuality Research & Social Policy*, April 2004, http://psychology.ucdavis.edu/faculty_sites/rainbow/html/Herek_2004_SRSP.pdf.

24.  LGBT-Sexual Orientation, American Psychiatric Association, http://www.psychiatry.org/mental-health/people/lgbt-sexual-orientation.

25.  Japhy Grant, "Perez Hilton's gay witch hunt," *Salon*, December 15, 2006, http://www.salon.com/2006/12/15/hilton_2/.

26.  Stone Martindale, "Perez Hilton outs more celebrity gays in media," *M&C*, November 4, 2006, http://www.monstersandcritics.com/people/news/article_1218294.php/Perez_Hilton_outs_more_celebrity_gays_in_media.

27.  Grant, "Perez Hilton's gay witch hunt."

28.  George Clooney, Oscar acceptance speech for Best Supporting Actor, American Rhetoric Online Speech Bank, March 5, 2006, http://aaspeechesdb.oscars.org/link/078-2/.

29.  Jeanette Walls, "Paula blames Simon for her goofiness on 'Idol' Plus: Spike Lee blasts George Clooney's Oscar speech," *Today Entertainment*, March 30, 2006, http://www.today.com/id/11878505/ns/today-entertainment/t/paula-blames-simon-her-goofiness-idol/#.VLVZ1phKHgw.

30.  Annie Proulx, "Blood on the red carpet," *Guardian*, March 11, 2006, http://www.theguardian.com/books/2006/mar/11/awardsandprizes.oscars2006.

31.  Ted Casablanca, "George Clooney Weighs In on Prop 8," E! Online, November 11, 2008, http://www.eonline.com/news/68336/george-clooney-weighs-in-on-prop-8.

32.  "Miss California Blows It with Her Anti-Gay Answer."

33. Carrie Prejean, *Still Standing: The Untold Story of My Fight against Gossip, Hate, and Political Attacks* (Washington, DC: Regnery, 2009), 4.

34. Ibid, 80, 77, 80–81.

35. Kristie Cavanagh, Carrie Prejean and Oakland Raiders quarterback Kyle Boller to get married on Friday in San Diego, *New York Daily News*, June 30, 2010, http://www.nydailynews.com/entertainment/gossip/carrie-prejean-oakland-raiders-quarterback-kyle-boller-married-friday-san-diego-article-1.179101.

36. "Former Beauty Queen Carrie Prejean Gives Birth to a Baby Girl! Congrats!" *Hollywood Life*, May 31, 2011, http://hollywoodlife.com/2011/05/31/carrie-prejean-gives-birth-baby-girl-kyle-boller-miss-usa-controversy/.

37. "Opposite Sex Husband Sells SD Mansion for Loss," *TMZ*, September 16, 2012, http://www.tmz.com/2012/09/16/miss-usa-carrie-prejean-kyle-boller-sell-san-diego-house-at-200k-loss/.

38. Janna Darnelle, "Redefining marriage hurts women, children," *Deseret News*, September 28, 2014, http://www.deseretnews.com/article/865611924/Redefining-marriage-hurts-women-children.html?pg=all.

39. Jeremy Hooper, "Gay man realizes he shouldn't have entered into an opposite-sex union—so no same-sex marriage for anyone, demands ex-wife," *Good As You* (blog), September 22, 2014, http://www.goodasyou.org/good_as_you/2014/09/gay-man-realizes-he-shouldnt-have-entered-an-opposite-sex-unionso-no-same-sex-marriage-for-anyone.html.

40. Rivka Edelman, "Ruthless Misogyny: Janna Darnelle's Story and Extreme LGBT Activism," *Public Discourse*, October 2, 2014, http://www.thepublicdiscourse.com/2014/10/13867/.

41. Andrea Peyser, "Couple fined for refusing to host same-sex wedding on their farm," *New York Post*, November 10, 2014, http://nypost.com/2014/11/10/couple-fined-for-refusing-to-host-same-sex-wedding-on-their-farm/.

42. Aaron Klein, phone interview with author, November 25, 2014.

43. "Sweet Cakes by Melissa, Oregon Bakery That Denied Gay Couple a Wedding Cake, Closes Shop," *Huffington Post*, September 3, 2013, http://www.huffingtonpost.com/2013/09/02/sweet-cakes-by-melissa-closed-_n_3856184.html.

44. Sunnivie Brydum, "Colo. Baker Who Refused Gay Wedding Cake Appears in Court," *Advocate.com*, December 5, 2013, http://www.advocate.com/politics/marriage-equality/2013/12/05/watch-colo-baker-who-refused-gay-wedding-cake-appears-court.

45. Nicolle Martin, phone interview with author, November 25, 2014.

46. Colorado Court of Appeals, Masterpiece Cakeshop and Jack Phillips appellants, Charlie Craig and David Mullins, appellees, http://www.adfmedia.org/files/MasterpieceAppealNotice.pdf.

47. "Leslie and Katina's Story," Why Marriage Matters website, accessed February 23, 2015, http://www.whymarriagematters.org/stories/entry/leslie-and-katinas-story.

48. Nicholas Riccardi, "Colorado Civil Rights Panel: Baker Must Make Cakes for Gay Weddings," *Huffington Post*, May 30, 2014, http://www.huffingtonpost.com/2014/05/30/colorado-baker-gay-weddings_n_5420252.html.

49. Todd Starnes, "Baker forced to make gay wedding cakes, undergo sensitivity training, after losing lawsuit," Fox News, June 3, 2014, http://fxn.ws/1kGIU0N.

50. "Two Ministers Told to Perform Same-Sex Wedding Face Jail, Fines," Alliance Defending Freedom, October 20, 2014, http://blog.alliancedefendingfreedom.org/2014/10/20/two-ministers-ordered-to-perform-same-sex-wedding-face-jail-fines/.

51. "City Backs Off from Forcing Idaho Pastors to Perform Same-Sex Ceremonies," Alliance Defending Freedom, November 3, 2014, http://blog.alliancedefendingfreedom.org/2014/11/03/city-backs-off-from-forcing-idaho-pastors-to-perform-same-sex-ceremonies/.

52. Sarah Pulliam Bailey, "Houston subpoenas pastors' sermons in gay rights ordinance case," Religion News Service, October 14, 2014, http://www.religionnews.com/2014/10/14/houston-subpoenas-pastors-sermons-equal-rights-ordinance-case-prompting-outcry/.

53. "Mayor Parker directs city legal department to withdraw pastor subpoenas, City of Houston website, October 29, 2014, http://www.houstontx.gov/mayor/press/mayor-parker-directs-city-legal-department-withdraw-pastor-subpoenas.

54. K. Allan Blume, "'Guilty as charged,' Cathy says of Chick-fil-A's stand on biblical & family values," Baptist Press, July 16, 2012, http://www.bpnews.net/38271.

55. Andy Towle, "If You're Eating Chick-Fil-A, You're Eating Anti-Gay," *Towleroad*, January 4, 2011, http://www.towleroad.com/2011/01/if-youre-eating-chick-fil-a-youre-eating-anti-gay.html.

56. Kim Severson, "A Chicken Chain's Corporate Ethos Is Questioned by Gay Rights Advocates," *New York Times*, January 29, 2011, http://www.nytimes.com/2011/01/30/us/30chick.html?pagewanted=1&_r=1&src=twrhp.

57. Felicia Sonmez, "Biden: I'm 'absolutely comfortable' with gay couples having same rights as straight couples," *Washington Post*, May 6, 2012, http://www.washingtonpost.com/blogs/post-politics/post/biden-im-absolutely-comfortable-with-gay-couples-having-same-rights-as-straight-couples/2012/05/06/gIQA59Wg5T_blog.html.

58. Edward-Isaac Dovere, "Book: White House scrambled after Joe Biden's gay marriage comments," *Politico*, April 16, 2014, http://www.politico.com/story/2014/04/joe-biden-gay-marriage-white-house-response-105744.html.

59. "Transcript: Robin Roberts ABC News Interview with President Obama," ABC News, May 9, 2012, http://abcnews.go.com/Politics/transcript-robin-roberts-abc-news-interview-president-obama/story?id=16316043.

60. Paul V., "Still Homophobic? You're Going to Have to Give Up the Following . . . ," *Huffington Post*, January 3, 2013, http://www.huffingtonpost.com/paul-v/still-homophobic-youre-going-to-have-to-give-up_b_2059510.html.

61. Blume, "'Guilty as charged.'"

62. Michael Foust, "Chick-fil-A interview with BR triggers media storm," BRnow.org, July 19, 2012, http://www.brnow.org/News/July-2012/Chick-fil-A-interview-with-BR-triggers-media-storm.

63. Thomas Menino letter, July 20, 2012, posted at https://www.facebook.com/photo.php?fbid=10151791883475752&set=a.336030020751.189466.64266725751&type=1&theater.

64. Michael Scherer, "Chick-fil-A Meets a First Amendment Buzzsaw in Chicago," *Time*, July 26, 2012, http://swampland.time.com/2012/07/26/chick-fil-a-meets-a-first-amendment-buzzsaw-in-chicago/.

65. "Mike Huckabee Calls for National 'Chick-Fil-A Appreciation Day,'" *Huffington Post*, July 24, 2012, http://www.huffingtonpost.com/2012/07/24/mike-huckabee-chick-fil-a-appreciation-day_n_1696648.html.

66. "Chick-fil-A plucks one-day record from gay marriage blowup," Reuters, August 2, 2012, http://www.reuters.com/article/2012/08/02/usa-gaymarriage-chickfila-idUSL2E8J28IL20120802.

67. "Former Lecturer/Corporate CFO Bullies Chick-fil-A Clerk," YouTube video, 2:21, posted by "u1oo," August 1, 2012, https://www.youtube.com/watch?v=Jg-jzlWcc0E.

68. Katie Pavlich, "Man Who Shot Up Family Research Council: I Wanted to Kill as Many as Possible and Smear Chick-fil-A in Their Faces," *Townhall.com*, http://townhall.com/tipsheet/katiepavlich/2013/02/07/frc-shooter-i-wanted-to-kill-as-mant-as-possible-and-smear-chickfila-in-their-faces-n1506908.

69. Joe Satran, "Chick-Fil-A Sales Soar in 2012 Despite Bad PR," *Huffington Post*, January 31, 2013, http://www.huffingtonpost.com/2013/01/31/chick-fil-a-sales-2012_n_2590612.html.

70. Sunnivie Brydum, "Nearly 65K Demand Mozilla CEO Come Out for Marriage Equality," *Advocate. com*, March 31, 2014, http://www.advocate.com/business/technology/2014/03/31/nearly-65k-demand-mozilla-ceo-come-out-marriage-equality.

71. Stephen Shankland, "Exclusive: Mozilla CEO Eich says gay-marriage firestorm could hurt Firefox (Q&A)," *CNET Magazine*, April 1, 2014, http://www.cnet.com/news/mozilla-ceo-gay-marriage-firestorm-could-hurt-firefox-cause-q-a/.

72. "Mozilla chief steps down after controversial donation causes uproar," CBS News, April 3, 2014, http://www.cbsnews.com/news/mozilla-chief-steps-down-after-controversial-donation-causes-uproar/.

73. This and subsequent comments follow Shankland, "Exclusive: Mozilla CEO Eich says gay-marriage firestorm could hurt Firefox (Q&A)."

74. Tony Bradley, "Backlash against Brendan Eich Crossed a Line," *Forbes*, April 5, 2014, http://www.forbes.com/sites/tonybradley/2014/04/05/backlash-against-brendan-eich-crossed-a-line/.

75. Drew Magary, "What the Duck?" *GQ*, January 2014, http://www.gq.com/entertainment/television/201401/duck-dynasty-phil-robertson?currentPage=1.

76. "Phil from Duck Dynasty Rips Homosexuals . . . Man Ass Can't Compare to Vagina," TMZ, December 18, 2013, http://www.tmz.com/2013/12/18/duck-dynasty-phil-robertson-vagina-better-than-man-anus-gq-homophobia/.

77. Ted Johnson, "'Duck Dynasty' Patriarch Draws Rebuke for Anti-Gay Comments," *Variety*, December 18, 2013, http://variety.com/2013/biz/news/duck-dynasty-gay-phil-robertson-anus-1200973197/.

78. AJ Marechal, "'Duck Dynasty': Phil Robertson Suspended Indefinitely Following Anti-Gay Remarks," *Variety*, December 18, 2013, http://variety.com/2013/tv/news/duck-dynasty-ae-suspends-phil-robertson-following-gay-remarks-1200974473/.

79. Liz Fields, "Cracker Barrel Flipflops on Nixing 'Duck Dynasty' Items From Shelves," ABC News, December 22, 2013, http://abcnews.go.com/Entertainment/cracker-barrel-flipflops-nixing-duck-dynasty-items-shelves/story?id=21302746.

80. Emily Yahr, "Phil Robertson back on 'Duck Dynasty' as A&E lifts suspension," *Washington Post*'s *Style* blog, December 27, 2013, http://www.washingtonpost.com/blogs/style-blog/wp/2013/12/27/phil-robertson-back-on-duck-dynasty-as-ae-lifts-suspension/.

81. Greg Braxton, "'Duck Dynasty': GLAAD responds to Phil Robertson's return," *Los Angeles Times*, December 27, 2013, http://touch.latimes.com/#section/-1/article/p2p-78697558/.

82. Magary, "What the Duck?"

## CHAPTER 8: AVENGING ANGELS

1. Tina Moore et al., "Two NYPD officers 'assassinated' while sitting in patrol car in Brooklyn by gunman who boasted on Instagram about 'revenge' killing cops," *New York Daily News*, December 21, 2014, http://www.nydailynews.com/new-york/nyc-crime/cops-shot-brooklyn-sources-article-1.2051941.

2. "Video Shows NYC Protesters Chanting for 'Dead Cops,'" NBC New York, December 15, 2014, http://www.nbcnewyork.com/news/local/Eric-Garner-Manhattan-Dead-Cops-Video-Millions-March-Protest-285805731.html.

3. Heather Mac Donald, "The Big Lie of the Anti-Cop Left Turns Lethal," *City Journal*, December 22, 2014, http://www.city-journal.org/2014/eon1222hm.html.

4.   "NYC protesters say they won't stop demonstrations despite de Blasio's wishes," Fox News, December 23, 2014, http://www.foxnews.com/us/2014/12/23/nyc-protesters-say-wont-stop-demonstrations-despite-de-blasio-wishes/.

5.   "Remarks by the President to the UN General Assembly," September 25, 2012, http://www.whitehouse.gov/the-press-office/2012/09/25/remarks-president-un-general-assembly.

6.   Phil Robertson, *UnPHILtered: The Way I See It* (New York: Howard, 2014), 20, 130.

7.   Drew Magary, "What the Duck?" *GQ*, January 2014, http://www.gq.com/entertainment/television/201401/duck-dynasty-phil-robertson?currentPage=1.

8.   Robertson, *UnPhiltered*, 131.

# INDEX

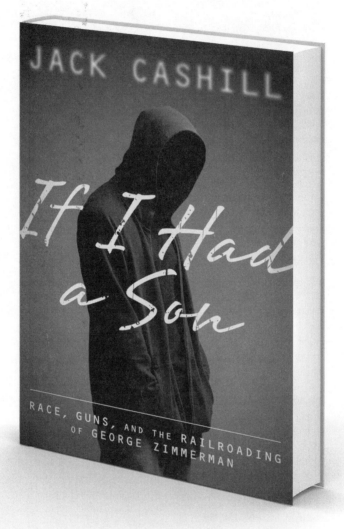

In 2012 when president Obama said about the shooting death of 17-year-old Trayvon Martin, "If I had a son, he'd look like Trayvon," he opened the floodgates of propaganda and vilification against an innocent man. The media portrayed Martin as an eleven-year-old cherub of a boy and Zimmerman as a white racist wannabe cop. Nothing could have been further from the truth. They ignored the fact that Trayvon was really into marijuana and street fighting and George Zimmerman was really a Hispanic liberal activist and Obama supporter. Now the truth is revealed.

WND Books • WASHINGTON DC • WNDBOOKS.COM

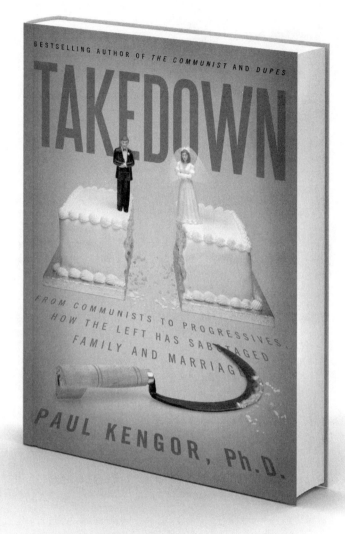

TAKEDOWN exposes how gay marriage is serving as a Trojan horse for the far left to secure the final takedown of marriage that it has long wanted, and countless everyday Americans are oblivious to the deeper forces at work. TAKEDOWN takes no prisoners and bluntly shows the reader that even Karl Marx and his more anti-marriage comrade Engels would be dumbfounded at the mere thought that modern Americans would gladly join them in their rejection of God's design for natural marriage and the family.

WND BOOKS • WASHINGTON DC • WNDBOOKS.COM

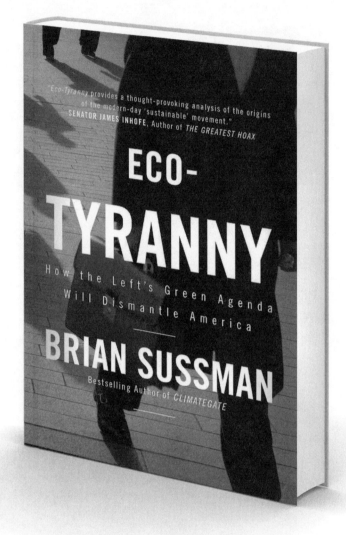

"Eco-Tyranny provides a thought-provoking analysis of the origins of the modern-day 'sustainable' movement."
SENATOR JAMES INHOFE, Author of THE GREATEST HOAX

ECO-
TYRANNY

How the Left's Green Agenda
Will Dismantle America

BRIAN SUSSMAN

Bestselling Author of CLIMATEGATE

In order to de-develop the United States, the left is using phony environmental crises to demonize capitalism and liberty and purposefully withhold America's vast natural resources – and the Obama administration is piloting the plan. ECO TYRANNY, by bestselling author Brian Sussman, presents a rational strategy to responsibly harvest our nation's vast resources in order to fulfill the future needs of a rapidly growing population.

WND Books • WASHINGTON DC • WNDBOOKS.COM

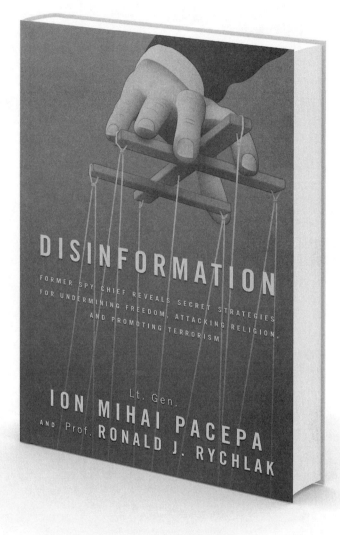

Today, still living undercover in the United States, the man credited by the CIA as the only person in the Western world who single-handedly demolished an entire enemy espionage service – the one he himself managed – takes aim at an even bigger target: the exotic, widely misunderstood but still astonishingly influential realm of the Russian-born "science" of DISINFORMATION. Indeed, within these pages, Ion Mihai Pacepa, along with his co-author Ronald Rychlak, exposes some of the most consequential yet largely unknown disinformation campaigns of our lifetime.

WND Books • WASHINGTON DC • WNDBOOKS.COM